T0283331

IN
GAD
WE TRUST

IN
GAD
WE TRUST

A TELL-SOME

JOSH GAD

GALLERY BOOKS

New York   Amsterdam/Antwerp   London   Toronto   Sydney   New Delhi

G

Gallery Books

An Imprint of Simon & Schuster, LLC

1230 Avenue of the Americas

New York, NY 10020

First Gallery Books hardcover edition January 2025

GALLERY BOOKS and colophon are registered trademarks of Simon & Schuster, LLC

For information about special discounts for bulk purchases, please contact Simon & Schuster Special Sales at 1-866-506-1949 or business@simonandschuster.com.

The Simon & Schuster Speakers Bureau can bring authors to your live event. For more information or to book an event, contact the Simon & Schuster Speakers Bureau at 1-866-248-3049 or visit our website at www.simonspeakers.com.

Interior design by Karla Schweer

Manufactured in the United States of America

10   9   8   7   6   5   4   3   2   1

Library of Congress Cataloging-in-Publication Data is available.

ISBN 978-1-6680-5052-1

ISBN 978-1-6680-5054-5 (ebook)

To my mother, Susan,
who made me stand up straight
and face my dreams head-on
instead of up and to the left

CONTENTS

FOREWORD

by Sacha Baron Cohen

I first heard that Josh was writing an autobiography in 2022. When he told me, I said, "Wow—so you must think that the actors' strike is going to go on for ages." He said, "No, I need to tell my story," and I said, "What?" and he showed me the advance he was offered, and I said, "Can you ask them if they'd like to hear my story as well?" and he said, "No, they wouldn't be interested." I said, "Can you at least ask?" Two weeks later he claimed he did. I was suspicious and asked for email proof, which he did not provide. He ghosted me for another two years until yesterday. Imagine my surprise when Josh asked me to write the foreword to his autobiography. I said, "Do I have to read it?" And he said, "Read two chapters and you'll get the idea." I said, "Fine, two chapters, that's nothing." And if I had bothered to read those two chapters, I'm sure it would have reinforced what I already know about Josh: that he is in the top three Afghan Jewish Floridians in the business. I learned so much about myself through the simple act of not reading this book.

Josh is not only one of the three funniest people I have ever met in my life, he is one of the most brilliant, with the effortless ability to create legendary comedy characters out of pure imagination (and sometimes a bit of snow).

He is also undoubtedly one of the kindest people I have ever met, someone who fights for democracy, liberal values, and the well-being of others. I hope you do enjoy this lovely book whose cover I admire and cherish, and that you leave it a better person, because you should know that whoever you are, you pale in significance compared to Josh Gad. It is likely that most of you reading this will conclude the final chapter and feel that you are miserable in comparison. That's how perfect he is. I love you, Josh. Very much.

—Sacha Baron Cohen

IN
GAD
WE TRUST

BOOK I

Of Childhood Dreams, Teenage Schemes, and College Themes

GADISM

Dreams can become reality and reality can become dreams. When you envision something long enough and work hard enough, the sky is the limit . . .

Unless your dreams are about being bitten by a bat. That's a sign of bad luck and/or rabies . . .

Then, please do not follow your dreams!

1
—

HOW I LEARNED
TO STOP WORRYING
AND LOVE TO CLOWN

I have very few vivid memories of my early childhood: being dragged to *The Karate Kid Part II* in a theater and screaming at my brother because I didn't understand what sequels were and thought we were just seeing the movie I had already seen a thousand times and then being so confused by the montage of clips from the first film and then overwhelmed with joy that there were all-new adventures for Daniel and Mr. Miyagi; being introduced to a game called "Doctor" by my friend and wondering why she didn't also have a pee-pee in between her legs; holding what I thought was a toy snake, only to have my mom pry it out of my hands as it started to slither and wrap around my arm; vomiting all over my mother and father on a plane after we landed in New York and saying "Oh God, I feel so much better" as they both violently gagged; but among the most vivid images I have is the day my mother threw my father out of our house.

My parents' bedroom had two mirrored closets that faced each other, creating an illusion of infinite reflections of whatever was positioned in front of them. On this one particular day, my mother was hurling my dad's luggage and clothes at him and he was laughing it off, with my brothers holding on to me as I bawled in a state of confusion and fear. I had never heard my mom scream like that and didn't understand why my dad would have to leave. After all, infidelity isn't usually a topic taught in kindergarten alongside hygiene and the alphabet. I didn't realize it then, but that would be our last day together as a family.

It was also my radioactive-spider-bite-inception moment. Like Peter Parker turning into Spider-Man, this was the moment I would turn into my equivalent of a far less physically fit and lacking-all-superhuman-powers version of Spider-Man. The trauma of going from a full family unit to a broken household in a matter of minutes was fairly earth-shattering to me, but it would also set me on a course to become the entertainer I would one day be. But every origin story has a beginning, and mine began like those of many before me . . . in a hospital, followed by a strange bearded man cutting off a piece of my dick as strangers clinked glasses to celebrate.

I was born on February 23, 1981. *Fort Apache, the Bronx* was the number one film at the box office, the number one song was "I Love a Rainy Night" by Eddie Rabbitt, and there was a failed coup d'état staged against King Juan Carlos I of Spain. Back at Memorial Regional Hospital in Hollywood, Florida, I was staging my own coup on my mother's uterus. On an unusually crisp winter night, I was born at twenty-one inches, six pounds, and ten ounces (the last time I had a reasonably healthy body mass index). In what is a perfect example of my parents' relationship in my early childhood, my father was casually finishing his dinner as my mother went into labor and pleaded with him to "Hurry up."

I was hardly an accident, but barely a victory. I think my parents, who already had two boys, Jason and Jeffrey, then ages ten and eight and a half, were desperately hoping for a little girl. They had even picked out a name . . . Jacqueline. Well, out I popped and my surprise penis made it slightly difficult to go with the pink layette they had confidently purchased for me. My older brothers were so annoyed that my mother and father were having a third child much younger than them that they insisted my parents at least give me a *J* name so that it complemented their first initials. My mother conceded, and that's how Joshua was chosen. After two nights at the hospital, my parents brought me home to their North Park Road house in the residential community of Emerald Hills, a house they had moved to only six months prior, after spending the previous few years bouncing between Rio de Janeiro, Brazil, and East Meadow, New York (the peanut butter and tuna of geographical crossovers). After lengthy research, they determined that the one place that could marry all things Brazilian with all things New York was South Florida . . . and, more specifically, Hollywood, Florida.

In the multiverse of Hollywoods, this is the villain one. Lacking the romantic hills and movie-star glitz, Hollywood, Florida, was the less exciting little sister of Miami and the more exciting big brother of Hallandale. What it lacked in marquee venues it made up for in 7-Elevens and rundown beachfronts. In all truth, I have very warm memories of my childhood in Hollywood. I loved my friends, I loved my community, I loved my neighborhood. And while Hollywood, Florida, is often a punchline, for me it was the perfect place to start my journey.

My parents had decided to settle in Florida because it was easier for my father's business commutes. Whereas most of my friends' fathers were in fairly pedestrian vocations (doctors, lawyers, business owners), my father was an emerald dealer based out of Colombia—not South Carolina's, South America's. My father and his brothers had a company called AmGad, which owned multiple emerald mines. They would mine the caves outside of Bogotá and then sell the refined jewels out of their offices in New York City. As you can imagine if you've seen *Narcos*, working out of Colombia in the early eighties was, shall we say . . . fraught. Bedtime stories were often a mix of which one of his friends had been recently assassinated and what new technology (my favorite being a night-vision goggle of sorts) his security was using to monitor his finca (a South American farm of sorts) and spot would-be snipers (a precision killer of sorts). Essentially, my father's life was Disney's *Encanto* by way of *Scarface*. My parents had as divergent upbringings as one could imagine. My father's upbringing is an *Onion* headline: a Jew born in Afghanistan. He was the son of a rug salesman named Nisan and his second wife, Rivka, and one of fourteen children (seven siblings and seven half siblings from Nisan's first marriage). According to my father, his family was nomads, escaping persecution from one part of the Middle East to the next. You can apparently trace my lineage back to the early tribes of Israel, where we were dislocated by the Assyrians (never a big fan) in 723 BC (tough year). Over the next two-thousand-plus years, we took up residence everywhere from Iran to India, ultimately settling in picturesque Afghanistan. Surprisingly, in the late forties when my father was born, there was a fairly sizable population of Jewish people in Afghanistan. He was born in a town called Herat, where life was anything but normal. Electricity was not an option. Instead of soccer, locals played a game called "goat pulling" that involved two teams essentially scoring points on each other, not with a ball, but by throwing a headless goat carcass into a goal post. (Imagine being that "soccer mom.") Meanwhile, school, usually a safe refuge, was also fairly unorthodox.

My father has a history of embellishment, so please take everything that follows with a very large grain of salt. Having said that, one distinct memory my father has is that at the age of four, he was outed by his classmates to the teacher for bringing a balloon into class. The teacher took him outside, tied his feet together, and ripped a considerable branch from a large tree. The teacher then had the students take turns beating my father until he could barely walk or see. When my father stumbled home, his dad was outraged. He gathered a mob, returned to the school, and told the teacher that if she ever allowed an assault on my father to take place again, the group would take a larger branch and beat the teacher violently with it (again, just as a reminder—as much for you as for me—this was all over a CHILDREN'S BALLOON). But, such was life in Afghanistan. At nine years old, my father and his family moved to Kabul by bus. (I'm fairly certain it was not a Greyhound.) If life in Herat was hard, Kabul wouldn't be much easier. My father recalls a story about him and a group of friends playing on a roof one day with a kite. A local boy begged my dad to borrow the kite and, having never flown one before, the boy lost control of the kite, chased it, flew it off the roof they were on, and plummeted to the ground along with the kite.

For the record, I tried several versions of that sentence, and yes, they were all equally insane sounding.

Growing up in a predominantly Islamic society as a Jew was, in many ways, culturally stimulating and rewarding for my father. He was able to learn about rituals and expand his knowledge beyond the traditions of his own Judaic background. Many of his friends were Muslim, and his father did business and shared friendships with many high-ranking Muslim officials and leaders in the community. That is not to say there wasn't the occasional incident.

On one occasion, my father was surrounded by a group of bullies and a Koran was shoved in his face. He was told that if he did not renounce Judaism, they would violently beat him. My dad, still just a child, was terrified. His dad, a very religious man, had told him that if he was ever in danger, he should close his eyes and recite the holy Shema prayer. According to my father, he recited the prayer and in that moment his father, who never in his life had returned from work earlier than six p.m., suddenly walked toward the mob at three in the afternoon. His father took his walking cane and started whacking all of my father's tormentors in the head (like something out of a Jewish *Karate Kid*). I myself am not religious and believe in my heart it was probably mere coincidence that my dad's father showed up at precisely the right time to save him, but man, do I love the beauty of that narrative.

Shortly thereafter, my grandfather and his wife decided that while Afghanistan had been their home for many years, perhaps it was time for a change. By this time, they had many friends and family in Israel and thought it was time to return to their ancestral roots. Sadly, a few weeks before they were to depart, my grandfather Nisan died of a heart attack. It boggles my mind that I have a grandfather buried somewhere in Afghanistan.

My father and his family arrived in Israel when he was around twelve and a half. With nothing to their names, they lived in government housing, and they all found work to pay off their accruing bills. My father soon got a job in which he learned how to cut diamonds. As another source of income, he became a bodybuilder at age fifteen (you can't make this shit up). He would also take classes when he could, in between his totally normal work obligations as teenage-child diamond cutter and would-be bodybuilder. Around this time, my father—who had never played the lottery—was convinced by a friend to buy some sort of lottery ticket where the prize was a car. Somehow, my father won the car!

Realizing he had no need for an automobile or, indeed, even a license to drive one, he sold it off and used the money to join his older brother Amnon, who was then living in Forest Hills, New York, in a studio apartment meant to house five men, including my father and his nephew, whom he traveled with.

Now sixteen years of age and the only money in his pocket that from the sale of his car, my father immediately tried to join the US Army, but was denied

because he was too young, flat-footed, and could speak less English than Beaker from the Muppets. Meanwhile, his brother and nephew also tried to sign up for the military, but they too were immediately turned down.

When they had eagerly gone to the recruitment office and begged to join the service with their broken English and Borat attire, the officer looked both of them up and down and said, "You want to join the US military? Are you serious?" They were flabbergasted and responded: "No! We're not *Syrians*. We're Afghanis!" Suffice it to say, the Gads would not earn their living by serving Uncle Sam. Instead, they eventually ended up servicing one of the largest markets of growth in the 1970s: fine jewels.

As the Middle Eastern immigrant side of my DNA stew was breaking away from the hardships of their past to forge a new identity and pathway to prosperity, the Eastern European part of the Josh Gad equation was also coming into focus.

My mother's story is less harrowing and more . . . well . . . traditional American Dream. My mother, initially born as Sara and later renamed Susan (to conform to more standard American monikers), was born in Germany at the end of the Second World War. Her parents, Joseph and Evelyn, had both recently and miraculously survived the Holocaust (something I'll delve into more later). Having lost the prime of their youth, my grandparents, who had both escaped during a death march, were looking to jump-start their newly liberated lives. The two of them found themselves post-war in a small village in Germany called Weiden in der Oberpfalz, where they attended an event organized for Holocaust survivors one night and immediately fell in love. In 1948, they had their first child (my mom) and soon booked passage on a transatlantic ship headed to America called the SS *Marine Jumper*. The boat ride over was straight out of *An American Tail*, with my mom filling in as baby Fievel in a wooden crib that would slide from one side of the women's quarters to the other during the two-week passage. When they arrived at the NYC Seaport (the now-decommissioned Pier 32), they were greeted by my grandfather's relatives, who had thankfully fled to America before the war and agreed to sponsor my grandparents and my mother.

My grandfather soon got a job as a tailor for the high-end-fashion Zuckerman House, who would later gain renown for, among many things, producing dresses for everyone from Grace Kelly to Jacqueline Kennedy. After a few years of living in a small apartment in Jackson Heights, my grandparents moved to the booming Long Island.

My mom was not one to go on dates, but one summer evening in 1969, she was dragged by her two friends to a mixer in Forest Hills. The girls had gone on a trip to Montreal, Canada, for Expo 67 and while there had met a group of Israeli men from New York whom they promised to meet up with when they all got back to the US. My parents shared a dance and, luckily for me, but horribly for their own relationship fate, fell in love. In 1969, they married and shortly thereafter had my two brothers, Jason and Jeffrey. Eventually, they would move to Florida, which brings us back to my favorite subject . . . me!

Growing up, I never wanted for money. We lived in a beautiful house in a beautiful place. While I wasn't born with a silver spoon, it would be fair to say I at least had half of a silver spork hanging out of my mouth. We would often travel as a family to exciting places including New York City, Las Vegas, and even Colombia, where, as a four-year-old, I sat in a helicopter with no doors above a massive mountain range and questioned my mortality before I knew what the word *mortality* was.

Despite my father not being around for weeks and sometimes months at a time, everything felt fairly normal. My brothers and I were very

close and they often used me as a prop in their eight-millimeter home-made films, pretending to be medics and pushing me (their dying patient) around in a mobile serving cart. We would watch *The Smurfs* religiously and eat cereal from a giant green bowl that my mother would confoundingly pour multiple cereal brands into, mixing things like raisin bran and Life for no good reason. We were also a fairly religious family, walking to temple every Saturday and attending Hebrew day school for our elementary education. My parents would also throw lavish parties, including one at our house that transformed our home into a working casino with blackjack and poker tables and saw our covered pool become a dance floor, with me as a five-year-old attempting and failing to breakdance. Suffice it to say, I was either too young or too oblivious, based on the seemingly blessed lifestyle we led, to see that there were any cracks in this family tale. That is, of course, until the aforementioned radioactive-spider-bite-inception moment of my world shattering in front of the dual mirrors. But, as the old adage goes, "Comedy equals tragedy plus time." Well, at five, having your mom throw your dad out of your house in front of you while everyone is crying and screaming is a pretty good dose of tragedy for a quintessential "comedian origin stew" recipe.

Those first few weeks after the separation, my mother was in a depression-induced coma. She would essentially lock herself in her room and cry all day long, which was very understandable given the circumstances. I, however, felt helpless and scared. It is incredibly difficult to watch the person who exudes strength and confidence and protects you from the harsh realities of the world appear so raw and vulnerable and afraid. Nothing, it seemed, would break her from this spell. But, I knew I had to try.

From the early age of four, I could understand the power of laughter. At that very young age, we took my grandparents on a vacation to the Catskill Mountains to celebrate their anniversary. One night we went to a comedy club straight out of *The Marvelous Mrs. Maisel* and watched some random Borscht Belt comedian with a name composed of mostly consonants perform his schticky routine. I was intoxicated. I couldn't understand a single joke, but it didn't matter. Every time the audience laughed, I would laugh harder, like the Star Trek android Data studying and trying to replicate human behavior. This powerful drug called *laughter* felt so good, and the idea that one could wield it like Zeus's lightning bolt was invigorating. If there was one way to break my mother from her stupor, dammit, it would be laughter.

And so, every day, I would wake up and make it my duty to try to make my mom laugh, or at the very least smile. I would do everything, from using crazy voices or contorting my face to repeating a joke I might have heard from a movie or show. It didn't matter. I was sharpening the blade of my skills and trying to use it to stab through the shell of trauma. Slowly, it began to work. She would crack a smile as I spoke to her in a strange hybrid Polish/Yiddish old-man voice as a character I called Professor Mahoney who would perform strange and useless experiments in his laboratory and be an expert on all things that weren't useful. I would pull my underwear up to my nipples and run around the house like a grown baby, letting out a creaky wail that sounded like an ostrich being strangled. The smiles became guffaws. I was suddenly so drunk with power that my mother got a phone call one day from my elementary school teacher saying, "We have a bit of a problem. Your son walked into the class after the bell and screamed, 'Lucy, I'm home!!!!'" I was not only suddenly waking my mother up from her slumber, but I was now trying to make everyone around me laugh at all times.

At the time, I didn't understand that the pain I was so desperate to overcome was not just my mother's and others', but my own. Despite my

newfound addiction to laughter and comedy, I was spiraling. My father would visit sporadically from Colombia, treat me to a fun weekend here and there, and then take off again almost as quickly as he arrived. On one of these weekends, he took me to a Sheraton hotel in Fort Lauderdale and told me he had a surprise for me. While I had been hoping for and slightly expecting a dog or a toy, I instead got a half brother from Colombia and the mistress responsible for breaking up my family. I was so confused and enraged. Unlike my mother and my brothers (who at this point were both in college and luckily didn't have to deal with his bullshit brigade), I was completely unaware of why my parents had separated. For starters, the idea that my father had an entire other family in South America was definitely not in the top two hundred reasons I would have suspected for their separation. And suddenly here I was at eight, with a little toddler and his Spanish-speaking mother whom my dad was thrusting on me, and I was completely lost. Not only had he left my mother and my family for his Colombian ménage, but he was now planning on buying them an apartment in North Miami Beach and apparently wanted me to chill with them on the few occasions he would actually come to visit me. Then, to add insult to injury, my dad told me I couldn't tell anyone he had introduced them to me.

This one moment would truly have lasting consequences. My schoolwork suffered. I would lie about everything, small and big. And I would use food to compensate for my feelings. This was the beginning of my lifelong struggle with weight. It felt easier to use carbs instead of words to express my grief. My mother quickly realized that I needed an outlet to focus my energies on before I was derailed by the chaos my father had introduced into my life, so when she saw a clipping in the local paper for a children's theater at the Hollywood Playhouse, she signed me up and I immediately became obsessed. While I was a goofy kid at school, formal acting wasn't something I had any experience or relationship with. I had dabbled with the occasional elementary school show, and sure, I had stolen the 1985 production of the Beth Shalom musical *Professor Green and the Simcha Machine* (*simcha* meaning "joy" in Hebrew), where I played the title character robot, not to brag. For this breakout performance, I wore a large cardboard box with Magic Marker–drawn buttons and knobs on it and sang lyrics such as:

> *I'm the Simcha Machine, I run loose in the city*
> *and no one can stop me, my songs are too witty.*

Truly groundbreaking stuff. But, other than that, the idea of acting as an art form was very foreign to me in those early years.

The Hollywood Playhouse was run by three older individuals who were local favorites in the Hollywood community theater scene: Deloris Miller (a crackly, fiery woman who looked like Madam Mim from the Disney animated film *The Sword in the Stone*); Ron Hendricks, who was the choreography teacher and the gayest man to have the hottest daughter I've ever met; and James Michael (the short, bald, and brilliant head of acting who would be my first true mentor). The three of them ran a children's theater, but you wouldn't know it based on the way they spoke to us and taught us. These days, they would probably be canceled for being so forward and adult with us, but back then, it just felt refreshing and titillating, like we were equals and not some little children who needed a silly diversion to occupy our time. James in particular treated us as if we were in a Stella Adler class. It didn't matter that we were doing a production of *Peter Pan* and I was playing Smee. He expected me to find that character's truth and not be generic in my choices (so, for the record—Smee is overweight because he has daddy issues and looks up to Hook as his surrogate father).

I remember one day we were doing an exercise that required us to get emotional. Most of us were in the single-digit age bracket, ten at the oldest, and he wanted us to tap into our inner Julianne Moores. I finally got frustrated because I couldn't bring myself to connect with my emotions. I asked him to do it, thinking I would get him to concede that it was too hard even for him to just burst into tears. Not five seconds later, the man full-on wept in front of a group of stunned children. When I asked him how he did it, he took a breath and said, "I asked myself, 'Why?'"

I was baffled. "Why what?" I responded.

He smiled and said, "That's for you to answer."

I couldn't for the life of me figure out what the hell he meant, but now, some thirty-plus years later, I ask "Why?" before every emotional scene I do and, like clockwork, the tears pour out. James had such an outsized influence on me because he could tell that I had something more than just funny in me—I had pathos, and he demanded that I tap into that well of vulnerability instead of just relying on being funny or goofy. He weaponized my talent in a way that would give me durability and sustainability as a performer and not make me a one-trick pony.

Among my colleagues at Hollywood Playhouse were two individuals who would also break out from the confines of the local Hollywood theater children's scene: Randy Rainbow and Seth Gabel. Before Randy was an outspoken political satirist and musical aficionado, he was a somewhat shy and flushed young boy who came to life every time he opened his mouth to sing. His supremely high singing voice put all of us to shame. He could sing notes that would make some of the soprano girls in our class blush. Randy and I became quick friends. We were both somewhat chubby, came from households that were anything but standard, and had a common love of musical theater. Seth, on the other hand, was already one of my best friends. At the age of four, he and I had attended Beth Shalom together. Back then, Seth had the much more ethnically unambiguous last name of Kirshenbaum (a name he would later change to the more Italian Cosentino, then the more elegant Gabel, then finally to the more Hollywood-friendly and definitely-not-ethnic Howard-Gabel). We would constantly film ridiculous comedic spoofs of our favorite Spielberg movies, like *E.T.*, with me on an exercise bike and him popping his head out of the basket, and *Back to the Future*, where we reenacted the entire "Earth Angel" scene, electric guitar and all.

One day, I brought him to the playhouse with me as a guest. The girls immediately fell in love with him and threw themselves at this debonair tween. Seth had zero interest in acting at that time, but I wanted him to come with me every week because nobody made me laugh more than him. During a break, he held up a bag of Cheetos and told me he had somehow stolen it from the vending machine by reaching his skinny little child hand in and grabbing it. (Thankfully, the statute of limitations has run its course, allowing me to disclaim this criminal anecdote.) I told him that if he didn't sign up for classes, I would tell the teachers what he did. Therefore, I feel safe in saying I guilted Seth Gabel into becoming an actor. You're welcome, America!

While I was excelling at acting, I was *de*celling at school. The stuff with my dad continued to really take up emotional bandwidth and as a result I was spiraling. My secret visits to be with his "other family" were eating me from the inside out. I would subsequently lie about doing my homework, I wouldn't listen or care in class, and I would flunk every single test because I never bothered to study. The school would call my mom in on a monthly basis and tell her I essentially wasn't going to amount to anything. This is also when my mother found out that they had put me in all basic classes without consulting with her. She rightly suspected part of the reason I wasn't attempting to do anything was because they were treating me as less than I was capable of being. She told them that at the very least they had to place me in regular classes, which were slightly more challenging in that they didn't treat me like a Neanderthal in need of daycare. A common throughline in this book is going to be the story of my mother advocating for me, even when I wouldn't advocate for myself, and this was the beginning of that journey.

By third grade I was an absolute train wreck of a student and my mom thought it was perhaps time for a change of scenery. As fate would have it, the headmaster of the Jewish day school, Rabbi Malofsky, had embezzled thousands of dollars and bankrupted the entire institution (a real heroic assist to the centuries-old cliché of antisemitic stereotyping). Subsequently, I would be forced to find a new elementary school. During the exodus from the Beth Shalom Hebrew Day School, all of my best friends were relocating to a non-parochial private school in Davie, Florida, called the University School. You had to take an admission test to get in, and let's just say I didn't do what you would call "well." In fact, I did so poorly that the head of the school, Mrs. Brennan, immediately denied my application. I was devastated. All of my friends would be there and I would be forced to go to a completely different school. My mother, however, was not going to let that happen.

She booked an appointment with Mrs. Brennan and insisted that they give me a chance to attend, under the provision that they could remove me if I didn't meet academic expectations. The principal, apparently moved by my mother's passionate plea or unwillingness to accept no for an answer, reluctantly gave me a waiver and admitted me into the school, albeit on a short leash.

The first few years, I did fine enough that they couldn't find the catalyst they sought to remove me, but by seventh grade, all bets were off. I was once again a disaster, only interested in acting and playing pretend with my G.I. Joes. After one tragic report card filled with enough Fs and Ds to give Adele a hit single, my mother told me she was pulling me out of the school and sending me to our local public school, which had metal detectors for decoration at every entrance because kids brought more knives than textbooks to school. As a single mother working day and night as a realtor and essentially using all of her hard-earned money to send me to private school, she was done throwing good money after bad. I begged her to reconsider. But, she went even further and told me she was not only sending me to this *Dangerous Minds*–themed school but also pulling me from the Hollywood Playhouse. I was devastated, I was furious, and I was determined to do everything in my power to prevent her from this miscarriage of justice.

I started by reaching out to all of my friends and telling them to get their parents to rally behind me and call my mother out. My mom was suddenly getting bombarded with phone calls from random mothers pressuring her to reconsider her rash decision. I then had the head of the Hollywood Playhouse get involved and tell her it would be a terrible decision to pull me from the program. Anyone I could unite around my cause, I got to intervene. My mom was livid, but also tired of having the entire neighborhood assail her for being a monster parent, a false narrative I had conveniently created to get her to reconsider. Exhausted from the barrage of calls but still furious at my academic performance, she gave me one last chance, and told me that if I didn't turn everything around by the end of the next semester, there would be no desperate phone call in the world that could save me. She was done fucking around and I could tell there would be no more second chances, despite my seemingly expert manipulation. So, the next day I went to school and allowed myself to fall in love with learning.

Within a month, the teachers were baffled by my miraculous turn-around. Not only was I suddenly engaged, but everything was coming almost too easy. They had assumed that I was an idiot not worth investing in and were suddenly genuinely surprised that not only was I achieving the goals teachers set before me but practically begging for more challenges.

I soon told the teachers I no longer wanted to be in regular classes but wanted to be moved over to honors. The first one I negotiated with was my history teacher. He was reluctant and dubious to move me, but after I harassed him for two straight weeks, he finally allowed me the rope to hang myself. What he did not anticipate, however, is that I would quickly conquer everything thrown my way and excel at it. Soon, I was moved to honors English, science, and Spanish. Math was never going to be an option. I was and still am incapable of even the simplest arithmetic and am a sworn lifelong enemy of geometry. But in every other subject, a light bulb had gone off. Eventually honors became AP, and every time a teacher would doubt my abilities, I would shove it back in their face with my efforts and hard work. My mom's gut had been right all along: it wasn't that I was incapable; it was that I was uninspired. My mother was and is my fiercest champion and she fought everyone who doubted my abilities, including myself. At the end of seventh grade, the head of the school gave me an honorary award for the most improved student of the year. Among all of my accolades and successes, I think that one in particular is still the one my mother is proudest of.

While things were finally clicking into place at school, the absence of my father was still taking an enormous toll on me. Not only would I see him very sparingly, but when I did, it was always with this secret brother along for the ride, whom I was still sworn not to tell my mom I had been introduced to. The two things my father taught me very well were how to expertly lie and how to have a fun time. I would never not smile and enjoy his company. Every time I would see him, we would always do something exciting. One year, he took me to California to visit my uncles and cousins, and we went to Disneyland and Universal Studios. Another time, he took me to Vegas and I went to a burlesque show, which at eight was not quite something I had the proper adjectives to describe, although, let's just say, much like the dancers that night, the inside of my pants also put on quite a show.

But perhaps the most seismic trip he took me on was a trip with my brothers Jason and Jeffrey. One year, when I was ten, he flew us out to New York City, where he had an apartment close to Times Square. Back then, this was not the ideal place to be staying in New York. The soundscape even at 2:00 a.m. was sirens and pimps and there was enough neon light breaking through the windows to create an indoor roller-skating rink. During the day, we would visit all of the big sites, including the Twin Towers, which to a ten-year-old was among the coolest and most impressive structures one could ever imagine.

And at night, he would take us to the theater. We saw two shows, an off-Broadway production of *The Rothschilds*, directed by renowned director Lonny Price, and the Broadway production of *Fiddler on the Roof*, starring the brilliant Chaim Topol reprising his role from the film. While I had been to other shows in Florida, this was the first time I had ever heard of or been to Broadway. Sitting in the cavernous and stunning Gershwin Theatre, future home to *Wicked*, I felt an urgency and a purpose. I would one day be on a stage like that. I didn't know when, I didn't know how, but I knew I would do it. I had to. Hollywood Playhouse was one thing, but professional theater was a whole different experience. From that day forward, I would ask my mom to take me to any and all shows coming through town. I saw Cathy Rigby in *Peter Pan*, Jerry Lewis in *Damn Yankees*, and Sally Struthers in *Grease*. *The Phantom of the Opera*, *Miss*

Saigon, and *Les Miz* were all part of my theatrical education in the early nineties, and with each show, I would grow more and more in love with the form. But in order to forge my own path in entertainment, I was going to have to move beyond children's theater and the pain of my early childhood and into a new phase of my life.

2

FORENSICS CAN BE
SO MUCH MORE THAN
CUTTING UP DEAD BODIES

Whether we admit to it or not, every school activity has an inherent connotation. The sports boys are jocks. The chess club kids are intellectuals. The Honors Club members are kiss-ups. The cheerleaders are the popular kids. And the Model UN students are insufferable. I was in none of these clubs. Never played sports, wouldn't know what to do with a chess piece if I had the entire cast of *The Queen's Gambit* using my hands for me. I was an honors student, but Honors Club was a distinction I only once qualified for but never joined, mostly out of laziness. The cheerleader outfits didn't fit, and about the closest I wanted to be to Model UN was putting together a LEGO model set of the UN. So, for me, there was only one option left . . . the very last option . . . the loser's club . . . Speech and Debate.

By the middle of seventh grade, I was way too old to continue the Hollywood Playhouse children's theater and slightly too young to join our school productions, which were lavish musicals that frankly had no business being as good as they were. Having no obvious outlet therefore to feed my performance itch, I was desperate and hungry for any alternative that could satisfy my insecure craving for attention. One night, as I was sleeping over at the house of my friend Matt Swerdlow (who had two pet ferrets that would traumatize me every night by nipping my toes like two long-tailed sociopaths), his brother Danny told me about something called forensics. Danny was one of the stars of our school's esteemed musical theater program. He had starred as the titular Charlie Brown in *You're a Good Man, Charlie Brown* and was gearing up to play the lead in the new school musical of *A Chorus Line*, which had fully kept the lyrics to "Dance: Ten; Looks: Three" (aka "Tits and Ass") in the show, giving real weight to the now-common phrase "It was a different time." Suffice it to say, Danny was one of my school heroes (the other being Scott Weinger, who was the speaking voice of *Aladdin* and graduated before I ever got there).

Danny knew I loved to act. He and I had shared the same singing teacher, Gene Putnam, a sweet older lady who desperately wanted me to be the next Pavarotti and forced me to sing Italian arias (a skill I would one day finally put to use as a fairy-tale snowman.)

Danny asked me if I had ever heard of forensics. I told him I had once, on TV. "Isn't that when they cut up dead people to figure out who murdered them?" He said, "That's a different forensics." He then asked me if I had heard of the NFL. "Of course," I said, "I watch football with my buddies Dave Lang and Brett Horgan every week." Once again he shook his head: "No, different thing." I had no earthly idea what he was talking about, but one thing was clear—whatever the hell this NFL forensics was, it needed some serious rebranding. This *other* NFL, it turns out, was the National Forensic League, and forensics, when *not* referring to dissecting the dead, was a form of speech and debate. Forensics included multiple categories including Original Oratory, where one writes a ten-minute speech about a particular subject matter, meant both to entertain and to compel an audience to agree with the clearly defined thesis statement at the top of the speech. There are categories like Extemp and Public Address, which include more traditional debate tactics.

Finally, there was the subsection that appealed most to me as a performer: Interpretation, or, as it's commonly called, Interp. There are three main forms of Interp: Humorous Interp, or HI; Dramatic Interp, or DI; and Duo Interp, or Duo. Humorous Interp requires a performer to interpret ten minutes of written material into a comedic performance, playing all the characters by "popping" in place from one to another. Popping is a form of movement where you shift in place in quick pops, changing your posture and the position of your feet to bring a character to life (a skill that would later come in handy for my third Broadway show, *Gutenberg! The Musical!*, some twenty-five years later). DI takes the same approach but substitutes a dramatic piece of material in place of a humorous one. Finally, Duo is a two-person performance that calls for two performers standing side by side and never looking at each other to act out a dramatic or comedic piece of content. I was immediately intrigued. Danny told me he wanted to personally introduce me to our school's head of forensics and theater, Brent Pesola, to get the ball rolling. Which is when my ass clenched like a Pacific Coast clam.

Pesola was a name that struck fear and intimidation into every would-be performer at my school. He had not only transformed our program into one of the elite performing arts departments in South Florida over a five-year span, but his drama students were superstars in and outside of our school walls. Pesola was also a frankly unapproachable mythical figure. He didn't have the time or desire to learn how to talk to kids; he only had time for kids who understood how to talk to adults. You didn't ask him if you could be a part of his orbit; he sought you out and knighted you, if and when he so chose (which was incredibly rare). Nevertheless, he always left an impression, for better or worse. To this day, my dear friend Craig, a successful lawyer and friend of thirty years, immediately says "Fuck that guy" when I mention Pesola's name because of the way Craig and most students were mostly shunned and spoken down to by the larger-than-life giant of a man.

Pesola's gruff voice, no-bullshit vibe, dry and highly inappropriate sense of humor, large, broad physique, and penchant for alcohol and hot sauce made him seem less like a teacher and more like a championship-winning SEC coach all out of fucks. He couldn't be bothered with small talk unless you were one of his prized performers. Once you got into that rare circle, however, you had an ally and friend for life who would serve you your dreams on a silver platter. His wife, Kristin, a beautiful blonde bombshell that every single hetero male student at the school had a giant crush on, was his creative and business partner along with being the choreographer of the school musicals. They had recently created a forensics program at the school and were almost immediately successful (mostly in debate and oratorical categories), winning local and national tournaments, including Harvard and Emory invitationals. If I could somehow finagle my way into the highly selective program, I was certain I could do big things.

My first meeting with Brent was not dissimilar to my first time having sex: quick, awkward, and leaving the other person completely unsatisfied. Talking to him for the first time was like the scene in one of my childhood favorite films, *The Goonies*, when the boys ask Mama Fratelli for a water and she gives them a brown liquid and forces them to drink it before threatening to cut off one of their tongues. About thirty seconds into the one-sided conversation, he handed me over to one of his older students, Seth Yankowitz, and told him to teach me the basics. Seth, who was probably not very eager to spend his free time with a random tubby middle schooler desperate to impress, showed me the bare minimum. He taught me the basics of HI and Duo, the categories he thought would suit me best based solely on my appearance and about two and a half conversations. He then illustrated how to maximize cutting a script down to ten minutes in a way that satisfactorily tells a story with a clear arc and well-defined characterizations. My first piece was a Duo with my friend David Lang, adapted from the play *Lone Star* by James McLure, about Ray and Roy, two brothers living in the backcountry of Texas. I was excited but didn't quite know what to expect at our first tournament, a weekend novice competition. Each round has six competitors and a judge. At the end of the tournament, the team with the lowest points (earning the most first places in each round) wins. At around 10:00 a.m., Dave and I took our seats at the school's tiny desks and watched as the first team was called up to perform. Two girls took the stage and began performing. Within a minute, they stopped. I was completely confused. Was this normal? Why was the girl standing there staring at us? A second later, the young lady ran out of the room and started heaving so loudly into a garbage can, I could barely contain my laughter. This was forensics?

Pretty quickly, Dave and I were getting good enough scores that the Pesolas, while not overly impressed, were curious enough to let me audition for the school play they were directing next: *Hair*, a perfect musical for tweens and teens, covering such topics as Vietnam, sex, and drugs (again, it was a different time). I was genuinely stunned when I found out not only had I gotten a role, but I was set to have my own duet, something I (and everyone else) was frankly shocked Brent gave to an underclassman. Over the next year and a half, I continued to earn as much respect as an insignificant pubescent middle schooler could, performing Duos here and there and getting ensemble roles in shows like *Dames at Sea*. It wasn't until the summer heading into my sophomore year, however, that everything would really begin to click.

The Pesolas had a summer program that was gaining national esteem called the Florida Forensics Institute, or FFI, where the most celebrated forensics coaches from around the country gathered in South Florida for a multi-week institute that helped students identify great material and shaped them into nationally competitive performers. My teacher the summer of 1996 was a man named Peter Pober, a renowned coach from the University of Texas at Austin, who primarily worked with collegiate forensics competitors. At the beginning of every summer session, the students would be asked to perform one minute of a piece in order to give the coaches a sense of what each individual could do. The previous year, I had performed a Humorous Interp from *Laughter on the 23rd Floor* by

Neil Simon, so I decided to perform a snippet of that. It absolutely killed. Everyone in the room was dying. I was certain that Peter and I were going to find a next-level comedy piece that could build on what I had already accomplished as a freshman. My first day in the room with Peter, he looked at me and said, "You're funny, kid, but you're doing a DI." I was completely baffled. "I'm a funny kid, so you're putting me in a dramatic event?"

That's basically like saying: "Hey, LeBron, you're great at basketball, which is why we'd like you to be the shortstop for the New York Yankees."

Not that I'm comparing myself to basketball/hypothetical baseball legend LeBron James (or any person who does exercise for a living, for that matter), but you get the point. It made absolutely no sense. The more I tried to push back on Peter, the more entrenched he became in his decision. Not only was he insisting that I do a DI, but he had also already chosen the piece for me: from the 1955 film *Marty* by Paddy Chayefsky. *Marty* is perhaps best known for winning numerous Academy Awards, including Best Picture and Best Actor for Ernest Borgnine, a fact I *only* know because Dustin Hoffman's Rain Man literally says: "Yeah, *Marty*. Best Picture in 1955. Ernest Borgnine. He was in *Marty*. Best Actor too." Beyond the one *Rain Man* reference, however, I knew nothing.

I was handed the script and told to go off into a quiet corner and read it. When I returned, I looked at Peter and said: "Did I do something to upset you?" He said, "No, why?" I paused, then said, "Then why have you insisted I do a dramatic piece about an overweight man who has no friends outside of his mother and can't get a date because he is unnaturally ugly?" Peter looked at me and responded, "Because you're going to do a great job with it."

I had never done anything even remotely dramatic in my life. I was "the funny guy." The class clown. Now, suddenly, I was being handed a piece so beyond my skill set and forced to get it up on its feet and in tip-top shape in two weeks. To get me started, Peter handed me a long list of questions to answer about the characters. The sheet read like a form you would get when applying to the CIA. I had to answer every possible biographical question about this character and, where there was no concrete information, make educated inferences.

How old was he? Where was he born? What are his likes and dislikes? How tall is he? What's his favorite song? What does he like to eat?

I mean, all I wanted to do was a funny little ten-minute comedy and now I was prepping for an interview with fucking *60 Minutes* about a fat, single butcher.

The more questions I answered, the more new questions Peter asked of me. After a few days of that, we started to cut the piece down to its essentials, creating a ten-minute dramatic arc that told the story of this overweight man who desperately wants to overcome his lot in life and fall in love. I was going to play the three main characters: Marty, his mother, and his date, Clara. Now, if you take a second to read that back, you will notice that two of the three characters I was being asked to play were women. At fifteen years old, I was supposed to inhabit an overbearing elderly Italian mother and a shy woman in her mid-to-late thirties who has never found love, but now may have found it in the form of a notoriously ugly man named Marty . . . Oh, and I was supposed to do all of this completely unironically and not at all for laughs.

After about a week of work, each of us in Peter's group, about seven in all, were asked to perform for each other. I was terrified. Everyone else was doing something they were passionate about and confident in. I, on the other hand, was doing a drama about an obese meat dealer who can't get laid. I got up, took a breath, and started popping back and forth between my three characters, telling the story of this sad man and his quest for love. When I finished, my colleagues gave me a healthy round of applause. I had somehow acquitted myself. Hell, I had even gotten a few laughs. It wasn't nearly as bad as I thought. Peter, however, was not impressed.

He told me that it was technically competent and that my character was well defined for the most part, but there was nothing more to it. "Where is the soul? Where is the pain? Where is the heart?"

Um, I don't know, Peter, let me get back to you when I'm thirty and have any earthly idea what the fuck any of these people have been through. I was livid. How the hell was I supposed to channel complex feelings and emotions about things that were so unrelatable and beyond my years? What did he want from me? Peter calmly looked at me and said: "I find it hard to believe that even at your age, you've never experienced heartache, pain, and loss."

I went back to the hotel and read the script again. I threw it down in disgust. I didn't know what it felt like to be broken up because you have nobody who wants to date you in your thirties. How could I? I was just a fifteen-year-old kid with few life experiences.

And then, almost like a wave, I started crying . . . We're talking rom-com ugly crying. It was like a dam burst open. It suddenly hit me. I may not have known the specific experience Marty was going through, but I knew the pain of being rejected; not by a woman on a date perhaps, but by a father who always promised so much and gave so little. I knew the desperation of a mother trying her best to shield her child from that pain and sometimes becoming overbearing in the process. Like Marty, I was overweight. And while I wasn't a butcher, I was certainly a fat kid dealing with the stigma and pain that comes with everyone's judgment and ridicule. I might not literally have been Marty, but boy, did he live in me.

I started working day and night, making every single moment of that piece count, doing more investigations to find the truth in each one of these characters. What were my own experiences that I could pull upon when playing a mother who cared so deeply for her son? What element of loneliness and despair had I experienced in my own life that could reflect the pain of a shy girl who just wanted to be loved? And when I needed to tap into the emotional well of these complex characters and, in particular, Marty, I would go back to that simple question that gets to the root of universal pain, the same question James Michael taught me to ask all those years ago at the Hollywood Playhouse: "Why?"

Once again, Peter's group gathered to perform. With a few days having passed between our last showcase, everyone was now much looser and less tense. I, however, was the exact opposite. I was laser focused and hungry for a second chance. I went toward the end of the group. With most of my peers performing either HI's or less intense Dramatic Interps, the room was fairly boisterous and full of energy by the time it got to me. I took the stage and within thirty seconds, you could hear a pin drop. Over the next ten minutes, every single person was in the palm of my hand, hanging on every word and even laughing their asses off at all the right beats, not because I was being schticky, but because I was being honest. Most significant, however, was that by the end of the piece, there wasn't a dry eye in the house. Including my own. Peter smiled at me. He didn't need to say anything. He knew it all along. He saw something in me that I was too blind to see in myself: an actor who was more than just the class clown. Like James Michael before him, Peter knew that with a little push, I could be molded into a performer with the ability to tackle more than one thing. He also gave me the confidence to never allow myself to be pigeonholed, which is why today I have done everything from *The Book of Mormon*, an R-rated musical about religion, to *Murder on the Orient Express*, a dramatic Agatha Christie adaptation, to *Frozen*, an animated fairy tale in which I play a talking snowman.

My sophomore year of high school was an explosion of dramatic growth for me. Not only was I suddenly winning or placing in every major national forensics tournament, but with my newfound confidence in drama, Pesola had decided to roll the dice and cast me as the lead, Tevye, in the 1997 school production of *Fiddler on the Roof*. This proved to be both a blessing and a curse. For starters, the juniors and seniors were not particularly ecstatic that the lead role in one of their final shows was going to be played by a sixteen-year-old with barely enough facial hair to pass for a teen, let alone a father of five. Secondly, Pesola was quite eager to remind me of my place, causing us to get into such loud and intense shouting matches that other kids would essentially hide or cry. Fun fact: this was the only time in my entire youth that I ever said "FUCK YOU" to a certified teacher. Brent was trying to remind me he was boss and I was trying to remind him I was still just a kid and the pressure he was putting on me was oftentimes too much. These tussles, while fairly traumatic, would also have a positive effect on me in strange and unexpected ways. For starters, throughout my entire career, I would have to find ways to cope with directors and talent who were anything but generous or sweet. Pesola in many ways hardened and prepared me for the dog-eat-dog worlds of Broadway and Hollywood.

As for *Fiddler*, despite our screaming matches, the show was a smash hit and I was suddenly a local star at our high school (which is really not saying much, considering our high school only had around 398 students in it). In June of that same year, I competed at the National Speech and Debate Tournament in Minneapolis, Minnesota, going up against thousands of students from around the country. After six primary rounds, two octofinals, two quarterfinals, and one semifinal, I somehow found myself in the final seven, competing for the national championship. Performing in an auditorium with close to two thousand people in it, I was beside myself with gratitude and joy. Here I was, a sophomore, going up against all seniors and juniors who were far more experienced than me. At the award ceremony I waited for my name to be called. I was fairly certain I would do better than seventh, but anything more would be icing on the cake. I came in third. I was in shock. Somehow, I had changed my entire category and was now the third-best Dramatic Interper in the nation. The actor who took first place was a brilliant performer named Michael Benjamin Washington, who would later come to fame in shows like *30 Rock* and *Unbreakable Kimmy Schmidt*. After the ceremony he walked up to me and said, "You're next."

I was ready to take the mantle. But, now that I had proven I could break away from what was typically expected of me and succeed at the highest of levels, I wanted to try my hand at a new challenge.

One of the great opportunities of the national championship competition is that students get to celebrate all the final rounds of each major category in a one-day period in a giant auditorium. After I had finished my final round, I decided to sit through the final category of the day, perhaps the most prestigious of the speech events, Original Oratory. I had very little knowledge of OO, as it is called. All I knew is that students had to write a ten-minute speech on a topic of their choosing and then persuade you based on their opening thesis statement. Topics could range from the national opioid epidemic and how to stem the tide of international drug flow to something as simple as why pets make us happy. The structure of the speech could vary but had to generally resemble some form of the typical persuasive-writing outline: introduction, thesis statement, body, transitions, and conclusion, or a call to action. As for performance, the speaker can transition by moving a foot or two to the left or right and is allowed to use various hand gestures to make points. Anything beyond that was not within the confines of accepted rules and regulations. Finally, the speaker would be judged on several criteria, including content, delivery, organization, and overall effectiveness in persuading the audience.

As I sat and watched my first-ever round of Original Oratory, I was floored by the power of the written word married to the power of voice and persuasion. There was no doubt about it: this was going to be my next category.

When I returned to FFI that summer, everyone was baffled. Why would I, a student who was now gaining acclaim in Interp, suddenly switch over to Oratory, a category mostly reserved for brainiacs and non-actors, like future president Barack Obama and vice president Kamala Harris, as well as many senators, television hosts, and Supreme Court justices? Granted, there were exceptions like former national champion Shelley Long and my future *Marshall* costar, the brilliant Chadwick Boseman, who placed eighth in OO at the 1995 national tournament, but they were few and far between. I was determined, however, and nothing was going to stop me. I recruited the help of a legendary coach named Bob Marks and my ferociously smart and terrifying sophomore English teacher, Linda Winrow. The three of us sat down and they started asking me questions about the kind of speech I wanted to write. I didn't hesitate: "I want to do a speech about the therapeutic nature of laughter." Just as I had called upon my emotional experiences in DI, I was now prepared to reflect on how humor had been weaponized in childhood to combat the sadness and pain of my own household. It was personal, it was familiar, and, most importantly, it was wholly me.

My first draft was all anecdotes. Bob and Linda took one look at it and said, "This is all useless. Where are the citations? Where is the proof of what you're saying? You can't just prove your point with anecdotes and funny quips. Get back to the basics. You have to do research."

"Research? What am I, a doctor?"

Suddenly, I was back to square one. Just as I had immersed myself in the biography and psychology of Marty the summer before, I now had to become an expert on the therapy and health benefits of laughter. I plunged myself into books. I spent hours scrolling though microfiche and doing searches on rudimentary mid-nineties web engines. Once I had my research, I suddenly had the power to do the previously unthinkable: prove my point with more than just bullshit. I sat with Bob and Linda and mapped out the foundation of the speech. Now that I had meat on the bones and a clear sense of structure, it was finally time to do what I was most excited to do—make it my own. I sat at the computer for hours on end, trying to come up with the funniest way in and out of every moment and making sure that if I was going to prove that comedy is indeed a great elixir, by God, I better be funny in the process. Finally, with the speech ready to go, I had only one thing left to do . . . give it a name. There was only ever one option and when I wrote it down, I knew it was just right: "Punchline." Along with "Punchline," I was also going to do another DI, this one based on the life of Groucho Marx, from *Groucho: A Life in Revue*, by Arthur Marx and Robert Fisher. I was so excited. I had a killer DI and a killer OO.

Except everywhere I went, my Oratory did middling at best, terrible at worst. Nobody could buy me doing an Oratory. The DI, on the other hand, was unstoppable. I won tournament after tournament, including first place at the Harvard, Emory, and Florida State tournaments, but if there is one thing that is certain about forensics, it's that nothing is certain.

In order to get to nationals, one has to first break out of their local district. While local districts aren't politically gerrymandered, they might as well be, as results favor not those who have the best chance at nationals, but those who have brought the most mommy judges to a tournament. "Mommy judging" is a term affectionately used to describe first-time judges who are being dragged by their son or daughter to a tournament in which they have no idea what they are doing and who tend to penalize competitors going up against kids from their own school. A mommy or daddy judge is also very frequently uninterested in content, choosing naps over watching performances (something technically not allowed) and generally moved more by broad and overwrought than subtle and nuanced. In South Florida, there was another fun factor involved: the lack of English-speaking judges. Suffice it to say, it shouldn't have been the shock that it was that the previous year's highest-decorated competitor from the district (me) did not qualify out of the same district with a piece that had won the same state's championship tournament mere weeks before.

Suddenly, I went from hero to zero. I may not have qualified with my DI, but I had managed to somehow squeak out of the district with my OO, a piece that had not done much for me all season long. Pesola, who had decided that I had no chance to final outside of DI, decided not to accompany me to St. Louis for the 1998 national tournament. Pesola was also pissed at me for quitting my junior-year show, *Pippin*, which for the record I turned down because I had an ego as big as my waistline and was bummed that I was relegated to the fifth or sixth lead after playing Tevye. Another fun fact: the title role of *Pippin* was played by none other than my best friend, Seth Gabel! As for nationals, I was fully on my own. Since nobody else from my school had qualified that year, I would have to bring my own chaperones: my mom and my amazing stepdad, Stan, who came into my life when I was eleven, turning my whole world upside down by introducing me to everything from fishing to the joys of cheeseburgers. He also provided me with something I had previously been desperately missing: a decent adult male role model.

Despite my enormous success the previous year with my DI, in the world of OO I was considered an imposter by other competitors and their coaches, and nobody was giving me a chance to go very far. I was also entering the tournament with my own level of neuroses because it was my secondary category all year to DI and now it was the only opportunity I had left; an opportunity my own coach didn't regard with much optimism. Regardless, I was determined to have the time of my life with my parents. I would finish competing by late afternoon and we'd go check out the zoo, which had a completely hairless chimp that ate his own shit in front of us (it turns out small, run-down, indoor habitats for primates may not be the healthiest environment for these incredible animals). On another day, we hit the world-famous Gateway Arch. I was determined to have a blast no matter what.

On the third day of competition, I was at the hotel taking a quick nap in between the end of the regular rounds and the first-break round, where they announce which competitors have broken into the top forty. The phone in the hotel room startled me awake. My mom picked up and looked incredibly confused. She hung up and said, "Get ready quickly. Something's happened and we need to go back to the tournament."

When we got to the school where the rounds were taking place, the head of the tournament walked out of the tabulation room and said to me, "We are about to announce the top forty. Unfortunately, you did not make it." I didn't understand. They had made me come back to tell me in person I didn't make it? He continued, "There is, however, a performer who is under investigation for plagiarism and on the off chance he is disqualified, you would be next up." So, essentially, I was now out of the tournament, and if I was even able (by some miracle) to get back in, I would be fighting for my life with the knowledge that I was dead last in the standings.

Great odds!

Just for some context, in those days, with very little online resources and databases, it was almost impossible to prove that any performer had plagiarized a speech. The only way to do it would be to have video evidence or a person with firsthand knowledge of said material. By some miracle, that very person walked by the tabulation room just in time. Julie Shein-man, a renowned forensics coach from Stuyvesant High School (and coach to soon-to-be-famous Billy Eichner) known for her no-bullshit-all-business attitude and near-photographic memory, had not only remembered the original speech this competitor had plagiarized but remembered the name of the person who originally gave the speech and the year it was performed. Since my coach wasn't there to launch a formal protest, Julie miraculously and graciously took me under her wing and went to bat for me in a way that changed the course of events at that tournament.

Suddenly, I was back in the game, albeit dead last, a fact only I knew (as competitors are not told placement until final tabulations at the end of the tournament). Whereas some might take the knowledge of being in last place as a fait accompli and a giant burden that was impossible to overcome, I saw it as a huge opportunity. I now had literally *nothing* to lose. Like the world's most famous Jewish speaker—Jesus—I was back from the dead! The fear that I had had going into every prelimi-nary round was now gone. I was playing on borrowed time and I was determined to enjoy every last second. What I did not expect, however, was to get to the quarterfinal rounds, or top twenty-four, so when they posted the names and I was on the list, I thought there must have been a typo. When I was assured that my name was indeed correctly listed on the roster, I was elated. Once again, I entered the room and gave it my all, holding nothing back.

On Thursday afternoon, the penultimate day of the tournament, the list of the top twelve was put up on the wall. I don't know that I've ever been more shocked to see my name in print as I was when I realized that I had somehow made the semifinals in a category that nobody, including myself, had given me a shot in. I truly didn't care what happened next. I had accomplished the impossible and had proven to myself that anything is attainable when you put your mind to it. Word was suddenly traveling very fast and I received a phone call from my coach, Pesola, telling me he always knew I could do it and was in the process of booking a flight to come and prep me for the final round, a very presumptuous statement given that this was the same man who had originally written me off.

I walked into the semifinals and every competitor was congratulating one another and high-fiving each other. I, on the other hand, was being completely ignored. The expectation was abundantly clear to me. In their minds, I had no chance of making it to the final rounds. I was an intruder. An inconvenience. A quick detour on their way to glory. I suddenly went from humble and grateful to vengeful and determined. I was not only going to make the final round . . . I was going to win the whole fucking thing. As I came to the front to perform, I could see their side-glances and smirks, but by the end of the round, I could see their shock and dismay. I came, I saw, I conquered. This time, when the highly anticipated posting for the final round was put up, I wasn't hoping and praying, I was expecting. Much to everyone's shock, except my own, I was in the top seven.

I celebrated briefly, went back to the hotel, and started prepping like a boxer getting ready for a marquee fight. I opened the speech back up and started to add new elements, making it funnier and sharper. I had Pesola, who arrived an hour after I got into finals, get me into the giant auditorium that night and help me walk the stage, getting comfortable with how I was going to play the massive space the next day. I was up bright and early the next morning, once again making last-minute changes and additions, laser focused on my task.

All seven finalists were placed backstage. Once again, each of them congratulated each other and shared pleasantries, leaving me completely out of the mix. As before, I clocked the disregard for my presence and vowed to use that slight to propel me to do the best job I could possibly do when I took that stage.

The speech, which you can watch online, brought the audience to its feet. From the moment I walked onstage and described an anecdote about being bullied by a very oversized girl on the playground as a child, they were eating out of the palm of my hand. The same things I had been told again and again would make me fail at OO in actuality made me soar. The audience had never seen something so unorthodox in the category. I wasn't there to play things safe; I was there to entertain and make a point in the process. The same speech that had struggled to work in the small stuffy rooms at the beginning of the tournament was now bringing down the house. The speech had been built for this moment. It was designed for a large group of people who could allow each other to laugh and go along for the ride. In fact, the audience was laughing so hard, I had to take long pauses so they could hear my next line, a danger to me because of the designated rule of not going over ten minutes, but one that couldn't be avoided because they—and I—were having so much fun. As I came to the final paragraph, everyone was listening in rapt attention:

> British novelist J. B. Priestley once stated, "Humor we may say is society protecting itself with a smile." Now I know what you're all thinking. "What does all this mean for me and my personal encounters with the BWOC?" Big Woman on Campus. Well I may still face bullies on occasion, but now I have two choices. Either to again deliver a scathing and demeaning punch line, or to face them, and to perhaps use humor to help them truly see themselves, identify their own insecurities, and maybe to laugh for the right reasons. And just remember, when using humor, it really doesn't matter what you say, or even how you say it, but what you mean by it. So, in the words of Charlie Chaplin . . .

And after a long pause, I silently walked off the stage as the audience leapt to their feet. That brilliant joke, pitched to me right before finals by my friend Brad Hornstein, was the perfect ending to a magical fairy-tale moment. I had performed a speech I had written on the biggest stage of my life and it had left the audience screaming like they were watching Daniel LaRusso come back from getting his leg swept out from under him by a bleached-blond asshole from Reseda. When the award ceremony happened that night, I left my body as they announced names other than my own from sixth to second place. I had somehow gone from out of the tournament, to dead last, to national champion. Just like my teachers in elementary school doubting I could accomplish anything academically in my life, I had once again overcome expectations and preconceived notions and achieved the highest distinction possible. A theme in my life that continues to present itself is the idea of making adversity a friend instead of an enemy. That lesson has served me well again and again and in many ways that journey began with the national championship I won in 1998.

The following year, I decided I just wanted to have the time of my life and go out doing everything my way. Man, did that pay off. Everywhere I went that season, I won, not because I was competing to be the best, but because I was being true to myself and taking everyone along

for the ride. I decided I didn't care as much about winning as breaking the mold. For my HI, instead of taking a traditional comedic piece of material, I reinterpreted *The Wizard of Oz*, playing every single character as an unhinged counterpoint to a terrified Dorothy Gale (including a psychotic Jack Nicholson as the Scarecrow). For my Duo with my best friend, Seth, we decided to forgo the standard fare that everyone else was doing and instead take an idea our other close friend David Lang had pitched us as a joke: a two-man performance of the Monica Lewinsky/Linda Tripp tapes that had just been released publicly. And finally, for my follow-up OO, I did a piece that I wrote called "Hoo Ha," borrowing from the Al Pacino catchphrase in the hit film *Scent of a Woman*. The piece was all about taking risks in life and not following the given or expected path.

In many ways, it has been the thesis statement that has guided me through decisions big and small. All three pieces were considered clinically insane by everyone around me, but I knew in my heart that as long as I was having fun, nothing else mattered. That June of 1999, in Phoenix, Arizona, I won two more national championships in Humorous Interpretation and Original Oratory, adding to my previous championship, and a third-place finish in DI. As of this writing, I am somehow the most decorated speech competitor in the country, a stat that still humbles me to my core and boggles the mind.

While those three national championships and numerous pieces of hardware are a great source of pride to me, the most special thing about my time in forensics is that close to twenty-five years later it still leaves an impression on thousands of students around the country. I am constantly surprised when I'm stopped by a young teen not to discuss my TV, film, or stage work but rather the impact my Oratories and other pieces have had on them as they study my tapes and carve their own paths. Having a legacy dating back to my high school years that continues to impact students to this day is beyond my wildest dreams.

At eighteen, I was on top of the world. I was a big fish in a small pond, conquering everything in front of me. I was class president, a genuine star in my school, headlining shows like *The Crucible* and *Guys and Dolls*. Having broken away from my own insecurities like Marty before me, I now had a beautiful girlfriend named Laura (a junior in my high school) whom I started dating my senior year, I was driving a spiffy silver two-door Honda Civic with manual windows, and, last but not least, I finally had a healthy home life with my mom and Stan giving me the confidence and strength to dream the impossible dreams, with my dad relegated to the position of a stranger whom I now saw less and less. The sky was the limit . . .

How truly and completely unready I was then for the wake-up call my fragile ego was about to get.

3

MAN UP

As a senior in high school fast approaching two hundred pounds, I was quite literally a big fish in a small pond. Metaphorically, I was also a big fish, having stood out in my rather small school for some of my extracurricular successes. I was, after all, the star of the theater department, a triple national champion in forensics, class president, and certain to get into one of my top two colleges: Northwestern or Juilliard—a certainty guaranteed by two of my closest high school companions, Sir Ego and Madame Id. What could possibly go wrong? As it turns out, anyone both stupid and naïve enough to ask that question is on the path to confronting some unfavorable answers.

My first hard dose of reality that year came when I received a very nicely worded, terse letter from my top school choice, Northwestern, informing me that as much as *I* thought I was Northwestern material, they in fact had not come to the same conclusion. Being one of nine students from my class to apply to this iconic Midwestern institution, I sought out my fellow applicants (positive they too had been rejected), to take comfort in that age-old adage: "Misery loves company." Coincidentally, the other eight applicants had *all* received acceptance letters, making it perfectly clear that Northwestern thought that in a field of shiny gold, I was a shit-stained, rusted, corroded piece of oxidized and decaying iron. *Screw them,* I thought to myself, trying desperately to contain my humiliation and shame. *I'll go to Juilliard, a* real *acting institution and home to the greatest American thespians of all time.*

Ah, yes, what could possibly be easier to get into than Northwestern for acting . . . Juilliard, of course, *the young schmuck from the flatlands of Hollywood, Florida, confidently told himself as he ate a leftover piece of a Carvel Fudgie the Whale cake that had been in the freezer three months too long.*

I prepared day and night for my Juilliard audition, choosing for my modern piece a monologue from *Marty,* which had served me so well in my Speech and Debate years, and for my classical piece, a soliloquy from Shakespeare's *Henry VI.* My mother, who accompanied me to New York for the audition, dropped me off at the building across from Lincoln Center and wished me luck. I was escorted to a large room where around eighty young actors, who were also possessed of the belief that they were God's greatest gifts to the world, were eagerly waiting, hoping to become the next students of the so-called Harvard of conservatories. For our first assignment, we were asked to each choose an animal and, over the course of the next five minutes, metamorphize from said animal to a character that retained the qualities of our chosen species. (I assume there are similar assignments when applying to med or business school?)

I soon found myself surrounded by peacocks, elephants, lions, and zebras. I myself chose to embody a gorilla, since it has appendages that resemble my own. Juilliard faculty walked around the room observing our embodiment of these creatures, all last collectively assembled by Noah for his great Ark. I could see my competition bravely committing to such tasks as picking fleas off each other's bodies, gathering water with their sturdy trunks, and craning their elegant giraffe necks to gather leaves with their long tongues. I, on the other hand, was incredibly self-conscious while acting the part of a silverback gorilla scratching his asshole with one finger, as I had keenly observed years back at a zoo. When the teachers had sufficiently observed our abilities to embody residents of the African savanna, we were next escorted to a waiting room where one by one we would perform our modern and classical monologues.

After about an hour, I was brought into a cavernous rehearsal room. At a table sat three professors all dressed in various shades of black, resembling the Nazgûl from *The Lord of the Rings*, but far less approachable. At the helm of these Dark Riders was the acclaimed head of Juilliard, Michael Kahn, who was also the renowned artistic director of the Shakespeare Theatre Company in Washington, DC. Kahn, with his sharp features and well-groomed bald head, immediately asked me to step back as I approached him for a handshake. Apparently, human interaction would not be a part of the curriculum at Juilliard. After a brief and unpleasant series of hellos, Mr. Kahn asked me to do my first piece. I was confident that despite his hard edge and apparent disdain for handshakes, I would certainly win over him and his Death Eaters with my monologue from *Marty*. I took a breath and began my one-minute tour de force performance: tackling the intricacies of this complicated character by showcasing my heightened grasp of text, emotional range, and humor. As I triumphantly brought the piece to an end, I awaited their collective gasps and applause. Perhaps they would even break with tradition and accept me right there in the room—

"Anything else?"

The crispness of Michael Kahn's question paired nicely with the boredom underlying his tone as he asked it. "Unimpressed" is not a strong enough adjective to describe his lackluster expression. He and his colleagues looked at me as if I was a server handing them a plate of uncooked half-eaten carrots after they had ordered a Royal Ratatouille Terrine. Any delusion that they were just playing it cool and not wanting to let on they had actually loved my performance was quickly deflated by one of them yawning and hunching over and another one clearly scribbling doodles on a piece of paper.

I quickly continued on to my classical piece and as my mouth opened, the darndest thing happened . . . I forgot every single word of my Shakespeare monologue. EVERY. SINGLE. WORD. My brain synapses, already under incredible fight-or-flight trauma by the collective ennui of these apathetic Ringwraiths, immediately began replacing the correct Shakespearean words with the words of an eighteen-year-old with no formal classical training. While I do not remember exactly what I said, it would be the equivalent of changing "To be or not to be" to "Maybe I am, maybe I ain't." Perhaps unsurprisingly, improvising Shakespeare in front of the head of one of the most renowned Shakespeare companies in the world is a surefire way to never be invited back to Juilliard. As I finished whatever it was that had shit out of my mouth, I looked at the three dead-eyed ring servants of the Dark Lord Sauron and said, "I will see myself out now." An hour later, my mother lovingly went back to the school to check what I already knew to be certain: I did not get a callback.

A young lady who did get a spot that year was a talented up-and-comer named Jessica Chastain, so in the end, Julliard 1, Gad 0.

I will never forget walking through Central Park the afternoon after my audition, as snow began to fall. I was truly deflated. How could I have been so confident and so sure that I would get into one of these two premier schools and then be so quickly rejected by both? I was a fraud, a nobody. My self-pity was soon broken by the words of a Jewish mother seasoned in the rich tradition of using clichéd idioms to talk sense into her anxious brood: "Sweetie, think of this as a blessing in disguise." I'd like to think at some point Mary turned to Jesus as he was having an off day doing carpentry or miracles and said reassuringly: "Honeybuns, take it with a grain of salt." As a safety measure and because my parents insisted on it, I had applied to a few backup schools, including NYU, Boston University, and

Syracuse. But there was only one other conservatory I really saw myself going to: Carnegie Mellon University School of Drama. I knew very little about CMU. In fact, the only reason I knew about it at all is that an ex-girlfriend who had broken up with me to instead date another friend of mine had gone to a summer program there and had been rejected for early admission, so I applied out of spite, hoping to get in to rub it in her face. Very healthy behavior, I know.

The process of applying to CMU was quite different from the other schools I was applying to. For instance, you could apply to one of three BFA programs as an undergraduate: actor, musical theater performer, or director. What intrigued me was that when applying for director, you still had to audition. On a whim—and off my broken confidence in not getting into my top-tier schools—I decided that I was going to apply as a director instead.

When I arrived for my audition, I was escorted away from the leotard-clad applicants and instead brought to the room with all the kids in tweed coats and ascots. The head of the director program, Greg Lehane, ushered me in and started asking me why I wanted to be a director. "Why be on the ground floor, when you can be the one with the thirty-thousand-foot view?" He looked as confused as I was confident about this statement. He took out his notepad and asked me to do my audition piece. He informed me that it was more a formality than anything else, in order to make sure the directors applying understood what it meant to stand in the shoes of their performers. I told him my piece was from *Marty* and then jumped into it. When I finished, he had a perplexed and bewildered look in his eyes. He said, "Would you mind if I bring someone in to join us?" I shrugged and said, "No, not at all." He then came back with the acting representative for the school, Anthony McKay. Once again, I was asked to perform my piece and once again the two men gave each other that same perplexed look.

Finally, they brought in one more person, Don Wadsworth, who was also there representing the acting department, and once again, I was asked to perform my piece. The three of them huddled and then asked me: "Are you *sure* you want to be a director?" I took a beat and, after some performative consideration, said, "I guess I could be swayed into trying my hand at acting." And that is how I got into one of the top conservatories in the country: by Trojan-horsing my way in as a highly decorated bullshit artist.

One quick addendum: They did also have me audition for the musical theater program but assured me that based on my lackluster singing and dancing skills, I would be better served pursuing a nonmusical path. It is safe to say that as someone who can't read music and can barely dance, I am as baffled as they must be that I have since done three Broadway musicals, two animated musicals, one live-action musical, and one musical television series.

With my school now secure and my ex-girlfriend adequately jealous, all I needed to do was graduate and get a summer job. It turns out both would prove incredibly difficult. For starters, the head of my high school absolutely despised me because of how many days I had missed for Speech and Debate tournaments throughout the year. There maaaay also have been some skipped classes to go to Chili's with my buddy Dave to watch ESPN highlights, but who can say? Whatever the case may be, she was essentially determined to be the Rooney to my Bueller. She finally got her opportunity when I failed my college biology final exam. Now, I had been required to take a makeup exam along with three other students who had also missed the original test date. For the record, all four of us failed that exam, because all four of us were already admitted into college and couldn't have given two shits how RNA functions outside of their nuclei and how methylation could affect gene expression. Furthermore, I'll have you know, of all the failing grades in my class, I had received the highest failing score, so there. But none of that mattered to the principal, who seemed determined to lay the hammer down by ensuring I could not graduate or walk with my class. To add insult to injury, I also wouldn't be allowed to give the commencement speech as class president. Realizing that I had nothing left to lose, I went directly to my college biology teacher,

Doc Schaum, who also happened to be an athletic coach (about as useful to me as college biology). I told him that if he didn't curve my grade, I would get an F in his class and not be allowed to graduate, forcing me to take summer school like some cliché 1980s comedy stock character. Schaum told me he couldn't make any promises but would consider it.

As the final day approached, the principal became more and more delighted that she had outfoxed me. I was done for. I was going to have to enjoy my summer from the confines of a local community school studying a subject I was literally never going to need for the rest of my life, outside of poorly diagnosing myself to staunch my lifelong hypochondria. Then one day toward the end of the school year, I received my final grade for college biology and it was a C minus. The way I celebrated, you would have thought I had been told I was graduating summa cum laude. I immediately sought out Schaum to say thank you, to which he responded, "I did it on one condition . . . that you *never* pursue a career in science for as long as you live." I gave him my solemn pledge. The next time I saw my nemesis in the hall, she looked like a person who has just been told there was a clerical error and that the $1.5 million she had been promised was actually one dollar and fifty cents. I have never been happier to get a C minus in my life.

Looking to make a little cash that summer, I decided to apply for a job at my favorite place on Earth . . . Walt Disney World. I went to the casting headquarters in Orlando, Florida, and filled out an application. They made me watch a video (the extent of which was that a guest is always right and you are always wrong) and take a quick company standardized test (thankfully with no biology questions), presumably to make sure I could do basic arithmetic and understand how to read. I then sat down with the interviewer, who asked me what I was looking to do at the parks. I told her that I would love to either be a Jungle Cruise Skipper or a host on the Great Movie Ride (a now-defunct ride from the glory days of Disney-MGM Studios). She looked me up and down and said, "Well, that won't be possible, but we do have some availability in Custodial or

Concessions." I said, "Well, I'm really better at throwing *out* trash rather than collecting it, and certainly better at *consuming* food rather than selling it, so I'm not sure it would be beneficial to either of us if I took those jobs!"

I laughed into a void of silence.

She looked at me and said she would get back to me if anything opened up. Suffice it to say, for the next twenty-five years apparently nothing ever opened up. But many years later I would tell this story onstage as I received a Disney Legends Award for my service to the company, and Chairman of Disney Experiences Josh D'Amaro immediately sought me out and asked me if he could make it up to me. A few months later, my dear friend from Disney Artist Relations, Tony Shepherd, handed me a Skipper's outfit and a Jungle Cruise boat for the day, finally giving me the opportunity to entertain dozens of unsuspecting guests, while also proving once and for all that Disney really does make dreams come true . . . eventually.

Seeing as the summer of '99 was not going to be spent working at Disney World, I instead decided to make some cash coaching Speech and Debate students and working for our family friend Jason Brown as an advertising consultant. I was promptly let go about two weeks into the job when the best copy I could come up with for a client named Tell-a-Mattress was: "Not getting enough sleep, tossing and turning all night, waking up with a sore neck? Don't tell *me*! Tell-a-Mattress." I still think the campaign would have done well, but my days masquerading as Don Draper were too short-lived to ever find out.

Around mid-August of that summer, my parents flew me out to Pittsburgh and, after a few days of IKEA shopping, moved me into my all-boys campus dorm: Hamerschlag Hall. Adding to the quaint German theme was my roommate Fritz, an outrageously tall non-drama major who pretty much never communicated with me unless it was through the moans and groans of his intercourse, three feet from my bed.

CMU is a fairly eclectic campus known for programs such as AI, computer science, and robotics. The drama department is equally renowned but slightly more insulated and separate from the rest of the school. For instance, around the time I was applying, there were two published lists I came across that illustrated this fact in a rather unfortunate manner. One of the articles listed the hottest and ugliest schools in the country, and CMU (unfairly, I might add) was listed as the second-ugliest college in the US, with the drama department specifically excluded. The second list outlined the collective SAT averages of the best schools in the nation, of which Carnegie was included, but the article explicitly went out of its way to state *in bold* that drama department majors were not included in the scoring (for the best, I might add). Anecdotally, there was one student in my class who had scored under 700 on the SATs, which I didn't think was remotely possible considering you receive 400 for just spelling your name correctly. Suffice it to say, our drama program was truly in its own bubble on the campus of Carnegie Mellon, which made sense given its conservatory status. For those who don't know, a conservatory is truly a fully immersive dramatic education where you are not required to take many academic classes, if any at all. A class day might look something like this:

8:00 AM—ACTING

10:00 AM—VOICE

11:00 AM—SPEECH

12:00 PM—LUNCH

1:00 PM—DRAMATURGY

2:00 PM—MOVEMENT

3:00 PM—ELECTIVE

Academically speaking, it's basically the collegiate equivalent to pre-school. That is not to say it was easy. At the time of my attendance, each class admitted only around twenty-five students or fewer, and of those, a few would ultimately be cut. The cut system, as it was called (which to my knowledge has since been excised), would ensure that only the cream of the crop survived the impossibly difficult four-year program. Actors who weren't growing could be cut for any subjective reason whatsoever, while others might be told to take a one-year hiatus and come back when they had grown more. It was not unusual to lose up to five of your class-mates every year (kind of like the military but with less combat and more Mamet). It was truly survival of the fittest, and whether you made it to the end or not basically depended on how much you were willing to give your all to your craft and how much the faculty thought of you as a performer. As the then head of the drama department Peter Frisch stated at our orientation: "You are the only students on this campus who aren't separated from their work by a pencil or computer. Your body and voice will be what you are graded on."

Who knew that grading could be so *de*grading?

Like quite a few CMU drama classes before and after us, the class of '03 was a future who's who of New York and Hollywood notables. Some of my classmates included a young nebbish boy from Southern California with a very rich singing voice named Josh Groban, a ferociously talented and fiercely confident kid from Philly named Leslie Odom Jr., and a fair-skinned Irish boy from Cleveland named Rory O'Malley. Other notables included Katy Mixon, who would go on to star in *Mike & Molly* and *American House-wife*, and Griffin Matthews of *The Flight Attendant* and *She-Hulk* fame. Our senior class ('00) was even crazier. My big brothers were Matt Bomer and Joe Manganiello (basically half the cast of *Magic Mike*), for God's sake. Suffice it to say, talent was not in short supply at Carnegie Mellon.

The faculty was essentially like the Hogwarts faculty, if the Hogwarts faculty lacked any magic skills whatsoever. Our teachers weren't so much professors as they were institutions. Many of them had already been there for years before we arrived and had taught iconic students like Blair Under-wood, Ethan Hawke, Patrick Wilson, Zachary Quinto, and Gabriel Macht. Still others had attended the school years before that, opposite other famed alums like Judith Light, Ted Danson, Albert Brooks, and Holly Hunter (who was almost cut because of her now-iconic lisp). The school exuded history and legacy, and everywhere you went there were reminders that you were following in the footsteps of greats. In case you *weren't* aware, however, the faculty was always there to remind you of your place and how tenuous it was.

Our education in the arts was anything but normal. One incident oc-curred on day one of freshman year. The teacher asked each of us to walk back and forth. One by one, we paraded by in unbreathable black leotards as the professor studied our gaits. When the time came for Rory O'Malley to walk, the teacher abruptly stopped him, paused, took a dramatic breath, and then casually told this shy and eager-to-please eighteen-year-old on his first day of school: "Very interesting . . . the way you walk . . . that's how I identified my rapist." Rory's face turned a mix of red and purple, his visible embarrassment competing desperately with his desire to not let out anything resembling a shocked and audible response. Another day on our first week involved two young actors walking through a door and starting an improv scene together. Barely twenty seconds into their ad-libs our acting professor yelled at the top of his lungs, "DO YOU WANT TO FUCK HER OR KILL HER? KILL HER OR FUCK HER?! MAKE UP YOUR GODDAMN MIND!" Yet another teacher, unhappy at a student's emotional connection to a scene, challenged her to "use her cunt" to guide her choices. And that was all WEEK ONE!

Life at CMU was a mixture of joy, anger, frustration, indoctrination, laughter, tears, growth, and sexual awakening. So . . . basically college. The teachers were outrageously opaque in how they graded us. They would also often pit us against each other, hoping to see us channel that anger and rage in our work. We would spend hours and hours breaking down texts, analyzing scripts, and then applying various acting methods to ap-proach our characters. I often found the analytical nature of the work at odds with my more gut-oriented approach to acting. I didn't necessarily gravitate toward breaking down scripts like they were math assignments, but I eventually understood the benefits, especially when approaching denser or more classical material. Some students, however, broke under the system and ultimately lost the very thing that got them into the school in the first place . . . their instinct. The philosophy of these types of schools is to essentially break the actor down and then rebuild them from scratch, destroying their bad habits in the process.

Just like chemo, however, when you destroy bad cells, you also inevitably destroy good ones as well. I cannot begin to tell you how many of my colleagues I watched get worse in college because they no longer were able to approach their work viscerally, but rather forced to tackle everything from an intellectual methodology. Acting, in my humble opinion, is not a one-size-fits-all method. There was one actor in particular who was a year older than me who I really thought was going to be the next De Niro. Eventually, he graduated and left acting altogether for a real-estate career. I always think back and wonder what might have been had he never gone to the conservatory in the first place.

The weight of the program started to make me consider an equally large and more personal weight. See, I had always been uncomfortable and ashamed of my overweight body. Drama school only added to that unease, so I decided during my freshman year to walk everywhere, work out every day, and eat pretty much only protein. I would walk a mile home from school, scarf down tuna and whole jalapeño peppers, and then walk back another mile to campus to lift weights. Over the course of my first summer home from college, I swam every day for hours on end. By the time I returned to school for my sophomore year, I had lost a hundred pounds, dyed

my hair Eminem blond, and decided to fuck my way through the entire drama school, as you do.

Shedding that skin, however, caused me a great deal of dissociation and unease. I didn't understand how to live in this new body. It almost felt like I was a different person. For so much of my childhood, all I knew was being overweight. I quite literally consumed my sadness and never stopped consuming it after my parents had separated. Now I suddenly found myself walking around in clothes that actually fit and getting looks not because I was heavy, but because people suddenly found me attractive, something I couldn't wrap my head around. I also coincidentally started to get more attention from my teachers who claimed they wanted different body types represented in the program, but sure showed me a lot more support and attention once I looked like everyone else.

Meanwhile, drama school was a Dionysian master class in bacchanalia. We would experiment on our craft by day, and then experiment on each other by night, often to the point of caricature. On one particular night, my friends and I had a party in our three-floor building, during which I managed to drink half a bottle of tequila, piss myself in my jeans, take a thirty-minute nap, clean myself up, fool around with one girl on the third floor, fool around with another girl on the first floor, and sleep with yet another girl on the second floor, during which her boyfriend (who I was incorrectly assured she had broken up with) walked in on us. For the record, I didn't get this much action because I was cool or hot. Rather, it was because I was one of the few heterosexual men in a sea of raging female hormones. But all of this seemingly innocuous and silly partying spoke to a much larger issue: instead of being addicted to food, I was now addicted to sex and alcohol. I had essentially replaced one approach to not dealing directly with my issues with a whole different approach of not dealing directly with my issues. Whatever I lacked in emotional intelligence, however, I more than made up for with my commitment to my craft. I not only immersed myself further and further into my work as an actor but also started to explore my efforts as a budding playwright. While I had dabbled in writing in Speech and Debate, I had never really explored the form beyond that.

One day during my sophomore year, however, I sat down at my computer and came across my *Wizard of Oz* Humorous Interpretation script, which had been composed from the 1939 classic MGM musical. As I stared at the screen, I started to write new characters built around the characters I had previously established for my forensics piece. Suddenly, there was an entire new narrative involving a detective, a fisherman, and others all interested in this story about a girl who disappeared in Oz and the aftermath of her absence and subsequent reappearance. The play was called *The Wizard of Oz: A One-Man Show with Other People.* At the end of the school year, I convinced my teachers to let me borrow the brand-new main stage and allow me to use its sets and lighting to put up this one-night-only spectacular. They were very hesitant but eventually gave in. A few weeks before the school year ended, my cast of twenty and I mounted this new musical with original songs by my brilliant musical collaborator Jonathan Putterman and my equally brilliant choreographer Will Taylor.

The show, which I had done as a fun side hobby because only juniors and seniors could be in mainstage plays, brought the house down. It was so antithetical to the kind of stuffy and avant-garde plays the student body was used to and instead was a celebration of insanity and lunacy gone wild. In attendance that night was famed composer/lyricist Stephen Schwartz, who was in town for the revival of his musical *The Baker's Wife,* which coincidentally was the same show whose sets we were now using for our production. Stephen was effusive and overly generous with his praise. I could not believe that the man behind such iconic musicals like *Godspell* and *Pippin* and Academy Award–winning films like *Pocahontas* and *The Hunchback of Notre Dame* was now telling me how blown away he was by my work. It was one of the first of many out-of-body experiences I would have in this career. He gave me his card and told me to be in touch. He then turned around and said, "Come to think of it, I should also tell you . . . I'm also working on a little something with the *Wizard of Oz* characters that I think you might enjoy!" Two years later, I got to see his little project at the Gershwin Theatre and while I know *Wicked* is based on a preexisting book, a delusional part of me would really like to believe I had some tiny part in inspiring one of the most enduring pieces of musical theater of all time.

I did not, *the author firmly reminds himself as he pours another scotch.*

Along with *The Wizard of Oz: A One-Man Show with Other People*, I would write two other insane original comedy musicals during my time at CMU: *Belle Reve Come and Gone*, an unauthorized sequel to *A Streetcar Named Desire*, and *Axis of E*, a giant political musical comedy featuring a singing George W. Bush and his pet clown.

From a creative standpoint, I was continuing to flourish and grow, but from a personal standpoint, the dam was finally done leaking and rapidly approaching full breach.

In the summer of 2002, about two months before I was to leave for a semester abroad at the National Institute of Dramatic Art (NIDA) in Sydney, Australia, I flew home to South Florida for the summer. My mom and Stan were in the process of selling my childhood home. I was given the opportunity to go room by room and weepily say goodbye to every last inch of it. A few days later, I woke up with shortness of breath and severe chest pains. The shortness of breath soon became a crippling inability to breathe. No matter how hard I tried, I could not inhale deeply enough. I told my parents I thought I was having a heart attack and they rushed me to the hospital. The tests came back negative and they sent me home. Over the next few days and weeks, the symptoms grew worse. I was going from appointment to appointment, doctor to doctor, but nobody could figure out what was going on. One doctor thought I might have MS, while another believed I might have cancer. Further tests disproved both theories, thankfully, but the crippling symptoms just continued to worsen. After a while, I couldn't even leave the house, I was so despondent. Not only was I incapable of catching my breath unless I was asleep, but I was now prone to breaking down into uncontrollable tears suddenly and without warning. Finally, my parents took me to a neurologist who looked me up and down, surveyed my scans and bloodwork, and finally leaned in and said: "Kid, I think you've got anxiety."

I had never heard the word *anxiety* outside of a Woody Allen film. *What kid in their early twenties suffers from anxiety?* I asked myself. There was no way that the severe and traumatic things I was experiencing could be something as simple as anxiety. It all felt far too intense and paralyzing to not be something malignant. He told me sometimes when we go through a period of big change, this kind of thing can suddenly occur. I refused to believe it. Yes, I had changed my entire body, yes, I was saying goodbye to my childhood home (a place associated with so much unsettled pain), yes, I was on the verge of going off to the other side of the world alone for the first time in my life, and yes, I was less than a year from having to be an independent adult, but what could any of that possibly have to do with anxiety?

Having no other answers, he gave me the name of a psychiatrist and I was prescribed an SSRI. Within days I could suddenly think clearly again. It was as if a veil had been lifted and I could suddenly breathe freely. Soon after, I started talk therapy with a brilliant psychologist named Dr. Joan Rosenberg and together we explored the unresolved pain of my early childhood and the uncertainty I was facing as an adult about to enter the real world.

I feel blessed to now be able to talk about this period of my life with clarity and confidence, but I am also very well aware that there are many reading this book right now who are dealing with the stigma of anxiety and/or depression and are afraid to either admit they have it or afraid to confront it with traditional medicine and therapy.

Know this: there is nothing wrong with you if you suffer from these very real and very crippling disorders. Also know, you are not alone. There are in fact millions and millions of people out there dealing with the same exact thing right now and every single one of them is no different than a person who is fighting heart disease, glaucoma, or an iron deficiency. You are not responsible for this condition. It is a product of chemical actors outside of your control and while there are certain things that can exacerbate and trigger further anxiety and depression, it is *never your fault*. I wish someone had told me that twenty-some years ago as I lay in bed scared and ashamed of the agoraphobe I had become; terrified that I would never again be able to function in society. So, let me be that person for you. Let me hold your hand right now and tell you there is light at the end of the tunnel and hope at the end of this journey.

With the tools now in hand to conquer my anxiety, including continued therapy with Joan, I was able to confidently fly off to Sydney for my semester abroad. Here I would attend the same conservatory that had produced Cate Blanchett, Hugh Jackman, Mel Gibson, and AMC Theatres spokesperson Nicole Kidman. I was fascinated by the Aussies and curious to understand how these folks from a reformed penal colony were now the most sought-after actors in the world. Whereas American drama schools prioritized a cerebral approach to acting, Australia seemed to approach it in a more primal way. At NIDA, I was able to marry the heady work I had learned at CMU to the more instinctive approach the Aussies took. In fact, by being away from CMU, I was finally able to understand the incredible foundation it had given me. I was also suddenly able to explore the world as an adult for the first time. While I had visited other continents like South America and Africa as a child, I had always gone under adult supervision. Here I was, suddenly a young man on my own, and I was intent on embracing the moment. Every weekend and holiday I went somewhere new: the Great Barrier Reef, the Whitsundays, Darwin, the Blue Mountains. I was adamant that I leave no stone unturned now that I was on the other side of the world.

With a holiday week approaching that October, one of my CMU classmates who was studying abroad with me discussed taking a vacation together. The two of us looked at various locales and decided that Bali seemed like a fun place to go. We planned out the entire week, booked some hotels and hostels, and created an itinerary for ourselves that included various beaches, temples, and bars, including a kickass party spot called Paddy's. A week before the trip, I'm not sure what came over me, but I told my buddy I no longer wanted to go to Bali because the itinerary we had carved out seemed so similar to what we had already been doing in Australia and instead thought we should go to New Zealand, which would involve more interesting sightseeing and less partying. He reluctantly agreed and we set off for Christchurch. Shortly after we arrived, we turned on the news and saw a breaking report that a massive suicide bombing had occurred at a bar in Bali, killing over two hundred people. My jaw hit the floor when I saw the name of the location: Paddy's. I often think about how fortunate I was and how all those victims were just like me—innocent kids looking to have a fun night on the town. There have been quite a few of those moments in my life where I was in the right place at the right time, and whether it was dumb luck or divine intervention, I count myself blessed to have avoided a very different and much less fortunate fate. I have never been a religious person, but I am a spiritual one and I do believe that there are simply things that have happened in my life that I may not be able to explain but would consider myself equally unqualified to write off. I park my spiritual car somewhere at the intersection of faith and science, with neither one being wrong nor right . . . but simply possible.

While in New Zealand my buddy and I rented an RV and drove the entire South Island. My friend was a New England native and was one of the sweetest guys I knew . . . except for when he drank. When he drank, he would transform into something unrecognizable and someone you really didn't want to be around. I would constantly apologize for him whenever we hit parties together in Sydney, but now, we were on our own in a foreign place. One night, while we were out in the middle of nowhere, he decided to start drinking early. I was not in the mood to watch him transform into Hyde from "Jekyll and" fame, so I distanced myself for the evening. At around 1:00 a.m., I heard a loud, thundering knock at the door. It was my friend, who had returned with a local he had met at our campsite. I opened the door and he pointed at me, laughing, after which he turned to the stranger and said: "This is what a kike looks like." Prior to that moment, I had heard anecdotally about antisemitism but had never encountered it myself. In many ways, I naïvely believed that antisemitism was a thing of the past, relegated to small and distant uneducated parts of society. But here I was with someone I had called my friend, who had openly used such a hateful and derogatory term for his own entertainment. I'm not sure what came over me, but I told his acquaintance to give us a minute. As my classmate stumbled up the RV steps, I grabbed him by the collar, threw him against the wall, and told him to apologize. He turned red and threw a punch, which I somehow dodged, and then I hit him multiple times in the face, knocking him to the ground. I looked at him and said, "If you ever call me a kike again, I will make sure it's the last thing you ever say."

I'm not sure how or why I suddenly became Jewish Batman, but that was the most rageful moment of my life to that point. Never before and never again have I gotten into a fistfight, but the hate I felt that night was all-consuming. It was a rage that had been dormant in my soul. It was a subconscious fight-or-flight response not specific to the moment necessarily, but to the trauma that had befallen generations before me, including my grandparents. This wasn't my fists fighting back . . . this was my DNA fighting back. It may sound crazy, but all these years later, I'm kind of grateful for that moment. It was, after all, the moment I woke up to the unmistakable reality that antisemitism never stops hiding out in the open . . . even if our eyes remain closed to it. The next morning, he woke up sober and uneasy and told me he wanted to leave New Zealand and go home early. I explained to him that as much as I wanted to accommodate him, I was not going to ruin my entire trip because he now wanted to escape the shadow of his own mess. He reluctantly stayed two more days, sharing nothing with me but awkward silence, which in a place as radiant with natural sounds as New Zealand was exactly what the doctor ordered. We got back to Australia and didn't really communicate the rest of our time there. A few weeks later we came back to the US, and we never spoke again.

The remainder of my senior year was a blur: parties, hookups, road trips, and of course mainstage shows (including a production of *The Skin of Our Teeth* in which the set broke during rehearsal, sending the entire cast plummeting twenty feet to the ground and causing the two lead girls to use wheelchairs and crutches for the duration of the run).

The only thing left was to prepare for our showcase—a multiday event held in New York and Los Angeles that allows for top agents, casting directors, and managers to assess new talent and potentially engage with them. Most of the top-tier conservatories offer a showcase, which is in many ways a huge leg up that affords students an opportunity to break through in what might otherwise be a very long and difficult process. Each performer is expected to do a monologue and a two-person scene, while the musical theater students are allowed to sing a song. Much to my teachers' chagrin, I decided to write both my monologue and my scene, which I would perform with a brilliant actor by the name of Ben Pelteson. The monologue was a one-minute variation of my *Wizard of Oz* piece, combined from my forensics version and the CMU play I had staged as a sophomore, while the two-person scene was an original piece in which I played an avant-garde director auditioning a very straitlaced performer as I encouraged him to do crazier and crazier things (meta, I know). The two pieces were a stark contrast to what most of my peers were doing, which were more traditional pieces. The results were mixed. While people laughed their asses off, they didn't quite know what to do with me.

After the showcase, each of us was given a list of people who wanted to meet with us. We also had been asked to set up phone services where other interested parties could call us. The hardest part of these things is to watch some friends get massive responses while others get literally nothing. I was somewhere in the middle. Two of my first meetings were with a lovely agent named Sarah Fargo from Paradigm and a manager from Brillstein-Grey Entertainment named Geoff Cheddy. Both of these representation firms were of great interest and excitement to me because they represented some of my favorite stars of all time. Brillstein housed everyone from Adam Sandler to Brad Pitt and was the former home of the late Chris Farley, while Paradigm (and specifically Sarah Fargo) represented my favorite actor of his generation, Philip Seymour Hoffman. Both meetings went great, but both ended in heartache. While Sarah wanted me, her partners didn't know what to do with me and told her that, respectfully, they didn't think I was a fit for the agency. While over at Brillstein, Geoff and his colleagues didn't really have the time to take on a brand-new talent like myself and told me to come back when I had a little more experience under my belt.

I ultimately ended up at an agency called Don Buchwald and Associates, who was perhaps best known for representing Howard Stern. I had one awesome agent in New York named Hannah Roth and one unhinged lunatic in LA whose name I won't even bother with because he is not worth the effort. Let's just say he is literally every character in *Entourage* rolled into one . . . without any of the talent. With the two of them by my side, it was time to figure out how I was going to break into the biz, as they say.

For some unknown reason, I believed that the best way to parlay my four years at a conservatory studying Shakespeare and Molière was to audition for *Saturday Night Live*. With the help of Hannah, I was told to film and submit a tape. I immediately employed the assistance of my best friend, Seth. Seth had begun dating a beautiful young redhead in college by the name of Bryce Dallas Howard. I initially hated Bryce because I saw her as a threat to my relationship with my buddy. One weekend during my senior year, I visited her and Seth at their small apartment in Chelsea, where they had a cat named Sophia who rubbed her tail in my face every time I attempted to fall asleep and a dog named Charly who ate my toothbrush so aggressively there was literally a trail of blood on the floor where he had

dragged it. On one particular night, we decided to go out on the town. I had gone downstairs without a jacket and quickly realized it was freezing outside. When I rang the bell to come back up, Bryce ran

to the window a few floors above and screamed, "Don't worry, I'll bring something down for you." When she and Seth came out, Bryce handed me her fluffy pink bathrobe. I asked what exactly I was meant to do with it, to which she responded, "Duh . . . use it to keep you warm." For the rest of the night, I wore a fluffy pink bathrobe on multiple subways, at dinner, and inside of a movie theater. And that is how Bryce and I became lifelong friends.

When I told Bryce I wanted to audition for *SNL*, she immediately called her father, a little-known director named Ron Howard, and told him how funny I was and that he should open the video for me. Suddenly, Ron freaking Howard was doing a taped sketch with me that ended with him yelling into the camera: "Live from your VCR, it's Josh Gad!"

I put together a few characters and a few impressions and submitted the tape to Lorne Michaels's right-hand person, Ayala Cohen. After a few weeks, I got a response saying that she wasn't going to bring me in for an audition, but she did give me a few suggestions for the following year. For the next three years, I put together tape after tape, desperate to get an audition for Lorne Michaels and his renowned institution, but every time I would get a rejection. In those same intervening years, I would get a few auditions here and there, including one for a brand-new MTV series that Ashton Kutcher was producing. Ashton and his producing partner had me improv a few scenes in which I would intentionally "punk" unsuspecting people and gaslight them into thinking there was nothing weird about it. While I got pretty far in the process, the job eventually went to a young actor by the name of Bill Hader.

Once in a while, I would book a guest-star spot on a TV series like *ER*, in which I played a medic on a mission abroad. I was so bad that the medical consultant would watch me aggressively pumping the CPR mask on a background artist and yell out to me that I was not helping the dying patient but in fact killing him.

Suffice it to say, my first few years bouncing between Hollywood and New York were incredibly tough. I would do things to keep myself busy, like the Groundlings, a famed comedy-improv program in Los Angeles. The program, famous for launching the careers of many of my idols, explained to me that I wasn't good enough or funny enough to graduate from the second level into the third (years later, coincidentally, they would finally invite me to pay them an exorbitant amount of money to join their level-three training, but I informed them I had to unfortunately turn it down because I had just been offered a spot on *The Daily Show* with Jon Stewart, which, unlike their offer, was going to actually *pay* me to do comedy), or try to put up one-man shows that would ultimately fail to connect and would cost me a fortune in the process. I couldn't even afford my own place. While in New York, I would stay on my buddy's couch in Queens, and then when I was in LA, I would share a large couch at Seth and Bryce's West Hollywood high-rise with two other people: a young actress named Katherine Waterston (daughter to famed actor Sam Waterston) and an interesting recent Yale drama grad who was working as an apprentice to Daniel Day-Lewis by the name of Jeremy Strong. Walking around the city, I would occasionally have an exciting or thrilling moment that would remind me where I was. For instance, one day around 2003, Seth, Bryce, and I walked into a coffee shop called The Coffee Bean on Sunset Boulevard. I immediately spotted Robert Downey Jr., whose performance in *Chaplin* had been one of the most inspirational I had ever seen. Bryce encouraged me to approach him and discuss our mutual admiration for the great Charlie Chaplin. I took a deep breath, tapped him on the shoulder, introduced myself, and for the next five minutes the two of us shared a beautiful and inspiring conversation about our admiration for one of the world's great comedians. I felt so moved. Here I was with an actor who was truly extraordinary, sharing a deep love of our craft on such a personal level. As we approached the cashier, he suddenly turned to me and said: "Hey, I forgot my wallet. Do you mind covering this?"

With no hope on the horizon and mounting debt due to covering coffee bills for famous working actors, I was beginning to rethink my entire career and life. Maybe I wasn't cut out to be an actor after all. Perhaps I should be a lawyer like my two older brothers. The only thing keeping me from spiraling into a deep, dark depression were my friends like Rory. He told me that I needed to pick a city and settle down or I would never feel grounded enough to succeed.

Or my buddy Ben Pelteson, who called me up one day out of the blue and said, "Hey, next time you're in New York, you have to see this off-Broadway show at Second Stage. It's about these kids competing in a spelling bee and I think it may go to Broadway. There is a character in it who steals the show, and I couldn't help but think of you." It was nice to have friends always thinking of me, but it didn't change the fact that I was still desperately alone, not only in my career, but also romantically.

That is until one day, when I received a call that would change my life forever.

INWARD

by Josh Gad's Inner Voice

Look, if it were up to me, you wouldn't be reading this or anything written by Josh. The truth is, I have never been a particular fan of Josh's work, other than occasionally enjoying what he orders off a menu at some higher-end restaurants. Even though Josh *can* write, I'm not quite sure any of us are better off after reading his words. After all, just because a parrot can speak does not mean you would choose to hold conversations about world affairs with it. In my humble opinion, Josh is the parrot of humans: loud and obnoxious and good at tricks. However, whether you or I like or approve of his decision to write this book, Josh's ego (as always) won this particular battle. I hold Simon & Schuster, whomever they both are, directly responsible for forcing all of us to indulge the whims of a forty-three-year-old straight white male who thinks he has earned the right to have a published memoir. As a result of Josh's entry into this once esteemed subcategory of nonfiction, the memoir world has taken a substantial hit, seemingly suggesting, since allowing Josh into its ranks, that anyone with Microsoft Word can now write and get one of these sold.

If you are one of the sad few who have been suckered into purchasing a copy of whatever this is, I truly apologize. A better use of your money might have been on dry cleaning or upgrading your garbage disposal. However, now that you have chosen, unwisely, to add what would have been better served as a tree to your library, might I suggest employing it as kindling for your fireplace or as a way to prop up your computer the next time you are using it to Zoom.

In a world of intellectuals, the mere fact that such a simpleton can get a book deal should terrify us all. As always, the conversation must inevitably revert back to education. If society spent more time teaching the words of Steinbeck, Hemingway, and Tolkien, there would be less impulse buying of books like Gad's, which make Dr. Seuss seem like Tolstoy by comparison. A résumé that features a talking snowman cannot be the benchmark by which we allow "celebrities" to get paid to write books that get sold at airports. We must and can strive higher. Hell, even Timothée Hal Chalamet at twenty-seven years of age is more deserving of a memoir, simply by virtue of his name sounding more like that of an author than "Josh Gad," which sounds like cough tonic.

Our children deserve better than what we are settling for here. I hope that in my lifetime, there are fewer books written by people like Gad and more books written by people who have actually done something with their lives, like cure cancer, fight poverty, or teach apes and elephants to paint. That is a world in which all of us should want to live. For now, however, it appears we must settle for one in which 2015 *Celebrity Jeopardy!* loser Josh Gad is enough.

—Josh Gad's Inner Voice

Note: All opinions above are solely those of author and writer Josh Gad's inner voice and do not reflect Josh Gad or any of the people associated with the publication of this memoir.

BOOK II

Of Growing Men, Mormen, and Snowmen

GADISM

A career is not built in a day, but rather in a string of days one might even call a lifetime. Over the course of that lifetime, a career may take many twists and turns, and ride the ups and downs of successes and failures. A successful career is often defined by a variety of metrics including but not limited to money, output, status, power, fame, return on investment, followers, and reputation. By those metrics, Benito Mussolini and Krusty the Clown have both had successful careers.

Coincidentally, it has never been a successful career that I have ever been interested in chasing. But rather something far more enduring, far more compelling, and far more difficult to achieve:

A legacy.

4

SPELL CHECK

"Hey, Josh! It's Ry. Any chance I could get you to come to LA for two months?"

My friend Ryan Dixon, who had graduated a year before me from the CMU directing program, had recently been hired by a small theater group to put on a show at a small local West Hollywood theater called *The Elephant Asylum*. He was now calling me to see if there was any way I could come out to LA for two months to do a production of *All in the Timing* by David Ives. I explained to Ryan that I was currently living on a small couch in Queens and had no place to stay in LA, because Seth and Bryce's one-bedroom apartment was currently fully occupied. He told me I could live with him and his landlord/roommate, a middle-aged single woman with a house in Burbank who had a spare half bedroom. I figured with nothing else on the horizon acting-wise and an opportunity to live with my buddy and this strange older woman who was weirdly comfortable having two twenty-two-year-old roommates, I had nothing to lose except plane ticket money and my pride, so I booked a flight and went out to LA.

Within the first few days of me being in LA, Ryan had put together a table read to figure out casting decisions. *All in the Timing* is a series of hilarious, existential, and surreal short plays that involve everything from Leon Trotsky getting assassinated with a pickaxe over and over again to a group of chimps named after famous authors who are expected to write *Hamlet*. I forced my best friend Seth to go to the table read with me and the two of us joined a group of people neither of us had ever met before (who were all part of a preexisting acting troupe that had already done a few other shows together). These experiences are always slightly awkward, especially when everyone else already knows each other and you are "the new guy."

One of the actresses in the room was a beautiful young woman with black hair, deep brown eyes, and a killer smile named Ida, pronounced EE-da. She was tasked with playing Mrs. Trotsky to my Leon Trotsky. I quickly threw together a makeshift Russian accent and jumped into the read. She laughed, and any initial attraction I had for her quickly extinguished as she let out a Fran Drescher–caliber cackle. After the read, we had a fairly quick exchange and went our separate ways. Later I would learn that she thought I was both arrogant as hell and gay, apparently because Seth and I talked exclusively to each other all night (which I guess makes people gay?). Nevertheless, as the weeks went on and we were officially cast in the roles of Mr. and Mrs. Trotsky, our casual disregard for each other soon became an intoxicating attraction. Half-Persian and half-Italian, she was unlike anybody I had ever dated before, which I think was part of the allure. She was fiery as all hell and had a wicked sense of humor that was both biting and sharp. She was an East Coast girl, having lived in Washington, DC, for most of her young life after relocating from Iran during the revolution and then Italy a few years later. Every time I was near her, my heart would beat through my chest. She and I were soon flirting nonstop during rehearsals to the point where Ryan would have to interject to keep us on track. But the more time we spent together, the more obvious it became that we had incredible chemistry.

There was only one problem—she had a boyfriend of five years . . . a fact I only learned about while eavesdropping on her and her friends in the alley behind the theater.

AUTHOR'S NOTE: Eavesdropping on someone you have the hots for is not a recommended tactic, for both legal and ethical reasons. I would advise readers to avoid this tactic unless sanctioned by the person in question. The second option, of course, is to put it in writing years later in a nationally published piece of tell-all literature.

Suffice it to say, I was shattered. She was legitimately the first girl I had fallen for in LA and it was just my luck that she had a boyfriend. Sure, I'd had dalliances here and there, but nobody I was serious about. In fact, LA had terrified me relationship-wise because everything about the dating scene in LA just felt bizarre and foreign.

Please allow me one brief tangent now where I take you on a slight detour to illustrate my point:

My first week out of school in Los Angeles, a girl I had casually hooked up with in college invited me to her boyfriend's house for an evening chill. She sent me an address in a hilly and wealthy district of Los Angeles called Mount Olympus, which is such a perfect name for the mythical level of strangeness that awaited me that evening. Back then, there were no real GPS devices, so I had to use this large book of maps called the Thomas Guide *as I made my way through the winding and arboreal terrain of the Hollywood Hills with a giant book of maps in one hand and my rental car steering wheel in the other. When I finally pulled up to the house, nestled high atop this hilltop befitting the gods, I got out of the car and approached an intimidating massive door frame that looked straight out of* Jurassic Park *(this will be ironic in a moment). I rang the bell and a few seconds later my friend, dressed in a bathrobe, answered the door. Before*

I had time to ask why she was in a bathrobe, her boyfriend, the owner of this monstrous house, strolled up beside her in a matching bathrobe.

It was Jeff Goldblum.

I was completely baffled. My friend was casually dating a superstar, which she had neglected to mention on the phone, and for some reason they were both dressed as if welcoming me into a Four Seasons spa instead of their home. I handed them the cheap bottle of wine I had purchased, and they invited me to sit on a short, round, backless seat opposite their two short, round, backless seats as the three of us sat in a triangular formation. We made small talk.

"So . . . uh . . . Josh . . . uh . . . what do you do?"

"Well"—(he hadn't introduced himself to me but should I still call him Jeff, seeing that I and everyone else in the Western world knew his name?)— "I'm an actor."

"Great. What . . . uh, do you . . . do?"

I was beyond confused. I thought the profession had given it away, but I guess he needed further clarity for some reason.

"I act," I answered, not quite knowing a better way to communicate whatever it was he wasn't understanding.

"No," Jeff Goldblum said, "what method do you practice?"

"Oh," I said, looking at my friend for some help but getting a sweet smile and nothing more in return. "Different styles that I learned at school."

He then leaned in and said, "Are you happy?" I said, "Yes." He repeated, "Are you happy?" Once again, unsure if I was on Candid Camera, I looked around the room and repeated "Yes." By the third time the question was posed, I realized that I was being engaged in a Meisner exercise, a method of acting in which you repeat the same phrase over and over again until it becomes fully lived in and believable. Why I was playing it with a robed Jeff Goldblum in his Mount Olympus home on a small, uncomfortable cushion, I had and still have no idea. By the end of the call-and-response, Jeff nodded and told me I had done a good job. I laughed, perplexed by the strange out-of-body experience I had just had, and asked to use the bathroom, where I splashed water on my face to make sure I wasn't dreaming. When I walked out, Jeff offered me an opportunity to audit his acting class. I explained to him that if I had not literally just finished four consecutive years of acting classes, I would absolutely take him up on his offer. I left shortly thereafter, completely mystified but also exhilarated that I had for some unknown reason just done a weird dramatic sparring with one of the greatest to ever do it . . . even if it was simply because he was trying to land a new customer.

I have since seen Jeff Goldblum at various functions and I cannot bring myself to approach him because I wouldn't know what to say and I couldn't act like we've never met before even though there is no way on Earth he would remember me.

So, suffice it to say, the LA social scene can be weeeeeeiiiiird! So, when I finally met this awesome down-to-earth chick, it was like I'd hit the jackpot. Except for that one small stumbling block of her having a boyfriend.

As the rehearsals progressed, it became known to me by other cast members in the show that things were not great between her and her then partner, so I waited in the proverbial and literal wings for my chance to swoop in. By the end of the run, she had officially ended things with her boyfriend and it was off to the races. For the record, her ex was an awesome guy named Adam, who was an actor by day/rapper by night who looked like a young Mark Wahlberg, only better looking, and who would also later attend my wedding, which totally wasn't weird at all for me (he says sarcastically and not at all still bitter at his wife for inviting her insanely sexy ex to our nuptials). Following in the footsteps of other classy timeless romantic dalliances like Romeo and Juliet, Jack and Rose, and Mark Antony and Cleopatra, our first hookup was in a public bathroom at the Universal Hard Rock, with very impatient customers not exactly thrilled that we were using the stalls for extracurricular activities. It was like a pent-up explosion of lust finally allowed to burst wide open. After that evening, she and I would spend every waking hour with each other, going to movies, concerts, dinners, and bars. The only problem was, I didn't have a place and she was in between places, so we would end up crashing with friends.

One brisk Fourth of July evening, she and I went up to Seth and Bryce's apartment rooftop. Seth and Bryce were out of town and we had no way to get into their apartment, so we decided to camp out on the roof. Unfortunately, the temperature dropped by thirty degrees and by the next morning, we were practically frozen as the morning shift finally came up to the roof and kicked us both out.

We were unhoused but in love. Of our many early romantic experiences, perhaps my favorite was the night I decided to rent us a movie that neither of us had ever seen but had both heard so much about. As the two of us cuddled on our friend Rosa's couch, I sat back and hit play. For the next two hours, any romantic expectations were soon squelched by the unexpected traumas of this little movie I had hand-picked called *Deliverance*. For a while, all we would say to each other every time we kissed was "squeal like a pig." Another thing I soon fell in love with was her gullibility. One day I convinced her that there were drive-through mammograms. Another day I had her believing that meteorologists were predicting a massive earthquake by the end of the week. The more insane the statement, the more completely she would fall into my trap. By early 2005, I was certain that I had found not only an amazing girlfriend, but somebody to build a life with. The only

problem was, I had no way to afford that life.

Other than coaching debate students at various schools around the country, I had no consistent source of income. One day I called my agent in LA and told him after a long period of no auditions that I needed to go out for something. Anything. He called me back and said, "Got you." An hour later I got an email that I had an audition for a live *Snow White and the Seven Dwarfs* stage show at Disneyland to play Dopey . . . the only dwarf who doesn't speak. It was not only such a dick move, but a really disheartening one as well. I basically had an agent who thought my career and ambitions were a joke and I was starting to wonder if he was right.

A few months later, I received a tip that the hit Broadway show *The 25th Annual Putnam County Spelling Bee* was holding auditions. By this point, numerous people who had seen it, including my friends Seth and Bryce, were calling me, telling me that I had to audition to play the role of William Barfée, a role made famous by the Tony Award–winning performance of the brilliant Dan Fogler. The show, which featured a group of adult actors portraying ten-year-olds all competing in a local small-town spelling bee, had had a hit run at the Barrington Stage Company, followed by another smash off-Broadway run at Second Stage. Now, almost a year into its run, it was holding auditions and I knew I had to get in on them. Seeing as my agency was useless, I asked my friend Ben if he could reach out to the casting director, who was a friend of his, and get me in the door. Ben, ever the loyal friend, called her up and got her to agree to see me.

The auditions were held at a local church in Hollywood. I sang an original song from a musical called *Fat Camp* I was working on with Bryce, Seth, and their friend Dane. The assistant director and the casting director then had me do a scene and a little choreography. They seemed very pleased and told me they would share my tape with the entire creative team and get back to me. About a week later, I received a phone call that they were going to offer me the role of Barfée . . .

In San Francisco.

On the one hand, I was thrilled that I had booked the role, but on the other, I had had my heart set on doing it on Broadway (an insane wish, considering I had no real professional theater credits to my name and no formal musical theater training either). Everyone I spoke to was thrilled for me but a little voice in the back of my head kept saying, "Aim higher." I was, after all, the same guy who had written that ten-minute speech about taking chances and risking it all in life.

Everyone outside of Ida thought I was crazy, but I had made up my mind: I was going to turn it down, even though I had no other opportunities on the table. "FUCK US? FUCK YOU!" While that wasn't verbatim what was said, it still captures the essence of the production's response. In what shouldn't have come as a shock, the creative team was furious and basically told me they would never see me for anything again. What the hell had I done? I had gone from getting a break to pissing a once-in-a-lifetime opportunity away. What was I supposed to do now? The reality of the situation hit me like a ton of bricks. I was never going to get a chance like this again. After falling into a depression, I decided to reevaluate my life. I was now about three years out of college with nothing on my résumé outside of an episode of *ER*. Who was I fooling? I wasn't cut out for this. My mother had always told me I would be a good lawyer, so that's what I would do. Like both of my older brothers, I would go to law school and get a good-paying job and start a family.

I told Ida about my plan and she was perplexed. "Why are you going to law school?"

"Because I want to take care of you."

She retorted, "I don't need you to take care of me and I certainly don't need you to give up on your dreams to do it."

I was dead set, however. This was my decision, and I was sticking with it. I next called my mom to tell her the good news. If my wife was baffled, my mother's reaction was even more shocking.

"I am truly disappointed in you."

I couldn't believe my ears. What Jewish mother hears their son say, "I want to go to law school," and responds with anything other than a massive celebration involving everyone in a ten-mile radius, including people they don't even know? She continued, "You've spent close to fifteen years dreaming about being an actor and after barely three years of living out that dream, you're just giving it all up?" I heard crying on the other side of the phone. My mother believed so fully in me that she was pleading through tears for me to start believing in myself as much as she did.

I had no response. She was right. What the hell was I doing? There were people who spent their entire lives chasing their dreams through thick and thin and here I was, giving it all up after two and a half years because of a little rejection. Was I not the same person who had just been offered a role in a national tour of a hit musical and turned it down because I believed I was capable of more? The only things standing in the way of my dreams now were me and my own insecurities. I told my mom "Thank you," hung up, and immediately called up my one decent agent in New York City, Hannah Roth, and told her that I wanted another shot at *Spelling Bee*. She told me that they had already cast the San Francisco role, but that Dan Fogler was going to leave the company in a few months and they were looking for replacements. The only problem with that piece of news was that they were absolutely not interested in me because I had already turned down the other opportunity they had presented to me.

"Shit!" What a moron I had been—but I couldn't let that get in my way. I was determined. There was an opportunity here and I had to somehow turn a *no* into a *yes*. Once again, I had my incredible friend Ben reach out to his acquaintance in casting and tell her I would literally do anything for one more chance to show them what I could do. But as expected, he was told there was no real interest after the opportunity I had already squandered.

Still renewed with energy, I told Hannah that I only wanted her repping me from now on and not that schmuck in LA. I immediately started going out for more auditions, including the role of Dwight Schrute in *The Office*, which made a very good impression on renowned casting director Allison Jones, who would later be responsible for a different breakthrough in my career. I didn't book a series regular on any sitcoms, but I did manage to get offered a guest-starring role in a short-lived sitcom (the name of which I and the cast of it sadly can't remember) that was going to bring me to New York. I called up Hannah to strategize and told her to let the folks at *Spelling Bee* know that I was going to be in town and would love the opportunity to come in and audition for them. We heard nothing back.

As the December date for my shoot approached, I received a call that the role I had gotten had been rewritten and they were no longer going to need my services. I was bummed. Figuring I was going to be alone for the holidays, I booked a flight to Florida to spend it with my family. When I landed on the tarmac, I opened my Motorola flip phone and saw that I had a few voicemails. "Josh, it's Hannah. It's urgent, call me." I clicked the next one. "Josh, it's Hannah again. Where are you?" I didn't need to listen to the third message. I knew who it was from. I immediately called her back while we were still taxiing.

"We just got a call from *Spelling Bee*. They are seeing a small group of guys in New York City tomorrow and asked if you are in the city, because if so, you can go to the auditions." I barely let her finish before saying, "Tell them I'm in the city and will be there." I immediately called my mother and Stan and told them I needed a flight out of Fort Lauderdale Airport to JFK as well as a hotel for one night. When I told them what it was for, they sprang to my rescue and booked the first flight out.

I arrived in New York City around midnight and drove in a taxi to the Hilton on 6th Avenue between 53rd and 54th Streets. I unpacked, got some rest, woke up at 6:30 the next morning to warm up, and went to the audition. It was held in a large rehearsal space, and about fifteen slightly overweight men in loose-fitting clothes were going over the lines in the hallway. I was brought into the room to do my song and a scene from the show. I sang my standard "Sit Down, You're Rockin' the Boat" from *Guys and Dolls*. I then did a scene between Barfée and Olive Ostrovsky, a female contestant in the show. The creative team seemed pleased enough and invited me to do the dance audition. Amazing!

It was an unmitigated disaster.

Everyone in the room had training except for me. I flailed around like a beached whale trying unsuccessfully to flop back into the ocean. I knew any chance I had was now over. There was no way they would invite me into the next round, having just seen me dance like a pirate with one leg.

Twenty minutes later they asked me if I could come back in and read for the director.

I was shocked. They were going to give me another chance, even though I had completely botched the dance call? *Okay*, I thought to myself, *don't screw this up*. The director in question was none other than one of the most influential directors/creative minds in theater history: the brilliant and insanely talented James Lapine. Lapine, who had a storied relationship with inarguably the greatest composer in musical theater history, Stephen Sondheim, had written the books for *Sunday in the Park with George*, *Passion*, and *Into the Woods*, all three of which he had also directed. He had also worked with the renowned William Finn, collaborating on the Marvin Trilogy and once again on the Tony-winning *The 25th Annual Putnam County Spelling Bee*.

He was a *legend*. And so, my heart skipped a beat as I entered the room. He was not eager for pleasantries and immediately disposed with the small talk, asking me to sing for him. I sang. He didn't seem very impressed. He asked me if I had anything else and I sang a ballad. Once again, he seemed nonplussed. He then asked me to do the scene, stopping me every few seconds to tell me something I wasn't doing right. He said a few casually cruel things to me and then at the end of the audition gave me a curt thank-you and sent me on my merry way. *Well, opportunity number two was a bust*, I thought to myself. As I walked back to my hotel, head buried in my chest to avoid anyone seeing my disappointment, I received a phone call. I was to be at the Circle in the Square Theatre at 5:00 p.m. for a final callback.

"A final callback?" Once again, I could not believe my ears. Twice today I had thought I had completely shit the bed, and now I was presumably one step away from achieving my dream of being on Broadway. I showed up to the theater, expecting multiple people in the waiting room, but it was only me and one other guy: Jordan Gelber, one of the stars of the new hit musical *Avenue Q*. The two of us made some small talk and Jordan was brought out first. For what felt like twenty of the longest minutes of my life, I listened from backstage as he sang and performed his scene. He finally came backstage and wished me luck.

When I walked out onstage, I saw twenty-plus people (creatives, producers, investors) sitting in the audience staring back at me. My nerves exploded in my chest. The layout of the Circle in the Square for *Spelling Bee* was interesting in that it was a thrust stage (a stage that extends into the auditorium), surrounded on three sides by audiences. The intimate seven-hundred-seat theater is cozy, yet incredibly intimidating because it is still a Broadway theater that has been home to many iconic performers (Dustin Hoffman, Al Pacino, Joanne Woodward, Annette Bening, and George C. Scott, to name a few). The craziest part of this whole experience was I *still* hadn't even seen the production (because I was broke) and was completely in the dark as to what the show and the performance originated by Dan even were. I had never even seen a clip of the show!

I stared out into the crowd. After a silent beat, I said: "I have about ten minutes. What have you all prepared for me today?" After a few laughs and some stern stares, I was told to sing a few bars of my song. Midway through I was stopped by James Lapine and told that Tony Award nominee Celia Keenan-Bolger (for her work as Olive in the show) would be reading opposite me. Celia walked onstage, kindly introduced herself, and the two of us began performing the scene. Midway through the dialogue I was once again stopped suddenly. James called out from the top level of the audience and said, "Can I please see you up here, Mr. Gad?" I was perplexed. I had done a total of about one and a half minutes of auditioning and was now being called up for a personal discussion with the director. When I got up to him, the others in the area dispersed.

IN GAD WE TRUST   87

James looked at me up and down and said: "I don't think you take this seriously."

"Excuse me?"

He continued: "Do you have any idea the kinds of people who would kill to be on Broadway? Julia Roberts is about to make her debut. Why should someone like you, who thinks this is all just a joke, get that opportunity?"

I was shell-shocked. "Someone like me?"

"You," James persisted, "are not a serious actor. This is the biggest moment of your life and you walk onstage and the first thing you do is crack a joke. That is what amateurs do." In that moment I knew that I had two choices. The obvious choice would be to kowtow and plead for forgiveness, hoping that by conceding to these wild accusations I could somehow win him back and beg to be a part of this award-winning production. Then, of course, there was the much riskier second option.

I'm guessing you know which one I chose.

"You can question my talent, you can question my singing, you can certainly question my dancing, and hell, you can even question my acting, but don't you dare question my commitment to my craft. For four years, I spent every last penny I had going to a conservatory to study nothing but acting. I have worked tirelessly to get better every day of my life at what I do. I live, breathe, eat, and sleep acting. This right now is indeed the biggest moment of my life, so forgive me if when I walk out in front of twenty people who are going to decide whether or not I get my big break, I crack a joke to break the ice, seeing as the other option would have been to projectile vomit on you all because of my nerves. I guess I made the wrong choice. Good luck with your show. I wish you the best."

I got up, stormed off, and grabbed my things backstage. I congratulated Jordan on getting the job and walked back to my hotel in tears and rage. I couldn't pack my things fast enough. My mother, of course, called to ask me how it went and it took everything to not let on how heartbroken I was, given her confidence in me. I simply told her I had not gotten the role. As I was heading to the door, bag in hand, I received another call, this time from my agent, Hannah.

"Hey!"

"Hi," I barely got out, "now's not a good time."

"Well," she continued, "James just sent two tickets to your hotel to see *Spelling Bee* this evening."

I couldn't believe the nerve of this guy. "Why on Earth," I hissed through gritted teeth, "would I ever want to see that show?"

"Because," she responded, "he figures you should probably see the show before you take it over in a month."

Everything stopped. Including my heart. "Wait . . . what did you just say?"

Hannah screamed back at me, as if trying to wake me up from a nightmare: "You got the role! You're going to be on Broadway!"

Never in my life had I been so incredibly certain of one result only to receive the complete opposite outcome. For the life of me, I couldn't comprehend how I had gone from practically the single worst audition of my life to the single biggest break I'd ever gotten. It was as if the universe was bored that day and looking for something fun to do. Any uncertainty I had about why James had said and done what he did would soon be answered over the next hellish year of my time in the show, but for now I was in blissful ignorance. I was going to be on Broadway!

That evening, I went to the theater and watched this magical and hilarious show for the first time, studying Dan's every brilliant move. Sitting there that night, I couldn't comprehend that in a few short weeks I was going to be up on that stage playing this iconic role. For the next three weeks, I would rehearse with the assistant director, musical director, and choreographer by day, and watch the show by night. I ate, slept, and breathed *Spelling Bee*. I even went to a school to spend a day with elementary-aged kids, studying their every behavior and gesture, hoping to incorporate them into my performance as a socially awkward ten-year-old master speller who uses his "magic foot" to spell out every letter of the word before he says it out loud.

On Tuesday, January 31, I made my Broadway debut. I was terrified standing at the curtain, waiting for the first chords to start. But as I took that stage for the first time, I became so unbelievably excited and grateful that I was finally being given the chance to do what I lived for and simultaneously get paid for it. Everything went great until toward the end of the show, I literally forgot how to spell my final word and needed the cast to help me improv my way out (much like an actual ten-year-old might). But, otherwise, it was a blast.

The next day, I received a dressing-down from James Lapine, who had notes on what seemed like every single line and every single choice I was making. I figured this was completely normal because I was (A) new to Broadway, and (B) replacing a Tony winner. What I did not anticipate, however, is that this would continue for the next few days, and then weeks, and then months.

During the course of my run, nothing I did would please Lapine. Even if I was doing what he asked me to do. The joy I initially had coming into work was soon replaced by fear. I was terrified that on any given night James would be in the audience, waiting with bated breath to tear me apart once again. The cast was also not particularly supportive. Apart from a small few, most of them seemed like they were annoyed by my mere presence. It's funny now because today I consider them all close friends, especially Jesse Tyler Ferguson, but back then I think they didn't quite know how to deal with one of their own leaving and a random new guy coming in to join their

long-running party. I can't really blame them, even though at the time I felt so alone and depressed. Dan was the first of "the kids" to depart and my suspicion is the others felt both abandoned and slightly jealous that one of

their own was now moving on to Hollywood while all of them were stuck with this random new guy. In the subsequent years, the cast has not only apologized to me, but has truly gone out of their way to tell me that it was completely shitty and uncalled for the way I was treated during that period.

Unfortunately, the feeling I had at the time was that of being an imposter. What should have been such a joyous moment in my life was just the opposite: toxic and brutal. Every day, I wasn't allowed to be funny or make spontaneous new choices—I had to make every single decision based on what I thought James would want, which isn't a recipe for success. As the show progressed, James became more hostile and more disparaging. Often, James would call a rehearsal and spend the entire time belittling me in front of the rest of the cast. By the six-month mark, I wanted out, but they had an option to extend me and unfortunately chose to do just that. I begged the producer, David Stone, to let me go for my own mental health, but he told me that it wasn't an option. He did agree, however, to let me audition for film and TV and offered to give me an out if I booked one of those gigs.

One of the first things I went out for was a new James Cameron movie called *Avatar*, to play the role of Jake Sully's best friend and translator to the alien race known as the Na'vi. I put myself on tape and shortly thereafter got a call that Cameron wanted to fly me to Los Angeles for a final callback at his Lightstorm production offices (a role I apparently did not get because, while James Cameron was said to be thrilled with my audition, when I was turned into a digital Avatar I supposedly looked like a tall, overweight Smurf). A few days before I was to leave for LA, we all went out to The Palm Restaurant near our theater to celebrate Celia's last show. James pulled up a seat next to me and told me that he heard I was going to miss a show to audition for the movie. I thanked him for letting me out for a day. He responded that he had told the producers not to let me out, but that they had done so anyway.

Attempting to once again assuage his ego, I said, "Well, just to be clear, I intend to finish out my run either way," to which he responded, "What makes you think we would even want you back?" I finally lost it. "Then fucking fire me, James. Fire me. But whatever this is, I'm done with it."

With James it was always a mind game. He fed on my insecurities and tried desperately to keep me under his control. Some described it as a way to reassert his authority over those lower than him, because Dan apparently did whatever he wanted and didn't let James push him around. Over the years, I have heard this time and again from others who have worked with him. Apparently (especially in the old days), James would home in on one person in any given cast and make that person his punching bag. I do not understand the psychology of this and therefore will not attempt to remotely analyze it.

Years later, James would apologize to me for his behavior, first during my run of *The Book of Mormon* and then again when I returned twelve years later to Broadway. One day during my *Gutenberg! The Musical!* run I took him out to dinner to have a heart-to-heart, because despite his abuse seventeen years earlier, I really do respect his talents and incredible legacy and wanted to put the past to bed. Toward the end of the dinner, he looked at me, fully knowing the answer I would give, and said, "Did you enjoy working with me?"

I laughed. "Are you kidding? No. I hated it. It was truly awful."

He smirked. "Why?"

"Because," I stated bluntly, "you were a dick to me."

He laughed and said, "In all fairness, you needed to get your ass kicked. Trust me." As insane as this may sound, I actually think he was absolutely correct, although I detest his approach. There is no denying that James prepared me for a career full of ups, downs, lefts, and rights, even though his methodology was frankly psychotic and unnecessarily cruel. While it certainly didn't help me during the run of *Spelling Bee*, it set me up to pretty much handle any adversity I would face during the entirety of my career.

One day during my *Spelling Bee* run, Ida and I attended Seth and Bryce's wedding. Like a schmuck, I had forgotten to write a speech for the rehearsal dinner and ran off to the bathroom to quickly jot a couple of things down on a used napkin. When I came out, I gave a speech (or rather a roast) that brought down the house, the details of which have been lost to time and the trash can that the napkin speech went right into after the dinner.

While I do not remember any of what I said that night, it was apparently funny enough that the legendary Henry Winkler came up to me after and said, "I am now coming to see you in your show tomorrow because that was one of the funniest speeches I have ever heard." Another person in attendance was an ICM agent named Meredith Wechter. Meredith had been Bryce's agent since college, and I had tried to sign with her as well years earlier, only to fail miserably when she attended a makeshift stand-up routine I had put up that had been an utter debacle. (Somehow, I thought it was smart to do a half-hour set without testing any of the material out ahead of time. Coincidentally, that would be the final time I ever performed stand-up.)

But on this particular night, Meredith approached me and said, "That was one of the most hilarious speeches I've ever heard. I would also love to come and see you in your show." After she saw the show, she took me out to dinner and told me why I needed to sign with her. I frankly didn't need an invitation, seeing as I was already desperate to work with her, but I was also fiercely loyal to my then agents at Gersh, whom I had signed with after Hannah, and was scared to fire anyone. After almost a year of courting, I finally acquiesced and signed with the person who would represent me for the rest of my career. To this day, it is hilarious to me that my TV and film trajectory can all be traced back to a makeshift wedding speech jotted down on a napkin in a bathroom.

As I finished my run on Broadway, I knew it was time to leave New York. Ida, who had patiently moved to the city with me and endured living on friends' couches for over a year (because even on a Broadway contract I still couldn't afford my own place), was beyond ready to head back to Los Angeles, as was I. With stellar reviews for my Broadway debut and a new killer agent, it was time to give Hollywood another chance. On my flight back home, I picked up a book to prep for an audition I had gotten. The book was called *Bringing Down the House* by Ben Mezrich, and it was a true story about a group of MIT kids who had swindled the Vegas casinos by counting cards while playing blackjack.

Little did I know that much like the characters in the book, I was about to hit the jackpot.

5

HIGHS AND LOWS

So, how exactly does one become a movie and TV star? Well, it would seem all you really need to do is get as far away as humanly possible from both film and TV.

After four years of desperately trying to break into the Los Angeles film scene by auditioning, doing short films, and meeting with casting director after casting director, begging them for a chance, it turns out all I really needed was a one-year detour doing a small musical about pre-pubescent children in what is essentially a Broadway black box theater.

I had gotten enough great buzz off the show that the second I arrived back in LA, I suddenly started getting in the room for some very high-profile projects, including a Doug Liman movie called *Jumper*; a J.J. Abrams–produced alien-invasion movie called *Cloverfield*; and the soon-to-be-iconic *Tropic Thunder* (an audition so insanely bonkers with me going full tilt—at a role Jack Black would later brilliantly play—that the video got passed around years later and got me into some more very high-profile meetings when I was just starting out).

There was one project, however, that I was aggressively pursuing more than any other, based on my deep admiration for the book it was being adapted from. Sony was assembling a young group of twentysomethings to play the real-life MIT whiz kids who had broken Vegas by mathematically counting cards at the blackjack tables (hence the title of the film, *21*). The two adult leads anchoring the film would be Laurence Fishburne and (the artist formerly known as) Kevin Spacey. After a few auditions and callbacks with the director and producers, I was finally cast as the lead character Ben's (played by Jim Sturgess) best friend Miles. The character was essentially a sidekick, but one that would allow me to bring some comic relief to the otherwise dramatic proceedings. The movie was set to shoot in Boston and Las Vegas, and I couldn't have been more excited to be making my film debut.

Technically, my real-film debut is the 1996 film The Substitute *starring Tom Berenger, about an ex-mercenary who goes undercover as a substitute to exact revenge on a public-school gang for breaking his fiancée's (a teacher at the school) kneecap. My best friend, Seth, who didn't bother to read the fine print, saw that a new movie was casting high schoolers for a Tom Berenger film and volunteered us to go to a shoot one Saturday. I was so excited. I figured it was going to be either a fun high school comedy or a cool drama like* Dead Poets Society. *All of that changed, however, when we pulled up at 5:00 a.m. to the downtown Miami set. From the second we arrived, it became fairly apparent that we were essentially the only two non-gangbangers who had shown up to work that day. Everyone else looked like they'd either killed someone or were in the process of killing someone. Seth and I were the only background artists without either gold on their teeth, platinum in their ears, or ink all over their faces. I am also fairly confident I was the only extra wearing prescription glasses. So, the next time you see a big outdoor high school crowd scene in* The Substitute, *make sure to look for a chubby Jewish fifteen-year-old with spectacles. Trust me, it will be the easiest game of* Where's Waldo? *you will ever play. Now, back to* 21.

The two months of filming *21* were basically an elongated bachelor party. I immediately connected with the younger cast, including Jim, Kate Bosworth, Aaron Yoo, Sam Golzari, and Liza Lapira. We were all around the same age and coincidentally loved the same two things: alcohol and partying. Not helping matters, the young cast was given a healthy per diem and encouraged to practice our skills at the various casinos on the Strip. On one memorable night, we were all handed a stack of chips and brought up to the Playboy Suite, where we were regaled with unlimited drinks, cards, and breasts. We all took a multi-day course in counting cards (keeping track of the cards played to calculate the probability of certain ones being dealt), which, given my horrific math skills, would prove fruitless in any future gambling pursuits. Our adviser during the shoot was one of the actual MIT card counters from the Ben Mezrich book, named Jeff. For a card counter, Jeff looked and acted more like a frat boy than a brilliant mathematician. He was ripped, with slick black hair and ready to party all night long everywhere we went (again, would not recommend Las Vegas when shooting a movie with and about young people). The hilarious thing was that anytime we would go into a casino, their entire security team would descend and ensure that he was nowhere near the tables due to his infamous history in Sin City.

But shooting in Las Vegas went from being a nonstop train of fun to a living nightmare fairly quickly. We were staying at and working out of the then brand-new Planet Hollywood Casino, and would be there for about a month. You could never tell if it was day or night, Earth or hell, fake set filled with drunk-looking extras or real casino filled with coked-up whales, and you would walk around the endless halls in search of just one solitary window, which was as elusive as ATMs were abundant. Boston, on the other hand, was a blast, not only because I love history and did endless tours of the city's most iconic landmarks, but also because we were there during Saint Patrick's Day, which was essentially like celebrating Halloween in Salem. Our cast took over a dive bar and the local Bostonians helped teach us how to pickle a human liver in one hour or less.

Wherever we went, we were treated like royalty and shown the time of our lives. For me, it was also a truly out-of-body experience. For someone who had always loved movies and the magic of moviemaking, I was suddenly getting to be in one. I was flying first class for the first time in my life (which I'm certain the flight crew was aware of, considering I had to ask how all of the seat mechanics worked). I was now making real money and trying to imagine all of the things I could do with the $75,000 paycheck I had received for my work (which coincidentally was $74,000 more than any other paycheck I had ever received). I was living out of luxury suites and being handed envelopes with cash with which to play blackjack. I was also getting to work with people I absolutely admired and looked up to. Our producers, the iconic Mike DeLuca and the insanely funny Dana Brunetti, fostered an environment that was equally fun and creative. Our director, Robert Luketic (of *Legally Blonde* fame), was equally supportive, allowing me to do pretty much whatever I wanted on camera, a far cry from the oppressive process that had been *Spelling Bee*. While socially most of my time was spent hanging out with the younger cast, there was one noteworthy exception.

For whatever reason, actor-producer Kevin Spacey took an interest in me.

For obvious reasons, the author feels the need to specify that "taking an interest in me" in this particular case does not in any way suggest a sexual or even flirtatious interest, not the least of which is because I am clearly not Kevin Spacey's type. This concludes the author's commentary on the current climate as it pertains to biographies with the words Kevin and Spacey next to each other.

What Kevin would do, however, was: take me out to dinner and force me to have an "impression-off" with him. No joke. We would sit across from each other at a small restaurant in Boston and Kevin Spacey would ask me to exchange impressions with him. He would do Jack Lemmon, I would then do Philip Seymour Hoffman; he would do Jimmy Stewart, I would do Jack Nicholson; he would do Katharine Hepburn, I would do Al Pacino, and so on. His impressions were truly killer and he was very complimentary and impressed by my impressions as well. That does not mean to suggest that the situation was not another out-of-body experience. For starters, it was just such an awkward assignment: sit across from a star celebrity and engage per his demands in impressions with him. It would be like two teachers going out for drinks after school and one suddenly turning to the other with a pencil and paper and saying, "Hey, let's both do a competitive math test right now!" As surreal as that episode was, the entire experience of making *21* remains one of the highlights of my career, marking not only an incredible milestone (costarring my first film) but also paving the way for what would be a seminal springboard for the rest of my professional life. The movie, however, was small potatoes compared to the next (far more personal) project I was about to jump into.

In the midst of shooting *21*, I had decided to propose to Ida. After three years of courtship, I was fairly confident I had a decent shot of not being rejected. The plan was to fly her to Vegas to visit me on set and then, in the middle of shooting the scene, do an elaborate scripted sketch with my fellow actors that would culminate with me proposing while she watched on the monitor. I bought the engagement ring, wrote the whole thing up, and got the crew to agree to partake. Then, four days before Ida was set to fly out, I got an unexpected phone call from my then TV agent Dar Rol-

lins. Prior to doing *21*, I had auditioned for a new multicamera sitcom from two of the star writers from *Frasier*, Steve Levitan and Chris Lloyd. The show, titled *Back to You*, was set to star Kelsey Grammer and Patricia Heaton, as well as the legendary Fred Willard and a

brilliant, fresh-faced, thirtysomething character actor named Ty Burrell, and was set to be directed by the legendary director of *Taxi, Cheers,* and *Friends,* Jimmy Burrows. It was about two news anchors who had previously had a relationship being forced back into each other's lives to do a local newscast, and it was hilarious on the page.

I had auditioned for the role of the uptight and sweaty news director Ryan Church, but had lost out on the role to another actor and had forgotten all about the project. Now, close to four months later, I was receiving a call explaining that the show, which was about to do its live taping, had had a dress rehearsal that was apparently disastrous, and they now wanted me to come in on one day's notice and take over for the recently fired actor in that role. As if that wasn't enough stress, I would also have to learn all of the dialogue, blocking, and how to perform in a multicam sitcom for the first time in my life, with basically nothing but a few hours of rehearsal.

So, of course I said yes!

Now I had to quickly figure out how to pivot from proposing on set to proposing at home, since Ida was no longer going to fly to Vegas and I didn't trust myself to hold on to an expensive engagement ring without misplacing or losing it for more than a few days. With just hours to go before my arrival, I called our then roommate Christy along with Seth and had them buy as many rose petals as they could find and lay them all out in front of and throughout the entire house. They also lit a dozen candles, because wax and fire were still romantic and not cliché in the early aughts.

Essentially, my plan was to go from an awesome, well-thought-out, memorable proposal on set to a cheap, makeshift reenactment of the poster for *American Beauty* or *Ghost*. Ida picked me up from the airport, we arrived at our rose petal–littered driveway, walked into the rose-covered living room and into our bedroom, which was also covered with yet more floral debris, and Ida looked at me and said, "Wait . . . you're proposing to me?"

It was truly the single most anticlimactic proposal of all time. I literally just took out the ring and said, "So?"

In my mind, I had always imagined something epic and memorable and romantic, and instead it played out like a *Seinfeld* episode wherein a thousand flower beds were murdered all for my would-be fiancée to ask me the question before I could ask *her* the question, after which we immediately had to clean everything up for the next two hours, so our cat wouldn't eat it all and puke. Although, when I think back to the alternative, I'm not quite sure that a Kevin Spacey wedding-proposal bit would have aged particularly well.

On April 13, 2007, after a day of rehearsal, we shot the pilot of *Back to You* at the Fox Studios lot in Los Angeles. The experience of getting to perform a sitcom opposite some of the heaviest hitters in television comedy history was equal parts intimidating and thrilling. I was basically shitting my pants backstage minutes before the live taping, thinking to myself, *Oh God, I'm going to look like an amateur opposite these titans.* As fate would have it, in the pilot episode, my character was meant to be sweating through his clothes in a recurring bit that saw him getting more and more nervous as he attempts to get these two coanchors (Heaton and Grammer) back on a local Pittsburgh station again for the first time in years after their infamous falling-out. The makeup team had planned to spray my pits more and more during the episode, but by the time I came out, my pits had already done all of the work for them. Never have underarms Method-acted as hard as mine. It looked like it had been raining from the ground up.

I have never been so nervous in my life. As I prepped in a state of abject terror to walk out onto the stage, I looked around and saw Fred

Willard backstage, anxiously
going over his lines again and
again, Kelsey Grammer and
Patricia Heaton both running
their dialogue through nervous laughter, and Ty Burrell
studiously doing the same. I
realized in that moment that
it doesn't matter how big or

small you are in your career at any given point; everyone has some form
of nervous energy before a live performance. With that calming realization, I walked onstage and had one of the best career moments of my
life: sharing equal laughs with these giants of comedy. It was thrilling.
Not only was I not letting the audience down, but I was making my
costars, director, and writers laugh take after take. Prior to that moment,
I had never had the opportunity to lob jokes back and forth with people
I had grown up revering. Little did I know, it would become a recurring
blessing in my career.

Kelsey Grammer in particular took a liking to me, and I to him. During a rehearsal he invited me back to his trailer. I was so excited. He then
looked at me with a twinkle in his eye and said in that familiar baritone
of his: "Kid, do you like money?" I laughed and said, "Sure." He then responded with: "When you make money, do you like keeping it?" I paused,
not knowing where this conversation was going, and responded with "Yes, I
guess I do." He then leaned in and said, "Then I'd like to talk to you about
what being a fiscal conservative means." For the next ten minutes, Emmy
Award–winning actor Kelsey Grammer shared the virtues of paying less
in taxes and encouraged me to join the cause (which, for the record, had
I not been brought up in a very liberal household, I probably would have
run with because, well, money *is* really nice to keep once you've earned it).
Alas, I have remained a steadfast tax-paying lackey who all too willingly
parts ways with his money in order to help fund social services. But Kelsey

and I remain incredibly close and I continue to support his position of keeping that hard-earned *Frasier* dough, as long as he pays for the dinners!

The shoot was a resounding success, and the next day I flew back to Las Vegas to finish production on *21*, now an engaged man with my first starring TV credit to my name.

Shortly after wrapping *21*, which was everything I had hoped and prayed my first-ever film experience would be, I got word that *Back to You* was being picked up by Fox to be a part of its prestigious fall lineup. I barely had time to celebrate when I was suddenly offered my next starring role in a comedy called *The Rocker*. I was elated. Everything I had dreamed of, everything I had envisioned for myself was finally coming true and at a pace I could barely keep up with. I felt like I didn't deserve any of it, but I was beyond grateful for all of it, and once again I was about to somehow work with some of the hottest people in town. The film, which was set to star Rainn Wilson, who had exploded out of the gate with his brilliant performance as Dwight Schrute on *The Office*—the same role I had ironically lost out on two years earlier—was about an out-of-work drummer who was trying for a second chance after infamously being fired from his band on the eve of their successful breakthrough. The cast was a who's who of future all-stars including Bradley Cooper, Jason Sudeikis, Will Arnett, Fred Armisen, Jane Lynch, Aziz Ansari, and already-known commodities like Christina Applegate and Jeff Garlin.

The one fresh-faced newcomer, however, who left the biggest impression on me was a young redheaded teenager named Emma Stone. Other than an upcoming release of a film called *Superbad*, Stone had not previously been on my radar. From the second we got on set, however, it was abundantly clear that we were looking at a future superstar. There was something about her that was so charismatic, so effortlessly funny, so confident, goofy, and nevertheless sexy that permeated every choice she would make as an artist. I would constantly pull Rainn aside and say, "I feel like I'm watching the next Julia Roberts."

The time we spent as a cast in Toronto was spectacular, with all of us essentially becoming a family and hanging out together day in and day out. The first few weeks were all about learning how to play instruments. Emma was on bass, Teddy Geiger on guitar, Rainn on drums, and I on keys. There was only one problem . . . I had no idea how the hell to play keys. The production hired an Eastern European man named Dimitri to teach me, and poor Dimitri might as well have been teaching a lizard to paint nudes. I was hopeless. While my costars all legitimately play their hearts out accurately in the film, if you ever actually watch what I am doing, it is pure nonsense. At night, the cast would all gather around and watch rock-inspired films or docs. One particularly inspirational one was the Wilco documentary *I Am Trying to Break Your Heart*. We also watched the brilliant Metallica doc *Some Kind of Monster*, during which I pretended to know and like Metallica music (something I have now come to *actually* appreciate and don't have to pretend to enjoy).

Once rehearsals were over and production began, our schedules became insanely stacked. We worked crazy hours and only had Sundays off. One particularly fun memory I have is all of us shooting a sequence that took place at an arena that was meant to be the big performance at the end of the movie. We only had access to the arena for twenty-four hours and not a second more. Unfortunately for us, the nature of our shoot allowed the filmmakers to keep us there shooting for all those seconds of those twenty-four hours. I'll never forget our producer, the incredibly gifted and renowned Shawn Levy, showing up bright-eyed and bushy-tailed at 1:00 a.m. after we had already been shooting for eighteen hours straight and playing around with a

scene we were blocking. By that point, Emma, Rainn, Teddy, and I were literally holding one another up in place for fear that our legs were about to give out, while trying to simultaneously please a very energized and enthusiastic Shawn. Our poor director, Peter Cattaneo, was so behind and despondent at that point, but all we could do was laugh because we were so deliriously tired and slaphappy.

Another great memory on that set was working with the late Howard Hesseman, who had been a staple in my household on classics like *WKRP in Cincinnati* and *Head of the Class*. All day long I would shower him with questions about his storied career and geek out on tales from his classic sitcoms and other iconic work, like his role in the 1980s Disney film *Flight of the Navigator*. On one particular night, I dragged him and his wife, Caroline, to see *Ratatouille* in the theater. Neither of them had ever seen a Pixar movie before and were reluctant to go. When the lights came up, however, they were both teary-eyed and euphoric. It was such a joy to see a grown man in his sixties be so taken aback and full of wonderment at an animated film, especially one that culminates with a grown man remembering wonder. Talk about art imitating life.

On the heels of shooting *The Rocker*, I started to find myself in more and more interesting casting positions. One film that offered me a small two-day role was a movie called *Crossing Over*, starring Harrison Ford and Sean Penn (an awful and unwatchable movie, by the way, if you unwisely decide to search for it). What was incredible about this experience, however, was getting to see a very likely stoned Harrison Ford (one of my absolute all-time idols) practicing his bullwhipping skills with some kind of bullwhip tutor outside of his trailer, in preparation for the next Indiana Jones film. He and I got a tragically bad photo together on the set, wherein I looked like I could be meat loaf's heavyset daughter. And by meat loaf, I am referring to the food.

Years later, I was at a party and Harrison was also present. That evening I was hanging out with a young Hailee Steinfeld, whom my agent also represented, when she approached him and got a selfie. After Hailee took the pic, I asked Harrison if we could also snap a picture together.

Harrison looked at me and
said in that iconic gruffy
snarl, "No." I pointed to
Hailee and said, jokingly,
"But you just took a picture
with this little girl." He
squinted his eyes at me and
responded again in his signature growl: "I know . . .
She's a *LITTLE GIRL.*" No

picture could ever equal the joy of that incredible exchange.

During the next year, I rode a seemingly never-ending high. *21* opened
number one at the box office on March 28, 2008, earning $24 million,
while *Back to You* premiered to almost ten million viewers and got an additional order of episodes for a total of twenty-four. And I prepped for my
wedding date, which was set for that May. It felt like there was no end in
sight for the series of highs I was experiencing.

Coincidentally, my mother has a saying that she always reminds me
of: "Never let the highs be too high and the lows be too low, because you
never know when the ground might fall out from under you." Little did
I know how relevant those words would become.

On May 2, 2008 (the week before my wedding), the ground fell out. I
received a phone call from my stepdad, Stan, at five in the morning. He was
sobbing. In the background I could hear my mother wailing. "She's gone,"
my mom was screaming through tears. "Who?" I desperately responded.
Stan softly answered: "Your grandmother, she's gone."

Nana, as we lovingly called her, had died peacefully in her sleep. My
grandparents lived literally next door to my parents. That morning my
grandfather woke up to find the love of his life had slipped away in the
middle of the night at eighty-two years of age and called my parents, hoping they could somehow resuscitate her, but she had already been dead
for hours. She hadn't been sick. She hadn't had a disease. She just went

to bed one night and never woke up. My heart was shattered. My grand-mother had been my very own superhero. She and my papa had survived the atrocities of the Holocaust and had built a new life out of the rubble, providing their children and their grandchildren with opportunities they themselves were robbed of in their childhoods. My grandmother, who had heroically escaped from the Nazis on a death march and had been so full of life, was now nothing more than a memory. And for me, the most heartbreaking thing of all was that she had been meant to fly out for my wedding that very week.

Ida, who was set to leave in two hours for her bachelorette party in Las Vegas, asked me if she should cancel. I said "Absolutely not" and booked myself on the first flight home, crying nonstop and feeling des-perately alone on the plane. The funeral was one of the hardest things I've ever endured, with my grandfather falling to the ground sobbing. I wasn't even sure how my parents could come to my wedding in three days given everything that had just transpired. By some miracle, my parents convinced my grandfather to fly out with them, which everyone knew is what Nana would have wanted. I'm grateful he was there because it was a good distraction for him.

I'm also grateful he was there because he was a good distraction for *me*. The night of my wedding, as I was surrounded by family and loved ones, Chris Lloyd and Steve Levitan, the creators of *Back to You*, delivered the news that our TV show, that had once been so promising, had just been canceled by the network. The show, which had premiered to great num-bers, had steadily declined in its run, finally losing all momentum during the writer's strike of 2007–08. I couldn't help but laugh at the insanity of it all. Over the course of one week, I had lost my grandmother, my job, and was now having a wedding I could barely afford. Yet somehow, the night ended up being one of the greatest of my life. I was surrounded by incredible friends from within the industry and from all parts of my life. I was getting hitched to a beautiful and way-out-of-my-league wife. I was watching as my grandfather, who had been paralyzed by sadness mere days before, was now bravely taking the mic and making the entire audience laugh their asses off while explaining to them that he wanted me to use my connections in Hollywood to get him a good deal on a Jaguar. Most importantly, I felt surrounded by the presence of my grandmother. My grandmother had loved butterflies, so we had decided to get a box of them and release them during our vows. My niece Sydney opened the box, and at first the butterflies literally all fell to the ground. My wife and I were mortified. My poor niece looked like she was going to cry. Then, all of a sudden, as if by a miracle, the thought-to-be-dead butterflies rose into the air and flew all around us, like a phoenix from the ashes. It was beautiful and profound. The rest of the wedding, everywhere we looked, we would see giant monarchs swimming in the air all around us, bringing smiles to our faces and peace to our hearts. That night, in the presence of family and friends, I was able to settle my fears, my nerves, and my sadness and instead celebrate with the people I loved the most, in a beautiful ceremony held at a stunning botanical garden in Westlake Village, California.

That week was a perfect guidepost to the rest of my life. It has been a cascade of highs and lows, sometimes happening simultaneously. I think a part of my ability to accept the often-tumultuous nature of what I do is that I can look back at the bravery and perseverance of two individuals, my nana and papa, and remind myself that there is no hardship I will ever experience that can possibly compare to the adversity they endured as children. They gave me a lot in our time together, but perhaps nothing more significant than the gift of perspective. If they could survive and endure after losing their families and the primes of their lives, there is simply no rejection or failure in my life or career that will ever have the weight and significance of anything that resembles that level of hardship.

Oftentimes, I will find myself on the cusp of bemoaning a bad review or losing out on a job and I will stop and remind myself of the gift of being able to simply do what I do and get paid and recognized for it in the process. The gift of life is a gift that I find we oftentimes all take for granted and I always try to remind myself . . . everything else is icing on the cake.

As my wedding concluded and my wife and I returned from an incredible honeymoon in Italy, I got back to work. I fulfilled a two-picture deal I had with Sony with a movie called *Mardi Gras* (the single worst movie I have made—and will hopefully ever make—in my life). Although I had the time of my life shooting in New Orleans with folks like the magnificent Regina Hall and our ferociously funny writer (and now lifelong friend) Josh Heald, who would later go on to cocreate *Cobra Kai*, the experience of making the film was a waking nightmare, with nonstop studio interference where we would literally have scenes written by the studio head sent for us to do the next day. Nothing made sense and, worse, it was all big, broad, unmeaningful comedy in which none of the creative team had any say. What was worse, however, is that I began to grow really concerned that I was going down a path of playing the loud fat best friend in every project I was doing. While it was certainly starting to pay me more money than I had ever seen before, I was worried that I was getting into a situation of being typecast. Any dreams I had of following in the footsteps of Philip Seymour Hoffman or John Goodman were soon going to be dashed if I stayed on this path. I knew I needed to branch out and attempt to have people see me in a new and unexpected way.

As fate would have it, shortly after *Mardi Gras*, I got a call in early 2009 that *The Daily Show* with Jon Stewart was looking for a new correspondent, and the casting director, Allison Jones, thought I would be perfect for it. I had always wanted to be on *SNL* and, in many ways, *The Daily Show* had become the new *SNL*, producing such iconic comedy stars as Steve Carell, Stephen Colbert, Kristen Schaal, Ed Helms, Samantha Bee, and of course John Oliver. I was excited that this was a complete pivot from the kinds of films and TV shows I had been doing, and it felt like a cool and elevated way for me to rebrand myself. I went in for the producers and was asked to write an original piece in which I was speaking to Jon, in order to showcase a "persona." The approach I decided to take was that of an oblivious correspondent who tackles issues in the country he feels are raging out of control and ignores a few of his own shortcomings in the process, including, in this case, being close to two hundred and eighty pounds. Here's an excerpt from my audition:

Jonny, today I'd like to talk about the people who are misrepresenting us as a country, the people who are consuming all of our resources. Today, Jonathan, I'd like to talk about FAT PEOPLE. This is a nation of fat. This is a fat nation. People like Jack Black and those who look eerily similar to Jack Black are just adding to the madness. Did you know that more than 20 percent of adults are fat in every state except Colorado and that's only because fat people can't breathe in Colorado because the air is so thin? Jon, I get that it's hard for these people. But you know what . . . deal with it. I have my own hardships. Thank God, weight or being compared to Jack Black isn't one of them.

As I struggled to breathe in my two-sizes-too-small suit, the producers were dying. I ended the audition by leaning in for an intimate moment and finishing with:

God, Jonny boy, I hope our metabolism never gives up on the both of us . . . or you and I will really be in trouble.

Within a week, I was offered *The Daily Show.* I couldn't believe it. I was also weighing significant offers for two different network pilots that were each going to pay me close to $50,000 an episode, but there was no way I was going to do them, because I *had* to be on *The Daily Show.*

And then I got the *Daily Show* offer . . .

Three thousand dollars a week to write and star.

While that was a lot of money on paper, I knew it would not be nearly enough to up and move to New York City with Ida and afford a place that could not only house us but also give us the lifestyle to start a family, which we were beginning to talk about. I was shattered. I had promised myself I would never make decisions based on money, but at nearly thirty years old, could I really afford to turn down life-changing money and instead take what would amount to around $4,000 a month after paying my agent, manager, lawyer, and Uncle Sam? I talked it through with my family and Ida and decided that there was no way I could make it work. I called Jon myself to break the news and thanked him for the opportunity. What happened next blew my mind. He said, "What if we allow you to be a guest correspondent? You can fly in and out when we need you and do as many pieces as your schedule and our needs allow."

I wanted to cry. "DONE," I screamed. I could continue to live in LA with my wife and do *The Daily Show*? Um, hell yeah.

My first appearance on *The Daily Show*, an in-studio desk piece with Jon, was, to put it bluntly, an unmitigated disaster. The bit was me sitting opposite Jon at his anchor desk, playing various characters in rapid succession. I was dry-mouthed, over-the-top, and dreadfully unfunny in every way, shape, and form. The laughs were few and far between and I felt like an absolute fraud. I was experiencing strong levels of imposter syndrome, and *I* would have fired me if I had had that power. I felt like I didn't belong alongside all of the iconic people who had graced these halls (especially Jon), and fully caved under the pressure. I remember hearing the silence of the audience and pushing the jokes harder, which made the whole thing collapse even more.

My stomach dropped. I was certain I would never be asked back. As I walked backstage, I avoided every single person on staff for fear of getting booed. After each episode, Jon would call everyone into the office to do an autopsy on what worked and what didn't. He was very kind that evening, but rightfully not very effusive, talking through the bit very articulately, telling me which parts worked (few) and which parts didn't (many), but offering suggestions for the next appearance that might help me settle into the role a bit more. I had a sleepless night that night, tossing and turning and replaying the whole horrible sketch over again in my head. The next morning, I woke up with new resolve. I had to get back on the show immediately. After some self-introspection, I thought the best use of my skills would be in a field piece, like *60 Minutes*–style segments, pitting *Daily Show* anchors against colorful interviewees and backdrops about various topics from the mundane to the insane. I knew in my heart that I needed to change the narrative both for myself and for Jon as well as the producers, and thought that the best way to illustrate that was in a completely different type of *Daily Show* appearance. I started to email all the field producers to see if they were working on anything that might give me a chance at redemption. I knew I needed to get back in the ring and show them they had not made a mistake by hiring me.

None of the producers seemed to want to engage with me, but after a lot of persistence, I finally got a bite. The show was looking to do a piece about people who were making long-term investments not in stocks and real estate, but in semiautomatic and automatic weapons. The absurdity of the premise was exactly what I had been looking for. We mapped out the piece, pitched it to Jon (who always silently read the outlines while chewing on a giant gumball from his office gumball machine), and with a couple of spot-on notes from him, went off to shoot. A few weeks after my disastrous first segment, the new piece aired and was a massive success. The segment was the perfect fusion of everything that I comedically hoped to achieve on the show, allowing me to improvise, showcase my absurd comedic voice, and play the faux passionate and devoted news anchor opposite equally passionate (albeit real) people trying to explain to me the benefits of invest-ing in an AR-15 over an AK-47 and vice versa, or buying those same weapons as gifts upon the birth of a child (go watch it if you don't believe me). The audience lost their minds and Jon raved about my performance. I had exorcised my de-mons, redeemed myself, and impressed one of the best comedy minds out there.

Once again, it proved to be a good reminder of my mother's favorite adage: "Never let the highs be too high and the lows be too low."

While bouncing back and forth to do episodes of *The Daily Show*, I was also filming a movie called *Love & Other Drugs*, directed by Ed Zwick and starring Jake Gyllenhaal and Anne Hathaway (who would remain dear friends long after filming was complete). One day as Jake and I were driving home from set in Pittsburgh, I asked him if I could play a demo of a new musical that I had recently done a workshop for in New York, hoping to get his advice as to whether or not I should pursue it further. He said, "Yeah, pop it on," and I played the opening number. Jake laughed his ass off. I skipped to another track on the album and his face slowly went from joyful enthusiasm to abject fear and terror.

He stopped the car and said, "Dude, you cannot do whatever this is. This will be way too controversial. Who the hell wrote this anyway?" I paused the music and looked over at him.

"The *South Park* guys."

6

HELLO!

Six words. Six simple words were now standing between me and my destiny. I had been waiting for this moment for four years. The trips back and forth from the West Coast, the vocal training, the decisions to pass on projects that would have made me a fortune. It was all leading up to this one moment. A moment I had dreamed about, fretted over, left my wife and baby three thousand miles across the country for. This was either going to prove me right in the eyes of many cynical detractors or be an epic fail and send me back to LA with my tail between my chafed thighs. And all it was going to take were six simple words to determine my fate . . .

Five Years Earlier—A Much Simpler Time

"Hello, Josh. Bobby Lopez."

That was the call that started it all. It was either the spring, fall, winter, or summer of 2007. My résumé had thus far been a smorgasbord of awkwardly fat, somewhere-on-the-spectrum, brainy stereotypes. In the eyes of the people who decide the fates of actors, I was a Chris Farley type by way of a Jewish banker/computer programmer. Who knew there was such a huge need for "that guy"? In Hollywood, once you have shown casting directors that you can play something fairly well, it no longer matters if you can do anything else. Hollywood is like Krypton as depicted in Zack Snyder's Twitter-bot-beloved masterpiece *Man of Steel*. Every actor is put into a huge, slick, gooey-liquid machine where their "fate" and "type" are predetermined and then shot out of this giant primordial vagina and sent on their merry way until a renegade creative, like Russell Crowe's Jor-El, comes along, swims up the vagina machine, and rescues the actor from his preordained fate. Well, luckily for me, Bobby Lopez was swimming upstream in the casting vagina. And luckily for you, *Man of Steel* is now streaming on Max, if you have no idea what I just said.

"There's a project I'm working on with the creators of *South Park*. It's about Mormons. We're wondering if you would be a part of the workshop for it?"

If there are three words you want to hear at the start of a sentence soliciting work, they're *South, Park,* and *Mormons*. I, like many in my generation, had been singing the "Dum, Dum, Dum" song from the classic "All About the Mormons" episode for years. *What an ingenious idea,* I thought to myself. Adapt that episode of *South Park* for the stage with music by the composer of the hit show *Avenue Q*. I asked Bobby, although it was already fairly obvious to me, if I was going to play Cartman.

"No"—he laughed (*you're a fucking idiot* being the implication)—"it's nothing like that." I told him that I was confused (*I am fucking confused* being the implication).

"It's about these two missionaries," he continued, "who are sent on a mission to Uganda. You're kind of the follower to this other guy until the second act, when you become the leader, but we haven't written the second act yet." I wasn't sure if I was being *Punk'd* or not. The idea sounded interesting, but what were the creators of *South Park* doing writing a Broadway musical about Mormons that had nothing to do with their TV show? That would be like Jerry Seinfeld, star of *Seinfeld*, writing and starring in an animated movie about bees. I was a little perplexed but nevertheless very intrigued. At the end of the call, Bobby notified me that he was going to send me a file with a demo version of himself, Trey, and Matt singing some of the songs.

Later that night, over a cup of black tea and some Metamucil, I downloaded the rather large file and listened elatedly to the first few songs. There was a splendid opening number, in which a group of happy-go-lucky Mormon missionaries practice their "hello"s in preparation for God's work. The follow-up song, "Two by Two," was even more resplendent and instantaneously catchy. Then there was a little number about the Mormon home life called "Family Home Evening," a song that, I might add, I am still sad few people were able to witness, as it was ultimately cut. And then it hit. *The* song. The song to end all songs. It started off simply enough. The boys were clearly sending up "Hakuna Matata" from *The Lion King*. But what was the translation of this strange phrase? I had a feeling it would be about suffering, or maybe about heat exhaustion. Nothing, however, could prepare me for what came next. "Did I just hear that right?"

About ten minutes later, after two subsequent rounds of listening to the song to make sure I was hearing what I thought I was hearing, I called my agent in New York, Adam Schweitzer. "Hey, bud, remember how I was going to do that reading of the new show from the creators of *South Park* and *Avenue Q*?"

"Yes," he said, "we're all very excited about it."

"Well, I'm no longer going to do the reading of the new show from the creators of *South Park* and *Avenue Q*."

He couldn't believe it. "What the hell are you talking about? Of course you're going to." I explained to him that in the pantheon of offensiveness, where Trey and Matt had already staked their claim at the top, this was the holy grail of fucked-up.

"It can't be that bad," he retorted. I then played him the verse in question. There was a long pause at the other end, followed by the now infamous question . . . "Wait, did they just sing: 'Fuck you God in the ass, mouth, and cunt' and talk about raping babies?"

"That would be correct," I said.

He took a beat and then offered his expert 10 percent–worthy advice: "Yeah, there's no fucking way on Earth you can do this reading."

It wasn't that the lyrics weren't funny. On the contrary, they were some of the funniest lyrics I'd ever heard. It wasn't that the message they were sending wasn't brilliant and expertly executed. It was a reminder of how masterful they were at satire. The issue at hand was how much I liked the idea of life and, accordingly, whether I was willing to get shot point-blank by a religious person for my art. You see, it's one thing for animated characters in their cute little celluloid and digital innocence to mutter the most offensive musical lyrics ever, but it is quite another thing for real people standing ten feet away from other real people to sing songs about what parts of God's body he can fuck himself in. I was terrified at the potential backlash and religious fervor this kind of material was bound to bring out. I like controversy as much as the next guy, but knocking on the doors of religious fanatics and telling them that not only does God have a cunt but that he ought to fuck himself in said cunt might be taking things a little too far, no?

I had made up my mind. I was going to pass on the opportunity to do this workshop because safety should always come first. I was resolved and steadfast in my decision. As hard as it would be to turn down the opportunity to work with my idols, I was not willing to put myself or my family in jeopardy for a few laughs. A day later Bobby called me and said, "So, you in?" And without a pause, without a hint of hesitation, and with all the courage of a man about to take a piss in a shark's mouth, I said . . . "Of course I am. See you in New York." Somehow my mouth just made the word *no* into a *yes*. I hung up. I'm not sure if I cried or vomited first. I do remember calling my lawyer later that day and initiating my will. But the rest of it is truly a blur.

The workshop would be held at the Vineyard Theatre, a stone's throw away from nothing. The intimacy of the space was ideal because the one thing you want when workshopping inflammatory material is to be within hitting distance of your audience. We all entered the small downtown lobby and greeted each other. When I looked up, I stood in shock as in walked two of my college roommates: Will Taylor and—one of my closest friends in the world—Rory O'Malley. I looked at both and said, "What the fuck?" The three of us had no idea the others had been cast in the workshop. We chatted for a few minutes and compared notes on the little we knew about the project: it was a musical, they were deciding if it should be for the screen or the stage, and producer Scott Rudin (of throwing-hard-objects-at-faces fame) was somehow involved. Beyond that, nothing.

Suddenly, a hush fell over the room as Trey fucking Parker and Matt motherfucking Stone entered it. You have to remember, these guys were basically gods to my generation. Beyond *South Park* and the *South Park* movie, they had also directed one of the funniest films of the twenty-first century: *Team America: World Police.* To this day, I cannot watch that violent and endless vomit scene and not lose my breath from laughing so hard. And now, they both looked . . . well, basically stoned. I'm not sure that they actually *were*, because having known them for close to two decades at this point, I am now aware that the general look of stonery is their standard. Anyway, the probably-stoned duo asked us to introduce ourselves and we went around the room. When it got to me, I looked directly at Matt and said, "I'm Josh Gad and I'm so thrilled to be here, Trey." I then looked at Trey and said, "Matt, you and Trey are truly two of my heroes and I am so excited to tackle this with you both." The two awkwardly laughed.

It wasn't until after an entire week of calling them both by the wrong name that they finally understood I wasn't doing it as a joke, but was truly just a fucking idiot. Matt finally looked at me one day from the back of the theater and repeated, "I'm Matt" three times before I realized he was serious and that I had been unironically calling him by the wrong name for seven full days. Suffice it to say, I now google people's faces before using their names in a sentence.

At the time of the first workshop, nobody was really sure what the endgame was. Readings and workshops like this are usually to give the creative team a sense of what's working and what's not. In the case of *The Book of Mormon*, however, there was an added element of what format and medium would ultimately best suit the material. In fact, rudimentary animation had been done and was going to be projected behind us as we performed, leading most of us to assume that there was still some thought of this ultimately being an animated film. There was also the small issue of the thing not being fully written.

That's actually a bit of an understatement. On day one we had about five songs, but only twelve pages of the script. For that initial workshop, we would only do the first act as a proof of concept, but getting that first act pretty much took all fourteen days. Trey would sit silently in the back of the room ferociously writing and rewriting pages as Matt would sit and laugh at us singing the same five songs over and over again as our music director, Stephen Oremus, would grill us on harmonies. We would then ask if there were any more pages to read and be told, "No, but you should be getting new ones tomorrow." *Tomorrow* ultimately became the day before the workshop, during which we suddenly found ourselves rehearsing forty pages of new dialogue with seventeen hours to showtime. Coincidentally, that would pretty much be the case for the next three years as Matt and Trey would play a game of script Russian roulette with us up until opening night on Broadway.

While the script would take some time to fall into place, it was pretty clear from the beginning that the songs were extraordinary. Matt and (even more so) Trey had been true students of musical theater. They had immersed themselves in everything from Sondheim (somehow a personal friend of theirs) to Rodgers and Hammerstein (too dead to be personal friends with them). It was never their intention to satirize musicals; they were setting out to fully write a traditional musical that could stand alongside the timeless hits that had inspired them. Hence the brilliance of teaming up with Bobby Lopez, who was one-half of the musical team behind the Tony Award–winning puppet extravaganza *Avenue Q.* Bobby was going to be the glue that would bind the irreverence of Trey and Matt's satire with a truly elevated and musically complex score. "Hello!" "I Believe," and "Tomorrow Is a Latter Day" aren't simply hilarious songs; they are breathtakingly memorable melodies that you can't shake after hearing only once. But fuck, are they hard songs to sing.

On the song front, we knew from the start that the real test for the workshop was going to be how people responded to the "Welcome to Africa" spoof of "Hakuna Matata." The number, "Hasa Diga Eebowai," was a true Matt and Trey special. It was that rare song that can somehow manage to properly offend every single demographic simultaneously while also daring the same offended parties not to laugh at the outrageousness of it all. If I thought I was nervous about the song's lyrics by simply listening to the demo, boy, did my anxiety reach a new historic peak once I was actually singing and dancing alongside twenty other New York City performers, all belting out "Fuck you, God" in a very small theater. As I had anticipated, this was going to be the test case for the whole damn exercise. Would the audience embrace the intention of the satire (dark and insanely twisted as it may be), or would the whole thing collapse, leading to a best-case scenario of the invited guests storming out of the theater and a worst-case scenario of the patrons rushing the stage and stabbing us with whatever props they could readily find?

February 22, 2008

It was an unusually snowy day; in fact, the most snowfall of that winter. I trekked through the soupy New York City sludge (a consistency, to the best of my knowledge, made up of cloud particulates, solidified car exhaust, and a fair amount of animal and human urine) and made my way to the tight backstage quarters, where a group of twenty-some other performers were already warming up. The dozen or so Mormon boys each wore white button-down shirts and uniform black ties that were handed out to us that morning. The rest of the cast wore loose-fitting nondescript clothes. There was an intoxicating buzz backstage: a mixture of anticipation, anxiety, excitement, and fear. My costar, Ben Walker (who would later come to fame in Broadway's *Bloody Bloody Andrew Jackson*), rehearsed some of the Elder Price/Elder Cunningham dialogue with me backstage, since a lot of it we had only received the day before. The audience was gathering at the front of the theater. There was no turning back now.

At around noon, they called us to our places and we walked out to our music stands to an audience of around 132 people (the maximum capacity at the Vineyard Theatre and most AMCs). The buzz in the room was equal parts excited and confused. Nobody quite knew what to expect. The lights turned down and the sound of a doorbell echoed over the loudspeakers, followed by a man with a high-pitched tenor voice and a smug smile greeting the excited attendees with an overly eager two-syllable word: "HELLO." Immediately, chuckles started cascading through the room. By the end of the number, the audience was erupting into applause. There was a "So *that's* what this is" quality to their response that thrilled me. The comedic momentum continued as we efficiently introduced them to the characters of Elder Price and Elder Cunningham and their respective families. From the beginning the Price/Cunningham dynamic was very clear:

One was the perfect specimen of the Mormon faith, exhibiting all the qualities of an eager missionary who would one day have many children of his own and a leadership role within the LDS ranks. The other was . . . me. More specifically, a slob with awkward social tendencies, a keen knack for exaggeration, and a tenuous grasp of Mormon concepts; again, me. Together, their pairing would be the perfect comedic odd-couple stew. Send these entirely unsuited Provo boys to Uganda and the show practically writes itself . . . unless of course it is written by three people who break every comedic norm for sheer delight and nihilistic joy.

At around 12:20 p.m., the moment of truth had finally arrived. Our missionary boys had arrived to their designated village in Uganda. As the insanely brilliant cast of Black actors (including future Tony winner Patina Miller) leapt up to the music stands to play the African villagers, a communal breath of "Here we go" transitioned us into THE song. Mafala, the town leader, gives a great big smile and leads us into the charming percussive rhythms of a song that will sound very similar to those familiar with the antics of Timon and Pumba, America's favorite warthog/meerkat pairing:

[MAFALA, SPOKEN]
In this part of Africa, we all have a saying. Whenever something bad happens, we just throw our hands to the sky and say Hasa Diga Eebowai.

[ELDER CUNNINGHAM, SPOKEN]
Hasa Diga Eebowai?

[MAFALA, SPOKEN]
It's the only way to get through all these troubled times. There's war, poverty, famine . . . but having a saying makes it all seem better!
(sung)
There isn't enough food to eat.
Hasa Diga Eebowai!
People are starving in the street!

[UGANDANS, MAFALA]

Hasa Diga Eebowai!
Hasa Diga Eebowai!
Hasa Diga Eebowai!

So far, so good. The audience understood the context of the spoof and the satire's message. However, only we knew what was coming next. In a fight-or-flight reflex, I clenched my jaw and my fists, preparing to white-knuckle my way through the next section of this soon-to-be-very-provocative song (perhaps the last song I would ever get to sing):

[ELDER PRICE, SPOKEN]

Excuse me, sir, but what does that phrase mean?

[MAFALA, SPOKEN]

Well, let's see. Eebowai means "God." And Hasa Diga means "Fuck you." So, I guess in English it would be "Fuck you, God!"

Suddenly, any and all laughter was replaced by one singular collective gasp. Audience members began turning to each other as if to subconsciously ask if they had just heard what they thought they had just heard. Some buried their heads in their clothing, as one might do in a horror film. A few showed more visible displeasure by shaking their heads in a definitive side-to-side "no" motion. I had known this was coming. My nightmare had come to fruition: I was about to die . . . in a 132-person theater. However, there was no turning back now.

[UGANDANS]

Hasa Diga Eebowai!

[ELDER PRICE, SPOKEN]

What?

[MAFALA]

When God fucks you in the butt . . .

[UGANDANS]

Hasa Diga Eebowai!

[MAFALA]

Fuck God right back in His cunt!

That collective gasp now had more audible sounds to them. You could really only hear a mixture of consonants and syllables, not representing any actual words in the English dictionary, but rather universal sounds of stunned shock and displeasure. The stunned response from the audience was a timely reminder that sometimes, very controversial satire might be better left to rudimentary animated characters on Comedy Central.

[UGANDANS]

Hasa Diga Eebowai!

Fuck you, God!

Hasa Diga Eebowai!

Fuck you, God!

Suddenly: a new sound broke through the gasps, shrieks, and murmurs. It was a sound I was loosely familiar with, and yet, for the last fifty seconds, a sound that had been so foreign. The English word for it is: LAUGH: *the spontaneous sounds and movements of the face and body that are the* instinctive *expressions of lively amusement.*Oxford [emphasis mine]

It echoed through the tiny house. Then, there was a second laugh. A third. And soon a cascade of laughter. We couldn't believe it. One brave audience member, who allowed themselves to go along on this insane ride, had suddenly and profoundly given the entire audience permission to join in. Now, instead of silence, you could barely hear the lyrics over the roars.

[MAFALA]
Here's the butcher, he has AIDS
Here's the teacher, she has AIDS
Here's the doctor, he has AIDS
Here's my daughter, she has A
Wonderful disposition
She's all I have left in the world
And if either of you lays a hand on her
I will give you my AIDS!

[UGANDANS]
If you don't like what we say
Try living here a couple days
Watch all your friends and family die.
Hasa Diga Eebowai!
(Fuck you!)
Hasa Diga Eebowai!
Fuck you God in the ass, mouth
And cunt-a.
Fuck you God in the ass, mouth
And cunt-a.
Fuck you God in the ass, mouth
And cunt-a.
Fuck you in the eye!
Hasa
Diga Eebowai!
Hasa
Fuck you in the other eye!
Fuck you!
Fuck you God!
Fuck you!
Fuck you God!

Fuck you!
Fuck you God!
Hasa Diga!
Fuck you God!
In the cunt!

As the song ended and the audience erupted into applause, we all knew we were sitting on something unique, groundbreaking, and unabashedly hilarious. Never in any of our wildest dreams did we think that would translate to a fifteen-year (and counting!) Broadway run that still sells out nightly and is one of the top earners in the history of musical theater.

But back to the reading. As we wrapped act 1 (the only act written), I ended with a solo version of "Man Up" that had not yet brought in the other characters and motifs. The audience gave us rapturous applause, and once people had exited, Trey, Matt, Bobby, and their amazing producer, Anne Garefino, huddled in the now-empty theater with then-titan producer Scott Rudin. Scott, who had produced *South Park: Bigger, Longer & Uncut* and *Team America*, agreed with their sentiment that this had to be a stage show. He was also insistent that he had to be involved. And, so with that, things suddenly fell into place. Over the next few months and years I would fly out to LA, do a workshop, wait for more info, and then be called back for yet another workshop. If film is a medium that operates at lightning speed once a cast is assembled, theater is a three-legged tortoise on an out-of-commission treadmill. Most shows take five to ten years to make it onto a stage. If you are insanely lucky, the fastest you can get something up is two to three years. And that was our timetable.

As with everything in life, however, it was not all smooth sailing. For starters, after humbly killing it at that first reading, I slayed at a subsequent second workshop opposite Cheyenne Jackson as my new revolving-door Elder Price. In the early days of the workshops, there would be a pattern of casting and recasting Elder Prices. Both Ben and Cheyenne were terrific, but Trey and Matt felt something just wasn't quite right for what they were imagining. On the flip side, I was getting rave reviews from both early workshops and couldn't have felt safer in the role. I was therefore quite confused and stunned when I received a shocking and unexpected phone call from the *Book of Mormon* casting director, Carrie Gardner. I was delighted to answer her call, as I suspected it must be about the next steps. What I did not expect were her next words.

"The producers have decided to go in a different direction."

My jaw hit the floor. "Excuse me?" I said.

Carrie, who is one of the most stand-up humans you could ever meet, said, "Josh, I truly do not understand this decision or how they think I will ever be able to replace you. I am so sorry. And for what it's worth, I truly don't think we'll find someone who can do what you do."

I felt ill. How could this happen? I had gotten such great feedback. I had done everything asked of me. Had I not done enough?

I reached out to my agent, Meredith Wechter, to try to understand what the fuck had gone wrong. She called me back and as calmly as she could, despite her own rage, explained that Scott, Anne, and the boys wanted to explore a celebrity name for Cunningham. A celebrity? So, they had used me to get the thing up and now, after my sacrifices, wanted to replace me with a bigger name? The name I later heard they were chasing was Jack Black. Like I said, Hollywood loves a type, and, boy, do they get horny when they can upgrade on that type as if they're trading in an older-model Lexus for a new one. Oftentimes, reps will advise you against speaking out from a place of anger. Apparently I didn't get that message because, in a blind rage, I sent Anne and Scott an email that can basically be summed up as: "FUCK YOU AND YOUR LOVED ONES. LOSE MY NUMBER."

I fell into a deep depression and decided that the only way to overcome my heartache and feelings of betrayal was to book a trip with my wife to Italy. A few weeks later, I was on a plane to Oklahoma for business (don't ask). When I landed, I opened up my black Motorola flip phone. I had ten messages. Each one was from the exact same young man asking me to return a call to Scott Rudin's office. I'm not quite sure why this poor assistant felt that leaving ten of the same message would not do the work of one clear "please call us back" message, but alas, when Scott wants something, he gets it.

In this case, however, I was not ready to call Scott back. He had chewed me up and spit me out and I was devastated. I opened up my email and saw a message that, to this day, I think may very well be the most heartfelt, kind, and lovely email Scott has ever sent anyone. Not only did he take full responsibility for what he claimed was his decision, but he fully owned being a complete fuckup and begged me to come back and see the show to its completion. A lot has been said in the press about Scott and his notorious behavior. I can only speak to my own experience, which is: he was the most difficult and awful negotiator I've ever dealt with, but aside from that one incident, he was truly one of the kindest and most caring folks during my *Mormon* run. He did things for me and other cast members that were not only above and beyond but genuinely beautiful, like paying in full for the medical care of one of our ensemble members who went through a very scary incident. That is not to excuse his behavior to others, but only to add personal color to the experience of working with one of the most feared people in Hollywood history. Funny side note: He did threaten to sue me once after I missed two shows with laryngitis. But then, when I called him out on it, he laughed and paid for my doctor's visits.

In 2010, after four workshops and yet another Elder Price, we were finally ready to make the leap to Broadway. The decision had been made to forgo the traditional out-of-town or off-Broadway tryout and instead go straight to the Great White Way. For those not in the know, that is basically unheard of, especially for an original musical not based on any preexisting IP. But Scott and the producers felt that the show was going to live or die on word of mouth, and why not make that bet on Broadway?

It wasn't my ten-million-dollar investment, so no skin off my back, but the pressure was definitely on. There were also two outstanding issues that would need to be resolved before we made the move. First, our brilliant director, Jason Moore, who had been with the project since the beginning, was no longer going to be with us. To this day, I am still not sure what the hell happened, but it was certainly not his decision. Alas, a new person was sought. Names for new directors, to the best of my knowledge, included my *Spelling Bee* director, James Lapine, as well as a few other big names. Ultimately, however, the team went with choreographer/director Casey Nicholaw, who had choreographed *Spamalot* and recently directed the brilliant *The Drowsy Chaperone*. Casey would be hired in a dual role as both choreographer and codirector alongside Trey Parker.

Finally, there was the very small, minor issue of who would be starring alongside me in the key role of Elder Price. We had now gone through three different actors, including Daniel Reichard (of *Jersey Boys* fame). From my perspective, all three had been wonderful actors/singers that landed all of the jokes and sang the hell out of the songs. But, for whatever reason, Trey, Matt, and Bobby weren't quite satisfied. Therefore, the team went back to the drawing board and after a wide casting search eventually whittled it down to three finalists.

At around 2:30 p.m. on June 2, 2010, I entered the small 3rd Street Dance studio rehearsal room in West Hollywood for what the industry refers to as a chemistry read. A chemistry read is an opportunity for two actors to showcase how well they work off each other and what, if any, "chemistry" they have. There were three actors I was going to read opposite. To the best of my knowledge, this is the first time their names have been revealed and since I have nothing but nice things to say about them, I hope they won't be pissed at me for disclosing this information. The first was the lovely T. R. Knight of *Grey's Anatomy* fame. He sang well and was excellent, but in terms of chemistry for these two characters, well . . . there was none. Part of the problem was his height. At five foot eight, he's basically my exact height, which almost makes Cunningham and Price equals. The second actor to read for Price was Nick Lachey (yes, as in the host of *Love Is Blind*). Funnily enough, this was the second time I had met Nick, the first being an audition around 2004 for the role of a heartthrob QB, for which we were both submitted. I fired my agents shortly thereafter. But now here he was again, this time potentially to lead this new Broadway musical alongside me. His singing was obviously great and his charm was exuberant. But something about the two of us didn't quite scream odd couple, which was essential to the show's success. He did all the right things, but even so, it still felt slightly off. As Nick left the room, I had a pit in my stomach. What if we were back to square one and couldn't find the right costar to build this entire thing around?

At around 3:15 p.m., the door opened and a tall, handsome Midwestern man whose face I had never seen before in my life walked in and smiled the biggest, whitest smile I had ever seen. "Hi, I'm Andrew Rannells." He looked like something out of *Mad Men* by way of an Alexander Payne movie. His hair is what men who stare at hair loss websites dream of when booking appointments. His boyish looks defied the unimpeachable fact that this was a man in his early thirties. His perfectly symmetrical facial features, eyes, and hairline looked like an ad for the Aryan race by way of Nebraska.

We exchanged pleasantries and then read three scenes together. The first scene was the moment when Price and Cunningham are paired up for the first time and forced to have a social interaction by themselves. Immediately, I was drawn to Andrew's incredible stillness and precision. His mastery of Price's confidence, pride, and self-righteousness instantly resonated with me as colors this character had long been needing but had never quite been articulated in the way Andrew was so effortlessly inhabiting him. We did the other two scenes and Andrew sang a song called "Something Incredible"

that eventually was re-purposed into "You and Me (But Mostly Me)." After he left the room, I looked at Trey, Matt, and Anne Garefino and said: "It's him. He's the one." They said they agreed but were curious why I felt so strongly,

and I responded with: "In three years of working on this show with numerous talented individuals playing that character, it's the first and only time I've ever been intimidated by an Elder Price." It was the first time I had understood why Trey and Matt had never settled on the previous three Elder Prices from the workshops. Andrew simply was this guy.

We moved to a studio space right above Juilliard and began our final backer's workshop, to close funding for the show. At this time, my wife, Ida, was around five months pregnant. My entire life was up in the air as I was about to move to a different city, become a father, and do a show that was clinically insane. So, why wouldn't I choose this exact moment to go off anxiety medication?

As you might recall, in college I had had what some might call a nervous breakdown and been on Zoloft for the better part of a decade. For whatever reason, I had bought into the stigma surrounding medication for anxiety and depression and wanted to wean myself off before the baby was born. So, I worked with my psychiatrist and started to decouple from my calming friend. The result was almost immediately catastrophic. I would go to rehearsal every day with Casey Nicholaw and learn the very complex and challenging choreography while simultaneously attempting to bury a crippling never-ending panic attack that would leave me breathless, scared, and alone. During that time, the two people whom I confided in the most were my friends Rory O'Malley and my incredible costar Nikki M. James, who would constantly comfort me and attempt to curb my anxiety. Unfortunately, I was in so deep, it wouldn't do much. On breaks, I would go into a corner and cry uncontrollably. On top of all of that, Casey never quite warmed up to me, which only added to my anxiety and stress. I was certain I was going to be fired. It got so bad that I had to fly my mother up to be by my side because I felt so lost and lonely. With the help of my brilliant therapist Joan, I talked through everything and found a new psychiatrist who was able to help me reintroduce the medication into my system, which I can safely say has saved my life and allowed me to feel like a normal human being again. But my God, was that period truly debilitating.

The investor's workshop was the final piece before our trip to Broadway and it could not have been more of a pressure cooker for all of us. We had a new director, we had to learn all-new choreography, I was having a complete mental breakdown, my costar Nikki James was having unexpected vocal fatigue and unfairly being made to feel like her job was on the line, Andrew was trying to play catch-up and become the new anchor to the show, and we were still learning all-new songs and cutting old ones. The biggest break-through was a second-act number that would be sung by Elder Price called "I Believe." The first time I heard it, I knew it was the missing piece. It had been written in a previous workshop, but reworked for Andrew. It was the perfect summation of everything the show had been trying to accomplish thematically and as sung by Andrew, it was nothing short of dazzling.

The big day finally came after four weeks of rehearsals. We were going to perform the show for the big guns with the even bigger wallets. Among those in attendance were theater god Stephen Sondheim and television god Norman Lear, along with some very high-profile investors. Unfortunately, there was one tiny hiccup. The day before, Heidi Blickenstaff, one of our two white female cast members, had a freak accident and ruptured her Achilles. So, we threw a wig on one of the boys and made him my mom. Sidenote: That would become the actual casting decision moving forward, as it creatively worked even better and supported the campiness to have the Mormon men playing the moms, unfortunately leaving Heidi on the sidelines because white women were no longer a part of the cast moving forward.

While the audience was very guarded and my mother (who was in attendance) thought everyone absolutely hated it, the response from the investors couldn't have been better.

The team had the pick of the litter, and while a few folks said "no thanks"—including producer Jeffrey Seller, who would have to settle years later for lead-producing a small historical musical about Alexander Hamilton—a number of other very smart folks jumped at the opportunity.

I flew back home for the summer and fall. Our beautiful baby girl Ava was born in early December 2010 (more on her later) and about a month later, I left my wife and my one-month-old and moved to New York, where they would meet me in two months for the duration of the show.

The show was pretty much ready to go. After a brief rehearsal period, we began previews on February 24, 2011, the day after my thirtieth birthday. We all went in not quite knowing what to expect. At that time, Trey and Matt had been threatened with a fatwa because of an episode of *South Park*, so we had a lot of security meetings. There was also an infamous article written by the notoriously gossipy Michael Riedel, who predicted that "Mormons and Catholic Leaguers would be storming the stage in protest." How does that saying go: "Other than that, Mrs. Lincoln, how was the play?" We entered previews confident, but still quite nervous.

Well, any doubts we had were immediately squelched by the near-deafening laughter and immediate standing ovation from that first preview audience, which included America's Dad, Tom Hanks. The response was

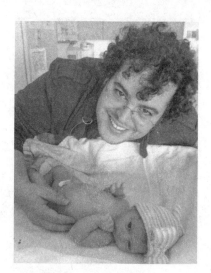

like a rock concert. People lost their minds. What I didn't anticipate, however, was how quickly word of mouth would start to spread. The next day we had forty people waiting outside for lottery tickets. The day after, over a hundred. By the end of the week, we had nearly five hundred people crowded around the theater hoping for any chance to see what the hell was happening inside of the O'Neill Theatre.

The only area I was still feeling uncomfortable with was some of the dialogue around "Hasa Diga Eebowai." I approached Matt one day and said, "Look, I think some of the raping-the-baby references are a little too much for the audience and it feels like we kind of lose them." He took me in and paused. He then nodded his head in agreement, suggesting that I was right, perhaps we needed to cut down the number of references. What I didn't expect was what he said next: "You're right—we're not going far enough. Because we're teetering on the edge, the audience isn't fully on board. We need to double and triple down."

That night, they added three more references to all of the horrible shit that goes on in Uganda and lo and behold, the audience went from gasping in shock to gasping with uncontrollable laughter. It was such a good lesson with regard to satire and one I have never forgotten. If the audience smells fear, they will run far away, but if you reassure them that you understand the discomfort and want to walk them headfirst into the commentary, they will join you all the way. It's what makes Trey and Matt two of the greatest satirists of our time.

On March 24, 2011 (four years after that first email asking me to do a reading), *The Book of Mormon* opened on Broadway. The *Mormon* after-party at Gotham Hall was quite an affair. To this day, it was the most impressive opening party I've ever attended. We all gathered around our rudimentary iPhones awaiting the barrage of reviews.

Traditionally, reviews don't start to come out until around 10 p.m., but there was one in particular that would make or break us. In those days, every show relied on one paper's review to decide its fate. And in particular, one man's. A seal of approval from the *New York Times* and its head theater critic could keep a show running for years; a

pan could close the show in a week. And now, six words were standing in the way of our communal fate and all of our collective efforts: "Did Ben Brantley like the show?"

I don't know who refreshed their phone first, but the review came popping up on our phones one by one and, as we all took a breath, our press rep read it aloud:

> *This is to all the doubters and deniers out there, the ones who say that heaven on Broadway does not exist, that it's only some myth our ancestors dreamed up. I am here to report that a newborn, old-fashioned, pleasure-giving musical has arrived at the Eugene O'Neill Theatre, the kind our grandparents told us left them walking on air if not on water. So hie thee hence, nonbelievers (and believers too), to* The Book of Mormon, *and feast upon its sweetness . . .*

There it was. The *Times* was a rave. Pretty much every single review was a rave. We were a pop-culture-defining hit. We were the new *Producers*, *Rent*, and *Wicked*. The kind of show that generally comes along once a decade and redefines everything. I couldn't believe it. Never in my wildest dreams could I have imagined all of my sacrifices paying off in such a cosmic way. I celebrated long into the night with my costars (perhaps the most brilliant collection of comedic and musical talent I've

 ever worked alongside), many of whom had been involved almost from the beginning, including Rory, Nikki, Michael James Scott, John Eric Parker, Brian Sears, Ben Schrader, Asmeret Ghebremichael, Kevin Duda, Rema Webb, and Maia Wilson. Along

with the newer cast additions,
including my missionary
brother Andrew, we partied
probably way too long into
the night, considering we had
a show the following day.

The next year was a blur of
unthinkable overnight success
and shoulder rubbing along-
side some of the most famous people in the world, from Oprah to Bono to
Springsteen to Streep. Every night was a star-studded event and a chance
to perform for idols. You name it: Jerry Seinfeld, Tina Fey, my old boss Jon
Stewart (whose show I ironically had to quit to do Broadway), the Clintons,
Sean Penn, Will Ferrell, Ben Stiller, Leo. It was a never-ending cascade. Two
of the most significant attendees were the late great Gene Wilder, whom I
had begged to come backstage but who sadly had to catch a train back to
Connecticut, and one of my true idols and inspirations, Billy Crystal.

*As fate would have it, years later I would perform "Man Up" at a gala honor-
ing Billy, after which he called me up and said, "How'd you like to do a show
with me?" The result was the short-lived but absolutely wonderful series The
Comedians on FX, one of the great creative experiences of my life, primarily
because it allowed me to spar with a living legend and, in the process, make a
lifelong friend.*

Now, perhaps the most significant celebrity experience I had was my
time with the man singularly responsible for my desire to one day be an
animated character in a Disney cartoon: Robin Williams. Robin, who was
serendipitously also performing on Broadway that year in the wonderful
Bengal Tiger at the Baghdad Zoo and living in the same apartment building
as me on 63rd and Riverside Boulevard, came to see the show on his night
off. When Robin came backstage, it took everything in me not to cry. I

could quote lines from pretty much every one of his films, including *Hook*; *Popeye*; *Good Morning, Vietnam*; *Good Will Hunting*; *The Fisher King*; *Mrs. Doubtfire*; and of course *Aladdin* (a film that, as I will later explain, would be very important in the trajectory of my life). Robin, sporting a giant, scruffy, Russian-looking beard for his stage role, gave me a big bear hug and said, "Kid, you're a genius! That was one of the funniest fucking things I have ever seen in my life."

What does one do when possibly the funniest person in the world tells you that you have delivered one of the funniest fucking performances they have ever seen? I could have died and gone to heaven. For the next ten minutes he regaled me with his favorite bits and conceded that he was so jealous that there could be so many "cunts, fucks, cocks, and buttfuck" references in a standing-room-only musical on Broadway. The next day I arrived home to a letter waiting for me with the doorman. The letterhead said *Robin Williams*.

> *Josh, it was a tour de force, a comedic colonic. You kicked my ass. I laughed so hard, I was sweating . . . Last night was a comedy revival meeting that gave me the spirit. Bless you brother Josh.*
>
> *Robin*

> *P.S. I'm thinking of changing the title of* Bengal Tiger in the Baghdad Zoo *to* Cocksucker in a Fez.

Had that been the last time Robin reached out to me, I would have literally lived the rest of my life in a state of never-ending euphoria from the ten-minute encounter and the incredible letter, but I was beyond blessed that many more nights would be filled with chance encounters with this beautiful soul. During the course of the next few months, Robin and I would constantly catch up after work in the lobby of our building. He would do bits about everything from the Yakuza to audience members' hearing aids ringing. It was like I would get my own nightly one-man show.

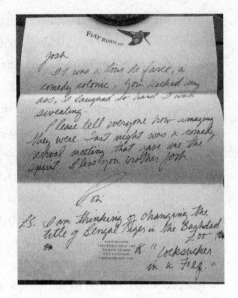

When Robin wrapped his production, he offered me his bicycle. Robin, an avid cyclist, told me he didn't want to bring the bike back to LA and was gifting it to me. I looked at him and then down at my body and said, "Robin, what the hell am I going to do with a $900 bicycle?" He laughed and said: "Well, you could start by riding it." I laughed my ass off and once again kindly told him to give it to someone who would truly use it. To this day, one of the greatest heartbreaks of my life is that I didn't take that bike. Not because it was a great bicycle, which it was, but because it was something to remember Robin by. There have only been a few times I have wept a deep and audible sob for the loss of anyone outside of my family. Robin Williams was one of those people. Unfortunately, he wouldn't be the last.

Back at the Eugene O'Neill Theatre, everyone and their mother wanted tickets and, boy, could you get them . . . if you were willing to pay $800. In fact, that was one of the hard realities of being such a smash hit: the very people we were initially targeting the musical for (students, younger general audiences, and lifelong Trey, Matt, and Bobby fans) were essentially priced out from day one. Ultimately, however, we did do a few "fan performances," which were chosen by lottery and, unsurprisingly, the greatest responses the show ever got. On the whole, though, everything I had worked so hard for had suddenly become a reality and it was beyond my wildest dreams. I even managed to fit in a movie during the run called *Thanks for Sharing*, opposite an incredible cast including Mark Ruffalo, Tim Robbins, Gwyneth Paltrow, and the iconic Pink, a brilliant actress as well as singer. The film is a little gem, but for the record, I would not recommend shooting anything while doing a Broadway show and raising a baby. I would wake up at 4:00 a.m. to go to set for hair and makeup, shoot until 6:00 p.m., get to the theater at 7:00 p.m. and then do a two-and-a-half-hour musical until ten thirty at night, fall asleep at midnight, and then start the routine again the next morning. All in all, however, everything during that time was pretty magical.

That is not to say that it was always easy or even pleasant. Our director, Casey, was a genuinely brilliant creative visionary and truly helped to make the show the giant hit it would go on to become. Having said that, Casey and I didn't always see eye to eye. For whatever reason, I think my choices were often too chaotic for his liking. He would try to steer me in a direction that didn't feel quite right to me, and I would usually push back, much to his displeasure. It takes two to tango, however. To own my part, I think I was, frankly, a stubborn prick because of what I went through with Lapine on *Spelling Bee*, and was therefore usually unwilling to concede to Casey's desires to steer or control my creative choices. After all, I predated him by almost three years and at that point felt very confident in the character I had created. As a result of my stubbornness and his clear displeasure with my choices, we would frequently butt heads and not engage in a creatively gratifying manner.

Years later, Casey would be interviewed for a *New York Times* profile about my return to Broadway with Rannells, and he had this to say: "Josh's comedy basically just says, 'Watch me. Love me.' Josh is just out there. Andrew knows how to hold himself with grace and dignity and just go for it."

To be perfectly honest, while at first I found this statement to be confounding and hurtful, the more I thought about it, the more I laughed at how accurate it actually is, and the truth is, I think Casey is right. I do approach my art with a degree of "watch me, love me," and at this point in my life, I'm at peace with that characterization. At the time of *Mormon*, however, I took such seeming slights personally and it caused friction, especially if I felt Andrew was not being fully supportive of me. After one particularly heated argument with Casey, I actually confronted Andrew and said, "I feel like you don't have my back." He didn't deny it, and that really hurt me. We didn't speak for almost two weeks, until I ultimately understood that it had nothing to do with Andrew and everything to do with the emotionally charged environment we were in. Years later, Andrew and I talked it through and realized in hindsight just how much we'd had to shoulder during that impossibly surreal period. At the time, it was a joy but also a huge responsibility. Now I understand not only his point of view but also that of Casey, who was simply trying to ensure all the pieces were in place for an amazing theatrical experience. Much like with Lapine, Casey and I have made our peace and are now at a place in our journeys where I think we finally understand and appreciate one another.

Another hard part of the *Mormon* experience, and I would imagine any Broadway experience, was Tony season. It is very hard to be part of a team and then feel like you are in competition with your costars. The producers certainly didn't help matters, and it felt like we were constantly having to work against each other instead of with one another. Perhaps the hardest pill for me to swallow was the decision to make "I Believe" the Tony number. I intellectually understood it, but would be lying if I said it didn't hurt to give birth to something and after four years not get to be a part of the biggest moment in the celebration of our show. It was painful for me to be excluded. It was also hard that nobody ever really said to the rest of us: "Sorry we are not featuring you at all on the Tony broadcast after your four years of contributions to our hit show." Having said that, I could not have been prouder of Andrew and can safely say he made that moment one of the defining moments in Tony history. Truly.

In the pantheon of iconic Tony performances, you would be hard-pressed to not include "I Believe" in the top five. While Andrew won the night for his performance, the two of us lost the Tony for Best Actor to the great Norbert Leo Butz. The irony was that both of us losing Tonys to Butz's *Catch Me If You Can* performance brought us closer together and made us once again realize how bizarre the whole Tony campaign season had been for us in the first place.

We recently had the great fortune of being nominated for Best Revival of a Musical and it was amazing to go back and share the stage for the first time at the Tonys . . . this time as a team.

After about fifteen months, I knew the time was right to finally hang up my shirt and tie and say goodbye to the show that made me what I am today. Frankly, I knew I was done, because after around five hundred performances of the same show, I felt slightly checked out and like I had nothing left to give. Not to mention, it was time to take my wife and baby back to our home in LA. I have such fondness in my heart for all of the people I took this journey with and for all of the incredible memories it brought me. My final performance was June 6, 2012. I gathered the entire cast on the balcony and said a teary goodbye. Afterward, I performed for the final time in front of an

electric audience. I think I cried through most of the final act. At the end of the show, I got a message that somebody wanted to see me.

It was my idol Philip Seymour Hoffman. He gave me a big bear hug and said, "You are one talented young man. I really hope we get to work together." We sadly never did, but that one encounter gave me more than he ever could have imagined. *The Book of Mormon* was a series of memories just like that one, memories that shaped my early adult life, shaped my artistic career, and shaped my vision for what I wanted to become. Together we made something that, nearly fifteen years later, continues to inspire and makes people howl, cheer, and applaud; an incredible feat when the average run of a Broadway show is less than six months long. Our producer Anne and her amazing team continue to keep the show fresh, exciting, and essential for audience after audience. It is always thrilling to stop in and see the show with a new cast every few years. I get asked a lot if I would ever return to the role of Cunningham, either onstage or on screen, and the answer is "In a fucking second." I love that show, that character, that crew, and my costars in a way usually only reserved for family. What an honor it would be to work again with such an amazing group of folks. Perhaps one day!

Now that I had conquered Broadway, I was interested in new horizons. More than anything, I wanted to do something that connected with people on a greater level; that's the greatest dream of a performer. Like many before me, I longed to do something that went beyond an audience of just over twelve hundred people a night and instead find an opportunity to entertain people all over the world. People young and old. People from all walks of life. People looking to connect with a universal character that transcends language, age, and class.

Never in my wildest fantasies did I think the path to such a dream would go through an enchanted fjord.

7

IT'S JUST SNOW, MAN!

APPOINTMENT—Thursday, September 9, 2009, 3:00 p.m.—SNOW

QUEEN READING—DISNEY ANIMATION BUILDING—ROLE OF "OLAF."

Back in 2009, *The Book of Mormon* was still more than two years away from opening and I wasn't quite a household name. As I've already recounted, I had a fairly healthy film and TV career with credits such as the hit film *21*, *The Rocker* (which randomly the late James Gandolfini called one of his favorite films), and *The Daily Show*, but I was mostly an "Oh, there's that guy" actor. This translates to: "I know him from somewhere, but I've never bothered to look up his name because I don't find it to be a worthwhile use of my time."

That is not to say, however, that I did not have fans! Two people who had taken notice of me were fellow actors and colleagues Adam Shapiro and his now wife, Katie Lowes. Adam and I had done a reading together of the horrible, unwatchable, please-don't-look-it-up film *Mardi Gras*, but I had apparently left a rather big impression on him somehow during the reading for that garbage can of moving images. Subsequently, Katie, Adam, and I had also done a few workshops together for our mutual friend Bryce Dallas Howard, and they were impressed enough to pass along my name to then Disney Animation casting director Jamie Sparer Roberts.

Adam and Katie had been doing a lot of readings and recordings for Disney Animation and had been asked to participate in a reading of a new project called *Anna and the Snow Queen*. The lead character was essentially the villain of the piece, and she had an army of snowmen. The commander of the army was a strange bucktoothed snowman with a significant lisp and an undying love for his evil queen. He was essentially the quintessential Disney villain sidekick, like Iago and LeFou (more on that guy later) before him. The character's Scandinavian name was derived from the Old Norse moniker Áleifr, which is a combination of the words *anu*, meaning "ancestor," and *leifr*, meaning "heir" or "descendant." In more direct terms, it translates to "ancestor's heir" or "descendant of the ancestors." In this case, the character, Elsa's loyal snowman, would use a more common and modernized form of the name . . .

Olaf. It had always been a lifelong dream of mine to be a part of a Disney animated film. In November 1992, I witnessed the brilliance and magic of Robin Williams as the iconic Genie. I turned to my mom and said, "I want to do that one day." A comic-relief character that could supercharge any scene by channeling impressions, going on wild detours, and delivering showstopping numbers—something that made the few hairs on my prepubescent body stand up. I was *going to do that* one day. I didn't know how or when, but I knew it would happen. Call it ego. Call it id. My brother Jeff called it "misplaced confidence" and told me I was far more likely to be the guy who places pimentos in olives than a working actor (even though I'm pretty sure machines do that). Nevertheless, despite the blood-related doubters, I had my eye on that prize from the age of eleven.

This is also a good time to admit that I had a bit of an . . . *unhealthy* obsession with all things Disney from a very early age.

Growing up in Hollywood, Florida, I lived just four hours from Walt Disney World in Orlando. When I was two, my family took me for the first time to the Magic Kingdom and Epcot Center, and it changed my life. I was addicted to the fantasy and escapism that these parks provided. Epcot in particular fascinated me as a child. It was a fever dream of 1980s corporate razzle-dazzle and a weird synthetic utopia built with concrete and geodesic spheres themed entirely around edutainment (I know, not exactly a kid's idea of a dream vacation, but for some reason it was my favorite theme park on Earth). From Horizons—a ride that explored the possibilities of humanity's future on land, under the seas, and in space—to the phantasmal dreams of Journey Into Imagination—featuring everyone's favorite purple dragon, Figment, and his professorial bearded caretaker, the Dreamfinder—the experiences and attractions of Epcot and its sister park, Magic Kingdom, became places where I learned to dream very early on.

On a deeper, Freudian, subtextual note, Disney World became synonymous with my absentee father. After my parents separated when I was five, my dad would visit every few months or so, and each time, he would

take me to Disney. These fantasy days with Dad would temporarily mend my broken heart and give me this sense of release from the enormous pain he had caused me and my family. It became a way of pretending that all was well, because the joy of Disney can do a lot to compensate for trauma and loss, especially when you are a five-year-old who doesn't yet have the tools to deal with such complex emotions and feelings, or an expensive Beverly Hills therapist to walk you through it. With the gigantic hole that it filled, those therapeutic visits to Disney World soon became an obsession with all things Disney. And to be fair, it wasn't hard to be obsessed with Disney in the eighties and nineties. It was the rock-and-roll era of Michael Eisner, Jeffrey Katzenberg, and Frank Wells. Every year, my generation was bombarded with a new Disney classic in the Second Golden Age of Disney Animation, from *The Little Mermaid* to *Beauty and the Beast* to *The Lion King*. And a few hours from my front door, the parks were exploding with growth, including two additional theme parks, MGM Studios and Animal Kingdom, which would open within a decade of each other. I frequently visited MGM and watched as young, up-and-coming performers by the names of Britney Spears, Justin Timberlake, Ryan Gosling, and Christina Aguilera sang and danced as official *Mickey Mouse Club* Mouseketeers. My obsession with Disney reached such a fever pitch that for my bar mitzvah, our dear friends and symbolic aunt and uncle, Edie and Irv Rubenstein, got me a signed letter from then Disney CEO Michael Eisner congratulating me on the milestone. What thirteen-year-old celebrates a signed letter from a chief executive officer of a Fortune 500 company? Apparently, this one. Suffice it to say, if Oprah is correct and *The Secret* is legit, then boy, did I secret my way into becoming a Disney Legend (an actual award I received in 2022 from the Disney company).

But, back to *Anna and the Snow Queen*. The table read was a way for John Lasseter, then head of Pixar and Disney Animation, to hear a script out loud and see what was working and what wasn't, much like the process Trey and Matt had utilized in those early *Mormon* readings. At the time, Chris Buck, director of Disney's hit film *Tarzan*, had been kicking around the concept for an adaptation of Hans Christian Andersen's 1844 publication *The Snow Queen*, a story about good versus evil that centers around two characters named Gerda and Kai. This certainly wasn't Disney's first flirtation with the Andersen source material. In fact, famed Disney animator and Imagineering Disney Legend Marc Davis had designed a never-built boat ride for Disneyland based on the Andersen work, and

Disneyland itself was in part inspired by Denmark's Tivoli Gardens, which was heavily inspired by the work of Hans Christian Andersen. Other directors had also pitched various versions based on the material throughout the years. But seemingly this was now the closest anyone had come to cracking the code. When I arrived at the large conference room, I met my costars. Ginnifer Goodwin was playing a character named Anna, the heroine of the piece; Jason Biggs was playing Kristoff, the traditional love interest; and finally, Megan Mullally was playing the villain and title character, the Snow Queen. With music by Alan Menken and Glenn Slater, the whole thing seemed like a no-brainer.

Due to the quick assemblage for the reading, all of the songs, written by the iconic duo, would be played intermittently on loudspeakers as we all would silently and gleefully listen. The songs included some Menken/Slater gems like "Love Can't Be Denied," a beautiful traditional love ballad; "Stop and Smell the Roses," a witty, charming song between Elsa and Anna; "Comin' in from the Cold," a jazzy and blues-inspired villain song; and "We're Having You for Dinner," a hilarious group number that is a mix of "Les Poissons" and "Be Our Guest." When the time came for me to bring Olaf's antics to life, I did not squander the opportunity. I channeled every single iconic comic-relief character before me and laid into every joke like it was my last. I played this version of Olaf like a mix between Buddy Hackett and Wallace Shawn's Vizzini, leaning into the character's prominent single-tooth-inspired lisp and his penchant for luxuriating in his post as a villainous henchman; a post he had no business serving in, mind you. Every once in a while, I would catch John Lasseter, in his signature Hawaiian shirt, cackling at some stupid thing coming out of my mouth. John is an animation legend, and I was a massive fan of what he had done at Pixar and what he was now trying to achieve at Disney, so seeing him seemingly gleeful with my choices filled me with joy. After the reading was over, John and the team went out of their way to tell me what a phenomenal job I had done and told me they would be in touch. The pieces were in place and it felt like I had put myself in a position to at least compete for the role. And then November 25, 2009, happened.

The early aughts had been a struggle for Disney Animation, to put it mildly. Audiences weren't exactly waiting in line around the marquee for titles like *Brother Bear, Home on the Range, Chicken Little*, and *Meet the Robinsons*, films that I don't think will be getting live-action reboots anytime soon. Pixar was eating Disney Animation's lunch and it wasn't even close. So, when Disney finally bought Pixar and put its head honcho, Lasseter, in charge of Disney Animation, it seemed like the time had finally come for the OG studio to regain some of its former glory. And what better way to return to form than by doing a princess film, the studio's bread and butter since Walt was king.

Under John's supervision, the first foray back into the princess territory was going to also be a return to traditional animation and center around its first Black princess, named Tiana, in an adaptation of the 2003 E. D. Baker novel *The Frog Princess*, which was itself adapted from *The Frog Prince* by the Brothers Grimm, which was in turn presumably inspired by one of the brothers watching a girl in their hometown kiss something in a local pond (none of which I knew before I googled these things for the book you are currently reading). The point is, the studio was hugely banking on the return of the Disney princess, as it would harken back to the first two golden ages of Disney Animation heroines, from Snow White and Cinderella to Ariel and Jasmine. The buzz was incredibly positive, as were the reviews, and while the film opened well, it was not the massive return to box office gold the studio had been seeking, given its rather healthy marketing campaign. It seems so bizarre now given the massive fan base and popularity that film has accrued since its release over a decade ago, but at the time, it was considered a disappointment (something I'm sure my brothers said about me when I first came out). Shortly thereafter, I received a call from my team saying that unfortunately, given the somewhat muted box office results, Disney would be shifting away from princess movies. They had one more project based on Rapunzel that they were going to try to salvage by doing it as a computer-animated film that utilized a more neutral, less princess-oriented style, but after that, they were going to shift gears completely. And so my dream of becoming a Disney character was dashed . . . or so I thought.

Meanwhile, during the run of *The Book of Mormon*, Jeffrey Katzenberg (then head of DreamWorks Animation and ironically the former head of Disney Animation) came to see the show and loved it. He offered me the opportunity of a lifetime headlining a gigantic new DreamWorks animated film called *Me and My Shadow*. The project was going to be groundbreaking in that it was going to mix both computer animation and old-school traditional hand-drawn animation. In it I played a character named Daniel, a pretty guarded and insular young adult, whose entire life gets turned upside down when his shadow, played by the brilliant Bill Hader, comes to life and recruits him to help fend off a nefarious force bringing the shadow world into the real one. Kate Hudson was to play my love interest. Bill and I did quite a few recording sessions together, and the animation tests I saw were absolutely remarkable and magical. DreamWorks was thrilled and they dated the film for December 2013.

Then, in late 2011, my once and future wish upon a star came barreling back down to Earth in the form of an unexpected turn of events. Disney, having renamed its *Rapunzel Unbraided* film to the more gender-neutral *Tangled*, had its biggest hit in years, once again proving that perhaps

princess films weren't as dead as was currently thought. Suddenly, *Anna and the Snow Queen* was back in business, now with another new gender-friendly title: *Frozen*. There would be some other big changes as well. For starters, a new director came on board opposite Chris Buck: Jennifer Lee, the insanely talented young writer coming off another up- coming hit film, *Wreck-It Ralph*. She would not only codirect but also rewrite the film. In addition, famed Disney Animation producer Peter Del Vecho would now oversee production. Finally, the new composers would be none other than Kristen Anderson-Lopez and her husband (my *Book of Mormon* composer), Robert Lopez. The entire direction of the story was also now shifting from a mother-daughter relationship to a story focusing on two sisters, a change precipitated by a new story team looking to break with traditional fairy-tale tropes.

And, unbeknownst to me at the time, another big wholesale change was the removal of that "annoying" snowman sidekick. On the page and in early scratch track recordings of Olaf, Jenn found him fairly insuffer- able and decided to "kill" the snowman, with a method stronger than melting . . . control/alt/delete.

By some twist of fate, however, an animator at the company had done a fifteen-second animation test using my vocals and Jenn was impressed enough to reconsider.

SIDENOTE: I have seen this test footage, which features Olaf doing dia- logue from my appearance as Bearclaw on the hit series New Girl. *And yes, it is as batshit crazy as it sounds.*

John Lasseter, who remembered my performance at the reading, also pushed to have her reconsider and try to save the character by getting me to play him. Well, luckily, Jenn and Chris were apparently delighted by what they saw and heard from the animation test using my voice. In early 2012, I was officially offered the part of the once villainous, then excised, now resuscitated comic-relief sidekick Olaf, the snowman.

Unfortunately, however, Jeffrey Katzenberg had other plans. With *Frozen* and *Me and My Shadow* now dated for release mere weeks apart, Jeffrey, whose greatest rival was Disney Animation, told my team point-blank that "under no circumstances could I be involved in *Frozen*." This information was relayed to me as I was literally on my way to my first recording as Olaf, and the car had to turn around and take me home. I felt ill. I called up my agent at the time, Tim Curtis, and said, "Please give me Katzenberg's direct number." I called Jeffrey directly and said, "Look, I really want to do both movies. I am the lead in yours and I'm just this side character in the other film." I also told him that I'd essentially be doing it as a favor to Bobby, whom I had just worked with on *Mormon*. Jeffrey reiterated that it would be confusing in the marketplace to have me headlining two simultaneous animated films (apparently a conversation no one has ever had with my buddy Chris Pratt). Not one to ever take *no* as anything other than a long-term-labor *yes*, I reiterated that this was really important to me and that I would do anything to make both films work. Katzenberg, eager to get me off the phone, I imagine, said he would consider the request and get back to me.

A few days later, I had my answer. I could do the film if . . .

- I did not promote it in any way.
- My name was not associated with the marketing.
- The film did not move off its date.
- All scheduling was done around *Me and My Shadow*.
- My involvement in the film was not announced.
- My second child would be named "DreamWorks."

Okay, that last one I made up, but the stipulations were so insane that there was no way in hell Disney was going to go for it. As my agent explained it to me, Jeffrey had basically sent a message to Disney akin to "Bring me the broomstick of the Witch of the West." I knew we were dead in the water. DreamWorks technically didn't have exclusivity, but if I did *Frozen* and ignored any of Jeffrey's demands, it was very likely he'd fire me, which I didn't want to happen. I asked my agent to call Lasseter and give him the news, which I knew was going to be the end of the journey.

And in fact, at this point in the process, hearing Jeffrey's list of demands, the *Frozen* team had indeed already moved on from me and offered Olaf to Christopher Mintz-Plasse.

Yes . . . Olaf was almost played by McLovin.

I was heartbroken. I had somehow snatched my Disney dream role back off the cutting-room floor and now the only way I could do it was if Mintz-Plasse passed and Lasseter somehow agreed to eat the pile of donkey shit (presumably from Shrek's sidekick's literal ass) that Katzenberg had sent first class to Burbank. I, who was generally able to always map out every angle, couldn't see a way out of this one. There was no way I was going to get to do *Frozen*. None. Zero.

And then . . .

"Josh, John Lasseter for you."

"Hello," I said, resignation already in my voice. I knew what this call was. I just didn't realize he was going to be kind enough to tell me no directly.

"Josh, we're gonna make it work. I spoke to the Disney lawyers and we are going to agree to Jeffrey's terms."

Was I in an alternate universe? What the actual fuck? I was stunned.

John continued, "It'll be fun. We'll have people guessing who played Olaf. We'll make it all work. We just want you to play this role."

Miracles can happen . . .

I could not believe it. Never in my wildest dreams was this even the remotest of possibilities. John and Peter had indeed delivered the broomstick, in the shape of a giant middle finger calling Jeffrey's bluff. And Jeffrey, who was just as shocked as I was that his bluff had been called, had no choice but to accept. In what had essentially been a dick-measuring contest between two kids'-content makers, I had somehow come out on top. (For the record, this is the only recorded time I have ever come out on top in a dick-measuring contest.) And to his credit, Jeffrey, whom I am proud to call a friend all these years later, never had to give any terms to begin with, and it was only due to his willingness to make me happy in some capacity that allowed me to take on the role that would in many ways change my life. The same can be said for John, who truly went to bat for me and fought a system designed to never allow for any legal leeway—let alone such prohibitive language—to be accepted under any circumstances.

DreamWorks also helped me in another, not-so-obvious way. Remember McLovin as Olaf? Well, apparently he had a very high animation quote (asking price) because of a little DreamWorks film he had done recently called *How to Train Your Dragon*. So, Disney moved on from him and back to me—all thanks to a DreamWorks deal. As Ian Malcolm so eloquently says in *Jurassic Park*: "Life, uh . . . finds a way."

Now that I was on board, the first task was to record my song. That's right. My very own DISNEY SONG! I couldn't believe this was how my Disney journey was going to begin. Talk about being shot out of a cannon. Not only was I going to get a solo number, but Bobby Lopez, who had spent the previous four years writing *Mormon* songs for me, was going to give me the gift of his music once again, along with his brilliant wife, Kristen Anderson-Lopez. I was shaking with excitement.

The song was hilarious. It was a love letter to summer by a snowman who had zero inkling that of all the seasons, this one would be the one most likely to vanquish him from existence. It had a rat-a-tat quality that harkened back to some of my favorite Disney songs, like Louis Prima's "I Wan'na Be Like You" from *The Jungle Book* or "Ev'rybody Wants to Be a Cat" from *The Aristocats*, but with the biting comedy of something like "Friend Like Me." Essentially, it was everything I could have ever hoped for in a song. We recorded it in one session at Sunset Sound in Hollywood on September 12, 2012. Chris Buck handed me a rudimentary puppet of the character so I could get a feel for what he was going to look like. I can still remember the feeling of pure euphoria holding that first makeshift Olaf, even though it looked like a broke-as-fuck snowman with a coke addiction and Marty Feldman eyes. It was, nevertheless, the full-circle moment that I had first dreamed of in that movie theater watching Robin Williams as the Genie.

When I got in the booth, we dove right in. Over the next four hours we recorded "In Summer," and Bobby, who knew what kind of stupid vocal hijinks my voice was capable of, decided to end the song with a version of me doing an Opera Man–style finale, something I had done comedically while we were doing *Mormon*. The song could not have turned out better and to this day is one of my favorite things I've ever recorded. BUT . . . if you listen very carefully, you will hear something that I have never mentioned before. It is very important to remember that I recorded the song before I recorded ANY dialogue as Olaf, and, because my last experience and memory of the character was held over from the original reading in 2009, I assumed he still had a lisp. Therefore, if you go back and listen again, you will hear a lisp on many of Olaf's *s*'s, something that we immediately dropped when the directors later explained to me that they had decided to lose the original character's lisp altogether. OOPS.

My first dialogue-recording session for *Frozen* was on September 15 at 9:00 a.m. at the Disney Animation Building in Burbank. Chris Buck and Jennifer Lee were there, along with their incredible team, including Peter and our editor, Jeff Draheim. Chris and Jenn talked me through the character and the essence of what they were going for (again, might've been nice had they mentioned losing the lisp *three days earlier*).

Since the idea of Elsa being a villain had been abandoned a few months earlier after the story team, including Jennifer Lee, pushed back on the main female characters being enemies, Olaf too was no longer villainous in any way. Instead he was now the glue between the two girls who had built him together as children.

There were three key words that Jenn used that I will never forget: *childlike, wonderment,* and *curiosity.* Those would be the key ingredients to the recipe to build this lovable snowman. Part of the reason I had wanted so desperately to create a Disney comic-relief character is it was a comedy sandbox in which I could play like a child, and here I was now playing in that sandbox, essentially getting to play a child. I immediately knew that the comedy of this character would come from that naïveté and desire to learn on the job. That would be the springboard for everything. The first dialogue I ever recorded for the film is literally the first Olaf scene in the movie. What is on-screen came pretty much verbatim from that September 15 recording. The mic was turned on and I read the first line: "Hi, I'm Olaf and I like warm hugs."

Jenn and Chris lit up. I don't think I've ever tapped so quickly into a character as I did Olaf. He was on the page, but he was also simply inside of me and when the two met, it was kismet. Chris and Jenn struck a match and let me set fire to the studio. Suddenly, I was talking about "yellow snow being a no-go." I was improvising about my little carrot nose looking like "a little baby unicorn." I was ad-libbing lines like "Who's the funky-looking donkey over there?" to which Jenn responded, "That's Sven," to which I responded, "Uh-huh, and who's the reindeer?" It was magic.

Chris and Jenn had unleashed me and let me essentially improv for four hours straight, and I am still in a state of shock about how pretty much all of my craziest stuff ended up in the movie. Our brilliant editor, Jeff, immediately tapped into my chaos and recorded every little thing, finding places for all of my scattered nonsense throughout the film. I have never had the kind of beautiful trust on any project that Jenn, Chris, and the entire *Frozen* team gave to me so immediately. It's like they had been waiting for me to walk in that door. And lord knows, I had been waiting for that invite through that door for over twenty years. And I was not going to let it shut on me now.

Over the next few months, I would make my way up to Burbank from West Hollywood, where I lived at the time, and record my bonkers dialogue opposite Chris and Jenn, who would stand in for Elsa, Kristoff, Anna, and all of the other characters I was paired with. Things I never imagined making it in the film like "Oh, look, I've been impaled" and "I don't have a skull. Or bones" came out of the constant trust-fall Chris and Jenn would do with me every time they were crazy enough to let me in the booth and just start running my mouth. But the truth is, it only worked because of the brilliance of the existing dialogue in the script.

In particular, there was the one line that Jenn wrote that was so profound and so brilliant, it would allow us to earn all of the comedic mayhem along the way . . . "Some people are worth melting for." The first time I ever read that scene and those words, I cried.

There is a reason that is the most-quoted Olaf line to this day . . . It captures the selflessness, the compassion, and most of all the purity of his heart and his love for Anna and Elsa. That is the genius of Jennifer Lee. Combine that with the brilliant mind of Chris Buck, and I knew from the beginning we were onto something very special. But, when you are working on a project like this, all you really get a glimpse of is what you yourself are doing. I never once recorded any dialogue with my castmates (and still haven't—two films and four shorts later), and was fairly clueless as to what the rest of the film was even about.

Apparently, that was for the best, as the early screenings of the film hadn't been exactly what the filmmakers had hoped for. One day, I was hanging out with Bobby Lopez in the back of a carriage in Central Park, as you do. We were filming an episode of a short-lived Anthony Bourdain series called *The Getaway* in which celebrities go visit different cool and exotic metropolitan cities and eat awesome food and take in the local culture. I said yes to the offer, thinking I would get a free trip to Italy or Thailand or Peru and instead somehow ended up with New York City. Go figure.

So, Bobby and I were shooting this segment and I asked him how *Frozen* was coming along. He told me in confidence that it was kind of a mess. Apparently, they loved the snowman, but some of the other stuff wasn't quite working. According to him, one of the big problems was that test audiences weren't quite getting the time to fall in love with the girls before they became grown-ups, and it was making a lot of the emotions in their eventual conflict fall flat. I asked if there was any kind of solution, and he said they were pushing to add a song that featured both Anna and Elsa growing up as they tried to recapture the thing that had brought them together as toddlers . . . building a snowman. That's how "Do You Want to Build a Snowman?" was pitched to me: in mid-April in the back of a carriage drawn by a horse that was taking a continuous shit while trotting in a man-made park. But there was yet another more significant song I knew nothing about that was soon to blow my mind.

Early that summer, Peter Del Vecho asked me if I wanted to see something. He brought me into his office and showed me a little number called "Let It Go." The song had been written by Bobby and Kristen in June 2012 and was in fact the impetus for shifting Elsa from a complete villain to a misunderstood young woman struggling with the weight of her own powers. This, however, was the first time I had ever even heard of it, let alone heard it. Peter disclaimed that the animation was not quite finished, but that it was pretty close to being done.

For the next three and a half minutes, my jaw hung fully to the floor.

The song ended and I said some form of "holy fucking shit" at least five times, which is probably a record in response to watching a nice princess (technically queen) song from an animated children's film. I said that they should literally release the song as the full trailer for the movie, something the studio had done years earlier with *The Lion King* when they released "Circle of Life" in its entirety.

But publicity was above my pay grade because originally the film was pretty much marketed solely on my character, ironically something they could do now because, oh yeah, I forgot to mention, *Me and My Shadow* had been officially killed by DreamWorks, clearing me of all the original provisions preventing my association with *Frozen*. After an extensive run of adult-skewing darker animated films that weren't performing well, Katzenberg had decided to pull the plug on our ambitious noir-style

CG/traditional animated hybrid. On one hand, it's a shame audiences never got to see it, but on the other, I'm not being sued for telling you now that I voiced Olaf. But, back to the marketing.

Disney was still trying to avoid the potential blowback of making their films appear too girly by overly relying on princess elements. The thinking went that girls would be drawn to the movie regardless be-

cause of the subject matter, but what would bring the boys out to a princess film? So, in an inspired and kind of bonkers move, they decided to do an entirely original animated short featuring Olaf and Sven, Kristoff's trusted reindeer. In the one-minute short, Olaf is sliding on a frozen lake as Sven desperately tries to eat his carrot nose. It was reminiscent of those brilliant wordless Scrat teasers that always preceded the *Ice Age* releases. For me, it was also unforgettable because the teaser accompanied the first film I ever took my daughter to see in a theater: *Monsters University*. In the teaser, Olaf simply makes a few funny silly noises and laughs, but somehow, Ava, at two years old, understood it was me and leaned over to me with wide eyes and said: "Dada. More Dada." I was so moved. My little baby would recognize my dumb voices anywhere. It's like those documentaries you see about a baby penguin recognizing its parents' singing scream squeals in the middle of the Antarctic as Morgan Freeman narrates their hardships.

On October 2, 2013, the day had finally arrived. I drove to the Disney lot from the set of my upcoming film, *The Wedding Ringer* with Kevin Hart, in which I had shot a scene the night before involving a dog biting down on my prosthetic penis, and now I was arriving to see my new Disney animated fairy tale (this job is really weird sometimes). The creative team invited us over to the Burbank lot to watch the completed film a month before its release in the Disney Animation Building screening room. John Lasseter, Peter Del Vecho, Jennifer Lee, and Chris Buck all met us in the lobby, where everything was decked out for *Frozen*, including a giant display in the atrium with all of our characters. We went into the theater and the creative team told us in very teary words that what we were about to watch was a source of great pride for all involved.

My barometer that evening would be my wife, Ida, and my then agent (now manager), Meredith Wechter Lane. Meredith is always very sweet and protects me from criticism while caressing my ego even if something is mediocre. Ida, on the other hand (who I do not pay 10 percent), is, shall we say, very honest. Sometimes to a fault. My ego and her honesty don't always go hand in hand, but because of that I know I can always go to her for an unbiased perspective. She will pretty much nitpick anything I star in and make sure I know all the flaws before she gets to any compliments. It certainly keeps me grounded—and sometimes even scraping to get off the ground. I had told her nothing going into the screening, because frankly, even that night, I pretty much still knew next to nothing.

As the film ended and the credits rolled, my very skeptical and highly critical wife leaned into me and said: "Josh. This one is special." I nodded. She looked at me again and said: "Like . . . very, very special." Meredith also leaned in and squealed, "Holy shit, Josh, that was brilliant." Two honest takes—both incredibly accurate, although stylistically on entirely opposite sides of the spectrum. But everyone felt the same electricity leaving the theater that night.

This wasn't just an animated film. It was something else. It made me feel the way I felt when I first saw *The Little Mermaid* or *Beauty and the Beast*. It made me feel the way I felt when I was eleven years old and first saw *Aladdin*. It felt like I just watched . . . a classic. We all had dinner afterward and Kristen Bell, Jonathan Groff, Santino Fontana, and I (Idina Menzel was sadly stuck in DC doing her production of *If/Then*, which was about to transfer to Broadway) all decompressed and shared thoughts.

None of us could quite wrap our heads around just how good what we'd seen was, but we all felt the same euphoria that whatever it was, it was beyond our wildest expectations. As we sat around the long

table opposite our filmmakers and Lasseter, we all knew we were about to share something "very, very special" with the world, but what the response would be, none of us could have imagined on that brisk fall evening.

On November 27, 2013, *Frozen* opened in North America and immediately crushed every single box office record for a Disney animated film Thanksgiving release, grossing $67.4 million over the three-day weekend, and $93.9 million over the five-day holiday period. Everyone was elated. At best, tracking had suggested between $60 million and $70 million, but nobody in their wildest dreams could have predicted the kinds of numbers the movie was putting up. But it was what happened next that truly stunned everyone involved.

The first time I realized something very crazy was happening is when I went online to buy my daughter an Elsa dress. There were none available. On the internet. You could literally not buy an Elsa dress anywhere. I didn't understand. I wrote a couple of folks at Disney to see if they could get me one since technically, I *was* Elsa's costar. They had none to offer. They told me my best chance would be to write Bob Iger. *Let me get this right,* I thought to myself, *in order to get a little toddler princess dress from my movie, I need to reach out directly to the CEO of the entire Disney company?* Being a father of a desperate little girl, I had no choice but to directly write the legendary Bob Iger like he was an Amazon vendor. He wrote me back that he was having the same problem and he pulled some strings and got the very last one in stock from Hawaii for his family.

Then, suddenly, everywhere I went I started hearing "Let It Go." At the mall, at restaurants, in neighbors' backyards, in abandoned alleys, in places of worship, on airplanes, in taxis, in gyms, in nightclubs, in doctor's offices (because there's nothing like being told you need immediate open-heart surgery while Idina Menzel belts high C's). I couldn't understand it. Everywhere I went, there it was, playing like an accompanying soundtrack to my life. But it wasn't just the song. Suddenly everyone also had an Olaf doll. With my voice. Poor Jonathan Groff told me a story about flying home with an Olaf doll in the compartment head and apparently, during turbulence, it got stuck on repeat screaming, "Watch out for my butt" and "Put me in summer and I'll be . . . a happy snowman!"

There was also the little problem of how I really hadn't changed my voice much for the film, and so now suddenly everywhere I went, from the grocery store to the gas station, kids would do an *Exorcist* slow turn when they heard me open my mouth. And not just kids. Random adults and celebrities too. Sacha Baron Cohen forced me into a kitchen at a holiday party and made me record a message for his kids four different times until it was to his liking. Adam Sandler was calling me to sing to his children. Melissa McCarthy was asking me to do "the voice" for her in a glitzy ballroom as I stood in a tuxedo doing my best impression of a grown man trying not to do character voices on a night out on the town.

And then there was the movie itself. It just wasn't stopping. Usually, after a movie opens, it has a fairly big drop-off the following weekend and then an even steeper one in the weeks after. But week after week, *Frozen* would stay on top. Insanely, *Frozen* remained in the top-ten highest-grossing films domestically for sixteen consecutive weeks, something that hadn't happened in over a decade. And abroad, it was an even bigger juggernaut. From Japan to India, from France to Brazil, from Korea to South Africa, there wasn't a part of the globe where kids weren't singing "Let It Go" and sharing warm hugs with their Olaf plushies. *Frozen* was no longer a movie. It was a phenomenon. A pop-cultural touchstone that connected with the zeitgeist in a way that nobody could have ever imagined.

To this day, I am often asked what I attribute the success of the franchise to, and in particular that first film. Honestly, I don't think it's simply one thing. Among its appeal is certainly the focus on two sisters, a dynamic rarely explored in similar films. There was also the disposal of the well-worn trope that was the previous traditional meaning of "true love." But, at its core, I think the reason audiences love *Frozen* and its characters so much is that there is a complexity to Anna, Elsa, Kristoff, Olaf, and Sven that feels unique and special. And that characteristic especially holds true in that first film for Elsa, a heroine for the ages that took something society called a weakness and turned it into her own strength. She wasn't just a warm and fuzzy protagonist, but a complicated young adult who was in many ways scared and bitter, desperate and alone, frightened and powerful. Those elements feel so familiar now, but in 2013, they were groundbreaking for the genre. And similarly groundbreaking was that she wouldn't be saved with a kiss from a male love interest, but with the undying love and potential sacrifice of both her beloved sister and the little snowman they built together for the first time as kids. A snowman transformed by the potent love of two sisters, who himself transformed me from a kid who grew up idolizing iconic Disney characters to somehow becoming one myself.

And what made it all the more special is that this story of two little princesses with a bond for the ages could in turn be shared with my own two daughters . . . two little princesses whose dad once upon a time wished upon a star and discovered that wishes really do come true.

BOOK III

Of Adulthood, Parenthood, and Avoiding White Hoods

GADISM

As parents of girls, who we are is defined not by the choices we make, the milestones we mark, or the paths we forge on their behalf.

Who we are is ultimately decided by whether or not our kids think we are slightly better than a piece of dog shit baking on a sun-drenched sidewalk and hopefully not much worse than a cringey embarrassment to their friends or the social media community writ large.

Knowing Taylor Swift song lists and having a basic comprehension of TikTok dance trends will be a good start on your path to acceptance.

8

JUST KIDDING

"Dada." The first time my daughter Ava said that word to me, it all made sense.

Life. I suddenly understood the meaning of it. It's all fun and great: partying, learning, working, earning, but none of it comes close to the euphoria and sense of responsibility that comes with an infant or toddler looking into your eyes and making claim to you as their caretaker.

It is a feeling of weightlessness. Of gratitude. Of love. Their undying trust that you will protect and nurture them gives you in return a sense of purpose and clarity. As they look at you with their big, helpless eyes and say that word, "Dada," you feel a desperate need to fulfill the promise of that title and all that comes with it. Just two syllables said in the tiniest of munchkin voices and I would literally cross oceans and deserts for them.

Until one day, in the blink of an eye, "Dada" becomes "SHUT UP, WHY ARE YOU ALWAYS SO ANNOYING AND EMBARRASSING, I HATE YOU," which for whatever reason, doesn't quite have the same ring to it. Alas, this, dear reader, is the saga of fatherhood.

I always wanted to be a dad. I think a big part of it was the absence of a real father figure for most of my childhood, until my stepdad, Stan, came into my life. I went from having a father who was never really there for me to eventually having a male presence who would take me out to talk through things, help guide me through socially challenging situations, and simply show me what normal dad-son activities should look like, from fishing to going to baseball games. I wanted to have a second chance at building such a relationship from the beginning.

Ava was born in December 2010, a month before I had to leave for New York City to start rehearsals for *The Book of Mormon*. The first two days of her life, I was terrified I was going to fail. I was shown by a nurse how to swaddle her like a burrito and when it was my turn to do it, I had her looking like an open-faced Reuben with every one of her tiny body parts dangling out of the blanket like pieces of pastrami. Washing her delicate little head in the sink was equally challenging, with me being terrified of letting her slip out of my hands, or getting soap in her eyes, thus blinding her for the duration of her life. The first time I had to put her in the car seat to take her home from the hospital, we all nearly died because I kept looking back at her every five seconds to make sure she was still breathing. In fact, for most of the first year of her life I was looking for signs of sudden infant death syndrome, since I had read one parenting book that made it sound like it was as frequent in newborns as the common cold. I would turn to my wife every few minutes and say, "Are we sure her chest is moving up and down? Feel her!" If God forbid she had sniffles or (far more catastrophically) a low-grade fever, I was convinced we were going to have to do final rites. I somehow transferred all of my self-focused hypochondria onto her and her well-being.

When I wasn't worrying about the ten thousand ways she could die, I was doing every form of bonding imaginable. We would do skin-to-skin in which I would put her small body on my chest and let her sleep, something I literally cry with joy thinking back on. I would sing to her, usually a mix of sleepy-time songs and eighties love ballads. I would walk her around the neighborhood in her stroller. And most frequently, I would simply endlessly stare at her, basking in the miracle of her being a part of me and yet something so much greater.

The day I had to leave home to move to New York was debilitating. I knew I wouldn't see her or my wife for two months, since Ava wasn't supposed to travel until month three. Every day I would rush home from rehearsal and Skype or call, asking my wife to put her on, which in hindsight did not make much sense. "Here, baby, your dad's on the phone, do some of those sounds you involuntarily make." Nevertheless, that ritual was the only thing that got me through those lonely and sad winter months. When they finally were able to come, it was such a relief. We lived in an eight-hundred-square-foot apartment with a tiny mutt named Didi (a ten-pound cutie we rescued from a kill shelter and who sixteen years later is still going strong and still looking like a baby sea lion), a tuxedo cat named Miles (who terrified me every day at 3:00 a.m. by clawing at my face and sounding like a small child in Vietnam screaming the word *meow* when he cried for food), and our newborn (a baby child I've already described to you and who never once clawed my face at 3:00 a.m.), but it didn't matter because we were together as a family. Unfortunately, the challenges of putting up a new show and doing all of the press that comes with an eight-show week proved very difficult, often keeping me from time with my baby girl, even though she was technically there with me.

That first year was impossibly hard on my poor wife, who essentially had to be a single parent while I was being pulled in every direction. Unfortunately, we didn't have any family in New York and while my amazing mom and awesome mother-in-law, Marisa (a strong and brilliant Italian woman whose expertise includes cooking, dissertations on Dante, and sixteenth-century Renaissance painters), would come once in a while and help with the baby, it was always a comedy show with the two of them basically standing in for Abbott and Costello in a nonstop comedy of errors. We also didn't have many close friends in New York who could help out. So, for the most part, Ida was frustratingly on her own in those early days. Every waking minute I wasn't working, however, I would spend with Ava, taking her to the park, restaurants, or music-related toddler programs. I would luxuriate in her gravitating to a piece of music or seemingly grasping what an instrument could do. Every milestone was a miracle. "Look, she's laughing." "Look, she's sitting up." "Look, she's pushing her torso up ever so slightly from the ground, implying that at some point in the near-to-distant future she might crawl." Crawling was its own stage of anxiety for me. First she wasn't crawling soon enough by what the books were saying, and then it was taking forever for her to walk. I legitimately turned to my wife one day and said, "What if she doesn't learn to walk until she's like ten?"

The first year of parenting was a series of anxiety-inducing make-believe benchmarks that various authors and experts put into books, which make it seem like if your child is slightly behind, you may want to just start over. By the time she was one, I finally settled into relaxing and feeling a great sense of accomplishment that she had simply survived; coincidentally the same feeling I had when I was able to successfully navigate my parakeet through its first year when I was a child. Ava finally walked and, more importantly, spoke. I became obsessed with spending day and night with her and course-correcting my own childhood relationship with my father. The joy of cuddling with her and teaching her at last replaced the void that I had felt as a child longing for the same love, adoration, and time commitment of a father unwilling and/or unable to give it to me.

Ida and Ava eventually went back to LA in early 2012 with our incredible new nanny McKenzie (or the baby whisperer, as we called her) and I followed just a few months later.

Part of my parenting schedule now included parent-and-me classes, which are very different in Los Angeles than they are elsewhere. One of the funniest and most bizarre moments at a parent-and-me class one day (around late 2013) was running into another parent who just happened to be famed director David O. Russell. He had recently been nominated for a slew of Oscars for his brilliant film *American Hustle*. When I congratulated him, he asked me what it is I do. I told him I was an actor. "Oh, what would I have seen you in?" I always feel so awkward listing off credits, but I felt obliged to answer. I told him a bunch of my work, to which he returned a blank stare. Long pause. I finally offered, "Your child may know me from [the recently released] *Frozen*."

"What's that?" he responded.

"Well, it's an animated film about two sisters and their undying love for each other."

"Who do you play?" he continued.

At this point, I wanted to crawl into one of the small cave-themed slides on the playground and hide. "A snowman," I half-heartedly responded to the Academy Award–winning director.

"Do it."

"Do what?"

"The snowman."

Having never before been asked to suddenly break into the voice of an animated snowman by a renowned filmmaker on a children's playground, I wasn't quite sure how to respond. If I said no, I would reasonably never be in a David O. Russell movie. If I said yes and immediately jumped into my snowman voice, I would reasonably never be in a David O. Russell movie. With my choices being evenly shitty, I opted to go for broke.

"Hi, I'm Olaf and I like warm hugs."

There was a pause. Neither of us quite knowing what comes next after one of two grown men (alone outside of a preschool) has just broken into a snowman voice. He cocked his head and studied me, like a coach might study a basketball player who has just used a baseball bat to hit a golf ball during the seventh game of the NBA finals. "Very interesting," he finally said, and walked away, leaving me alone with my thoughts, which ranged from "Am I on ketamine?" to "Is there a subset of the world that has a similar David O. Russell story?" to "Maybe we do live in a simulation." I finally caught up with my wife inside. My daughter was of course playing with David O. Russell's child.

As of this publication, I have not yet done a David O. Russell film.

By the time Ava was close to three years old, we decided that we wanted a second child. Having grown up with two siblings, I had always imagined three total, but as my wife explained to me, we were leasing *her* uterus, so it would be two. Isabella was born in early 2014. Our family was now complete. Whereas Ava was quiet, thoughtful, introspective, and the sweetest bunny you have ever seen, Izzy came out of my wife channeling Gilda Radner. Her energy, even as a baby, was chaotic, hilarious, and off-the-charts bonkers. I could not believe two human beings made from the exact same genetic recipe could come out so completely different. Ava loved her binky; Izzy hated hers. Ava loved to be swaddled; Izzy hated it. Ava would fall asleep in ten minutes; Izzy would literally twerk herself to sleep over the course of an hour. They were like DeVito and Schwarzenegger in *Twins*.

Another thing I had always pictured was being a dad to boys. Having only known growing up with brothers, it was a completely new experience to be surrounded by nothing but estrogen. When they are still little and not battling raging hormones, the relationship between dads and daughters had been described to me by many fathers as being one of the most profound and beautiful relationships you could ever imagine, but man, you do not get it until you GET IT. The "Daddy's little princess" phenomenon is a real thing, in which the father of girls is given a full pass while the mother is given whatever is left over. I don't excuse it, I don't understand it, and I don't condone it . . . even though I selfishly love it.

Little girls (not always, but often) tend to give their daddies nothing but love while showering their moms with whatever the atmosphere of hell is made from. To be fair, this is a very general statement, so please forgive me, as it only reflects my own experiences and I in no way mean for it to sound heteronormative. It is simply to say that in *my* household there was undeniably a bias. Having said that, my wife, who was always rightfully pissed by that disparity, is now equally joyful that I too get to bask in the shitstorm that is the early female teen years.

Now, please let me state with conviction that my wife is ten times the mother and father that I am. She literally keeps our children alive, thriving, and fed, while I do funny noises, show them movies, and fart out loud to make them laugh. If she is the president, I am a clown brought to the White House once a year for sick kids. That's truly our dynamic. I cannot do any of the things my wife does. She is miraculous, bouncing them from one activity to another, juggling their academic needs with their extracurricular needs, and making sure they have the resources they require to become exceptionally strong and strong-minded young ladies. If they were left solely in my care, they would undoubtably end up selling bagels out of a bicycle basket . . . which, for the record, they would kill at.

That is not to say I am not a present or fully engaged parent. It is simply to say I am useless next to my wife. So, I truly feel terrible every time one of my kids shows a bias, even though deep down inside I feel giddy. To be clear, the ONLY reason they sometimes favor me is because the word *no* does not come easily to me. I am what you call a "good cop," if there were cops who allowed inmates to go on monthlong vacations out of

the country while incarcerated. About the most discipline I show my kids is forcing them to watch *Jeopardy!* with me instead of *The Kissing Booth*. My wife, on the other hand, is amazing at keeping the home from becoming an insane asylum, specifically with regard to their exposure to screens and social media apps. The two of us agreed early on that we would not allow them to engage in social media until they were old enough to comprehend and deal with the incredibly complex factors that come with having such access. While I tend to cave, my wife puts down the kibosh, even if the children tend to respond to this with something that resembles the third act of a Rocky film.

As I stated earlier, now that my children have gone from very little girls to suddenly now young women, the introduction of hormones has certainly tempered their formerly ever-present enthusiasm for me. Excited shouting has morphed into unspecific aggressive grunting. "That's funny" is now more commonly replaced with "That's so dumb." "Why can't you be home tonight?" has turned into "Do you have to be here tonight?" I will say that I take sadistic pleasure in embarrassing them in front of their friends, but it is only because they constantly make a point of telling me how much I embarrass them in front of their friends. I recently attended a bat mitzvah for one of my daughter's classmates. When I approached the dance floor to start dancing with her, she took off at lightning speed, which made me pot commit to the bit even more, tearing up the floor with my wife to the point that her friends were cheering us on as my daughter looked on through a gaze of shame and awe.

As I now enter this new phase of my daughters' childhood development called puberty, there are endless new challenges, verbal landmines, and trigger-warning situations that I must heroically navigate while simply trying to survive the emotional shrapnel. I wouldn't trade it for the world, however. In a life of incredible milestones and achievements, my daughters are perhaps the greatest achievement of all.

There is so much that we teach children, but what isn't often stated is how much children teach us. My kids, even when they were little toddlers, would teach me something about the world or myself on a daily basis. I'll never forget Ava, at the age of four, crying one day at the dinner table. It was such a deep and heart-wrenching sob that came out of nowhere. As she put her little spoon down to catch her breath, I asked her what was wrong, and she looked at me and said, "I don't want to grow up." Our nanny at the time, Sara, immediately began guiding the conversation, helping to get deeper into what that meant, asking her why she didn't want to be a grown-up. And through snot, tears, and a squeaky voice, she said: "Because I'll never get to be a kid again." Every time I watch the video of this moment, which we miraculously recorded, I cry. I cry not only because of the pain of the realization in that moment that none of us can forever stay a child, but also because of the realization these days that my baby is no longer a baby—and is fast becoming the grown-up she once so desperately feared becoming, and the one I never imagined she would so quickly become. I forever thought I'd be a child.

I similarly fell into the same trap of believing my kids would forever be children, but one day you wake up and realize they are quickly becoming your height. They are going from saying "Dada" to "Dad." Ultimately, you realize no matter how hard you try, there is nothing you can do to stop the inevitability of them one day taking all of the work you have put into them and the thousands of mistakes you have made along the way and becoming an adult in their own right that will one day presumably take care of you. My younger daughter, Isabella, still believes in Santa and elves and magic. I am so scared of the moment she learns none of it is real. Not even because she will stop believing, but because I as her father will stop believing on her behalf.

As hard as we try to shield our children from reality, however, sometimes there is simply no shield big enough to protect them from the unexpected twists and tragic turns of life. On June 24, 2022, I received an earth-shattering call from my wife. Her nephew, Marco, had died in his sleep at twenty years of age. Marco was an honors student at the University of Miami, preparing to pursue international law after graduation with an eye toward Harvard Law. Marco was quite simply one of the most brilliant young men I have ever met. His fierce advocacy for those without a voice was inspiring and invigorating. He was so full of life that there was no way to imagine him ever being lifeless. Yet that is precisely what happened. His sudden death was not only catastrophic for his parents, Saadi and Mimi (whose only child was now tragically gone), and for us as his relatives but also for the two young cousins he left behind. Then aged eight and eleven, they had never had any reason to question their mortality to that point.

In what was one of the hardest days of my life, we sat them down and explained as best we could that their cousin (one of only three they had) was now gone. My younger daughter screamed and cried until she fell asleep from exhaustion. My older daughter let her tears openly flow down her face and asked for privacy. She then went into her room, closed the door, and wrote a letter to her beloved Marco. They both grieved in their own unique ways. Nothing my wife or I did could blunt or take away the pain they felt, but we remained steadfastly by their side to hold them, to love them, to answer their questions as best we could, and to provide them the space to grieve and heal.

Watching them work through that process was and still is the hardest thing I've had to face as a parent. It wasn't even guiding them through the turbulence of their loss that was the scariest part of the process; it was the fear as to whether or not we had done enough as parents prior to the loss to give them the resources they needed in order to guide themselves through the pain. I sobbed watching them both experience grief in their own ways, not only because I was so devastated for (and alongside) them, but also because I was so profoundly proud that they were processing their anguish in their own time and in their own ways. My daughters have and continue to impress me on a daily basis, but the way they worked through this unthinkable incident makes me proud to be their father. In many ways, I think they were able to find their own peace with it far faster than my wife and I did, who, now two years on, are still having a hard time comprehending Marco's absence from our lives.

Fourteen years in and all I know for certain is that being a dad is simultaneously both the greatest gift in the world and the greatest challenge. Every choice you make in turn shapes every aspect of who they will eventually become. No matter how big or how small, every ripple leads to a wave. From the types of movies they watch, to the kinds of musical artists they listen to, to the way they carry themselves in times of difficulty, to the way they show modesty in times of success; from prepping them for camp to sheltering in place from viruses, the work of a parent (and in my case a dad) is all-consuming and often terrifying.

Now, every father has their own observations, lessons, and rules of parenting. For me, there are many lessons that I wish other fathers would have shared with me before I became a dad or even now while I continue to navigate the choppy waters that is fatherhood. I therefore decided that, for the purposes of this book, I would share some of my own observations in the hope that they may be useful on your own journeys. Here now is a list of some of the things I *think* that I think about parenthood. Hope it's helpful:

1. Just because your child tells you they want ice cream on a Tuesday night at 9:00 p.m. doesn't necessarily mean you have to give it to them. You do have the option of saying no. Sure, it may mean that they say, "You are a bad daddy" or cry with great vocal effort within your line of sight, or vow to "not love you anymore." All of those cons, however, must ultimately be weighed against the potential fallout of being their twilight sugar dealer, namely, turning them into a leprechaun-sized monster who traffics in spazzing, jumping on beloved furniture, and licking things like air and walls.

2. Six is too young for John Hughes films. I know this is a controversial statement and I know a lot of readers will find this to be deeply divisive, but it takes an exceptional father

to answer questions about Judd Nelson's questionable stances on companionship or Ferris Bueller's clinical destruction of educational norms. Yes, *Home Alone* may seem innocent enough for your six-year-old, but do you really want to plant the seed in a six-year-old's head that when faced with armed assailants, they too would be able to whip up some DIY paint bucket Molotov cocktails and use the family's handy-dandy staple gun to assault said assailants? More importantly, do you even own a staple gun?

3. Love comes in all shapes and viruses. By committing to having a child, you must be willing to not only share your love and your home but also your immune system with them. You see, while a child may not love to share their toys or anecdotes about their day, the one thing they absolutely love to pass along are infections. Be prepared to have sounds come out of your body you have never imagined possible and sputum that runs the gamut between every shade of yellow and green on the color spectrum. The really fun part, however, is that once you have finally overcome one infection, another will be eagerly brewing in your upper-respiratory tract.

4. Tears for fears: be prepared to become a full-grown hypochondriac on behalf of every sniffle, pain, fall, and medical incident your child endures. Never in the history of self-care have I ever been so concerned as I am when any little thing makes my girls cry. Their pain is my terror. These precious commodities seem so fragile, but in reality, they are truly resilient. In fact, it takes a while to learn that it is we who are far more fragile than them. For example, when my daughter has a nosebleed, she simply puts a tissue on it, washes it off with a little water, and goes about her business, while I throw myself into the deep recesses of WebMD, call our pediatrician multiple times until

I get her, research nosebleed specialists, and keep myself up all night staring at my daughter's nose, looking for further signs of something she forgot even happened thirty minutes after it was done.

5. How to tackle bullying without literally tackling a bully. It is a fair assumption that in the course of child-rearing you will encounter an adversarial foe who focuses unwanted attention on your child. If that happens, it is best not to do what I did when a third-grade boy called my child ugly and made her self-conscious about her looks, which was to publicly shame and lightly threaten him on my social media platforms. I know now, with the help of my very angry wife, that that was not the ideal way to confront an issue like eight-year-old bullying. Instead, it is important to give your child the resources they need to deal with little fuckers like ██████████, so that they can learn how to navigate those issues for themselves throughout life. And while I know I could confidently kick the shit out of that prepubescent punk, it is apparently not within societal norms for a grown man (who also happens to be a public figure who does kid movies) to threaten a mean little boy. Fine, lesson learned . . . so long as he doesn't go near my baby girl again.

6. Do not project your own issues and insecurities on those tiny carbon copies of you. Each of us comes with baggage. I have a plethora of issues relating to food, abandonment, and self-worth (which we've now discussed ad nauseam). As much as I try not to, I often feel myself worrying about my girls encountering those same demons along the way. As a result, I will occasionally put unwanted attention and/or pressure on them to steer them away from these concerns. In so doing, however, I may run the risk of giving them *different* issues based on my own issues. Sometimes,

we have to trust that our children will have their own shit to deal with that they in turn can pass on to their children without also carrying our burdens as well.

7. Birds and bees don't do missionary. My first encounter with intercourse was discovering *The Joy of Sex* and *More Joy of Sex* illustrated books in my parents' bedside table drawer at the age of five. (For the record, I am now forty-three and still don't understand how most of those positions feasibly work.) I made a vow to be much more open and forthcoming about sexual education with my children than my parents had been with me. So, one day, after hearing from my wife that my oldest (then eleven) was hearing things about intimacy at school, I sat down with her and said, "I want you to know that I am here to answer any and all questions about sex and your body to the best of my abilities." What transpired was the single most uncomfortable conversation between two human beings in the history of the world outside of Kennedy and Khrushchev circa 1961. What I learned the hard way based on my daughter's facial reactions (which for the record I've never seen another face do before or since), is that there is such a thing as "oversharing." My lesson here is that, when in doubt, let the skilled professionals and educational literature available on the subject do the talking. Another word to the wise: always make sure your bedroom door is locked before performing any chapters from *The Joy of Sex*, as you never know when your six-year-old, wearing a Hello Kitty nightgown, is going to saunter up to you both like a terrifying apparition and say, "What are you doing?"

8. Lessons in empathy: it never occurred to me how blessed I was growing up in a household that wore its emotions on its sleeves. While it was often quite difficult to watch my mother openly sob

after my father left us for his "other family," I am grateful that she didn't try to shield me or protect me from that emotional wreckage. It gave me permission to also grieve and not be ashamed to share my own confused and raw feelings. The idea of openly crying is seen by many to be a weakness or a social flaw, but I would argue that it is in fact a strength and a power. If we can bestow that element of emotional intelligence onto our kids, imagine how much less chaotic and cruel this world would be.

9. In a one-on-one match, imagination can kick the shit out of an iPhone any day of the week. Trust me, I know how easy it is to hand a crying child an iPad or plop them in front of a TV to simmer them down, but over the course of my parental journey, one thing has become clear to me: nothing you hand your kid can ever replace the power of what they are born with. The potential of imagination and play is greater than any app or any device. I cannot imagine, nor can I stomach, the thought of being born now in the digital age. When we are constantly bombarded by ones and zeros and have a screen in front of us at all times, it is hard to remember just how much the computer chip called our mind can achieve and create when left to its own devices. I have been very fortunate to have a partner who from the very beginning understood that in a universe in which our children would eventually be inundated with technology, it was beyond important to place an emphasis on tactile and creative play over Minecraft and TikTok. In so doing, our kids can now just as easily keep themselves busy writing songs on the piano or cooking a feast in a mini kitchen (complete with a functioning sink and fingernail-sized toaster) as they can playing on their iPads. There is no right or wrong answer, but for us, that balance has been hugely beneficial in building their confidence and creativity, so that eventually they can have a stable and healthy

relationship with the rabbit holes known as social media, the internet, and whatever AI has in store for us.

10. Love and be loved. It is still relatively difficult for me to process the literal loss of almost a year and a half of normal life to a global pandemic. Yet, despite the sacrifices, the hardship, and the tedium of staying home for weeks on end, there was one shiny piece of silver lining: the time I got to spend with my daughters. It was the closest thing I had ever experienced to the 1950s idea of a nuclear family, and it suddenly occurred to me that I no longer wanted that to be the exception, but the norm. In our hustle-and-bustle lives, it is sometimes all too easy to get lost in work and life, but it is important to remember that our kids only get to be little once and when that ends, there are no do-overs. I have never loved anything quite as much as I love my two girls. But it is the love I feel from them in return that drives me every day and makes me want to be the father I know I am capable of being—the one I myself never had.

9

HATH NOT A JEW
BOOK-WRITING DEALS?

My relationship to faith is a tricky one. While I consider myself to be spiritual, I have never considered myself to be religious. For starters, the hypocrisy of my own father going to temple every week and then casually cheating on my mother and starting a second family while we were desperately longing for his presence at home kindaaaaaaa tempered my relationship to the religion he hid behind.

In many ways being Jewish was divided into two parts for me as a kid: the intense traditionalist and rigorous approach my father took to it (making us walk to temple every Saturday, forcing us to keep a kosher house, celebrating all eighty Jewish holidays, attending six years of Hebrew day school) and the more guilty associative and painful reverence that my mom's side approached it with (presumably to honor my grandparents and all of the loved ones they lost during the Holocaust). Neither of those things is particularly excitement-inducing. I guess most religious upbringings are based on a no questions/all devotion mentality, but it doesn't exactly foster a healthy relationship with faith when you're born into it at gunpoint.

Even as a child I would gravitate less to the tenets and more to the traditions. I loved the food, the gathering of family and friends, and the communal environment each holiday and tradition fostered. There is something beautiful and profound about simply doing the same ritual or saying the same prayer that your ancestors did and said three thousand years ago. In a way, it gives you a cosmic sense of place and purpose. Like anything else, however, when it is driven more by dogma and fervor, it becomes something far less emotionally appealing and far more task-oriented and therefore constricting. I was thus always divided between two feelings with regard to my faith: feeling inspired and feeling strangled.

It was only after my parents divorced and my mom allowed us to break with the more conservative approach to faith that I felt liberated from the constraints of my piety. For starters, I could have a cheeseburger. The first time I tasted one, I did fear I might be struck down, but was so enamored by the flavor that I felt it was probably worth it. Secondly, I could start to do religion on my own terms, like not going to temple because I had to, but because I wanted to. When my relationship with being Jewish became less about edicts and more about introspection, I came to really appreciate Judaism and its deep levels of mysticism and history (two things that endlessly fascinate me). Thus describes the journey of my relationship with the religion part of Judaism. What it does not account for is my identifying as a Jew.

Being Jewish has two meanings: one describing a faith and the other describing an ethnic group. The history of these (my) people as an ethnic group is tumultuous at best and horrific at worst. While the paternal side of my family was a minority group subjected to basic humiliation and subjugation at the hands of more dominant Middle Eastern factions, my maternal family was not faring much better in the West. My grandparents Joseph and Evelyn were both Polish Jews. Living as a Jew in Poland in the early twentieth century meant relative peace as long as you didn't cause trouble and knew your place. However, after the First World War, a scapegoat was needed as a result of a failing economy in nearby Germany and a radical turn toward populism and fascism across Western Europe. Thus, my grandparents went from simply having to stay out of the way to quickly being rounded up and sent to concentration camps. Both of my grandparents lost their parents at the start of the war. Barely teenagers, they watched as their families were dragged away from them and they were put to work at the cruel hands of the Nazis. Both of them were branded with numbered tattoos on their arms, designating them as nothing more than livestock. Their lives became a carousel of forced labor, humiliation, torture, fear, and, when they could fit it in, sleep and food.

The sights and sounds of their new lives were frighteningly unfamiliar and terrifying. My grandfather once described arriving in Auschwitz as confusing and surreal. As the train doors opened and he was forced at gunpoint to disembark, he "looked around and saw emaciated bodies which resembled a herd of human zebras in striped thin garments." He was then required to have his head shaved, and when he looked at the Nazi officer overseeing it, he was hit in the head with the butt of a rifle and told, "Eyes front, Jew." In an ironically grim twist of fate, my grandfather may have escaped the gas chambers thanks to one of the most notorious agents of death in the history of mankind. When he first arrived at the camp, a high-ranking official looked up and down at a row of men, splitting them up into two groups. The healthy-looking group would be sent off to work hard labor, while the weaker-looking group would be sent off, never to be seen again. Years later, after my grandfather had escaped, he saw a picture of the most-wanted men in the SS, and the Nazi officer who had sent him off to labor was among the faces. His name . . . Josef Mengele.

Like most Holocaust survivors, my grandparents were resourceful, resilient, and just plain lucky (as lucky as one can be when they are forcibly put in a death camp). What skills they had, they used. What skills they didn't have, they quickly learned so as to make themselves less expendable. For instance, my grandmother applied her rudimentary bilingual skills to translate Polish into German and vice versa for the primarily German-speaking Nazis. My grandfather, on the other hand, quickly learned how to work with iron and was put to use on the construction of the Autobahn. Working for the Nazis did not, however, translate to working *with* the Nazis. Oftentimes, the slightest thing would trigger a violent response—like my grandfather not screwing in something correctly and in turn getting his face beaten with a wrench. As he put his hand up to block the wrench, it broke his finger, resulting in a digit that would remain slightly mangled for the remainder of his life. As a result of the assault, his fingernail was broken and quickly resulted in infection. When he went to the infirmary, the medic ripped his nail off without any anesthetic and gave him an aspirin. He had to hide the swelling and discoloration to ensure the Nazis wouldn't think him incapable of doing his job.

With both grandparents having already lost nearly half a decade to Nazi subjugation, there seemed to be no end in sight to their trauma and pain. As fate would have it, however, the Nazis devised a plan to march the remaining survivors to their deaths while simultaneously attempting to use them as collateral and human shields along the way. By some miracle, Joe and Evelyn both escaped on their respective death marches. My grandfather used overhead gunfire from Allied planes to run into a forest with a group of friends, while my grandmother and a few others broke away from the troops and hid under a railway.

These harrowing stories defined my childhood. My grandparents were open books when it came to describing their nightmare experiences during the war, both to enlighten me and more importantly to warn me. The sad truth is, I never took much heed of their warnings. To me, Jews during my lifetime were living in a time of prosperity and freedom, a rare distinction the diaspora hasn't had for over 2,600 years, previously being exiled, enslaved, converted, slaughtered, "inquisitioned," or pogromed. The end of the Second World War seemingly meant a fresh start and a new understanding that after the massacre of six million, there was no way Jewish people would ever be subjected to that kind of bigotry, bias, and hatred again. I therefore always looked at my grandparents' warnings as more of an intellectual exercise than a practical concern.

Never in my wildest dreams could I have imagined both a return of Nazi rhetoric and self-identification along with a rabid disregard for anyone and anything Jewish. From chants of "Jews will not replace us" at marches like the one in Charlottesville in 2017 to massacres in Jewish places of worship like the Tree of Life synagogue massacre in 2018 to the romanticizing of terrorist organizations like Hamas in 2024, the twenty-first century has been an eerie return to the kinds of rhetoric that once felt so safely steeped in the past. It is once again popular to blame Jews, a favorite pastime for so many looking for a useful scapegoat to the world's problems. This has been a difficult realization.

While I rarely pray, practice, or even identify as a Jew, I feel an innate burden and expectation to protect and defend my identity against those who would try to disparage or destroy it. Generational trauma will do that to you. I have been fascinated and disturbed by the endless Jewsplaining I have experienced as of late, with people trying to lecture me as to what does and does not constitute antisemitism and the subsequent categorizing of acceptable Jews from non-acceptable Jews. I can only imagine how it must be for those who aren't public figures and don't have a platform with which to fight back. To my mind and to so many people like me, it has always been a zero-sum game to take a position on any geopolitical issue that directly deals with the one Jewish homeland in the modern world, but somehow it is now also a zero-sum game to beg people weighing in on these geopolitical issues to not simultaneously be antisemitic as they offer their expertise on what constitutes a good Jew from a bad one.

I personally try to avoid the Middle East issue altogether, as the middle ground involving humans peacefully coexisting is apparently not available as an option, leaving people like me who still enjoy nuance and critical thought to tribal up and pick sides. I am sadly grateful that my grandparents are no longer with us because I don't think they could have seen what has happened over the last decade and feel anything but the same fear and anxiety they once felt in the days leading up to the Holocaust. My great-aunt Fay, another survivor, now tosses and turns at ninety-eight years old as she watches the news and says to anyone who will listen, "It's happening again, isn't it? Why must they always hate us?" I truly wish I could answer that question. I don't know why she must fear going to temple on a high holiday. I don't know why she must incur the wrath of both the radical right and the radical left, leaving her once again feeling radically isolated and alone.

Think about this: When your history is one of being singled out and blamed for everything from the death of Jesus to the downfall of the German economy, there really isn't much left for my people to achieve, is there? We are only 0.2 percent population of the world, which is significantly less than those practicing voodoo, but apparently still powerful enough to run the world. If there is a secret cabal of Jews puppeteering all of humanity, I certainly have not been invited to the party. I would happily welcome the opportunity to drink goats' blood with George Soros and Steven Spielberg as we plot out which world bank to control next. On the flip side, I would equally love to not have to play Whac-A-Mole with antisemites parading as activists and neo-Nazis posing as patriots.

I don't anticipate that this chapter or this plea will change hearts or minds. In fact, I know the opposite to be true. Those who wish to use my faith and my identity as a cudgel for their cause will continue to do so and hide behind misinformation and disinformation, salivating for more opportunities to froth at the mouth and scapegoat a familiar foe. What I do hope, however, is that one kid who fears identifying as Jewish reads this and knows that while you should be vigilant, you should not fear or be ashamed of who you are. Your identity is one that has never been extinguished despite a multigenerational attempt to do just that. I often wonder if my grandparents didn't constantly repeat the words "Never forget" solely to scare me into thinking the same thing could happen again if we let it, but also to inspire me to never forget our resilience, our tenacity, and our perseverance as a people; our traditions; and above all else, the nihilistic acceptance of our almost hilarious (if it wasn't so damn sad) never-ending plight. To sum up my relationship with Judaism, I'll leave you with this:

I once asked my grandfather if he believed in God. I assumed because he always went to temple every Saturday and kept a kosher house for most of his life, the answer would be obvious and in the affirmative. However, less than a second after I asked the question, he tersely answered back . . . "No."

I stared at him in disbelief. "Why?"

"Because," he continued, "no God would have put me through the hell that I had to endure. No God would allow my family to all be murdered in cold blood for no reason. No God would have taken my entire youth from me as I fought to simply not starve to death or be shot or gassed." The answer was both shocking and yet so obvious. I had always taken for granted that his mere survival meant a renewal of his faith, never once contemplating that the horrors he had to endure to survive could simply mean proof of an absence of God in his weary eyes.

As I pondered his answer, however, I suddenly became incredibly confused by a set of simple facts: Why, for ninety-plus years, had he continued to worship if he felt this way? Why would he go to temple every week, celebrate every holiday, insist on his children and grandchildren doing all of the traditional Jewish rites of passage from brises and baby namings to bar and bat mitzvahs? How could a person who didn't believe in God pray to him publicly and celebrate in his name again and again? I couldn't for the life of me understand. "Papa, why then, if you don't believe in any of it, do you continue to do all of the things that identify you as being a practicing Jew?"

He looked me square in the eyes and smiled a crooked grin. "Because, Josh, it's all I know . . . so, what the hell else am I going to do?"

Tradition, identity, and guilt: the perfect recipe for a card-carrying Jew. I am destined to never fully embrace and never fully withdraw. My and my descendants' journey with Judaism is inevitable and familiar. It will be the same as those who for thousands of years have asked similar questions and arrived at similar answers. Despite the pain, despite the aggravation, despite the never-ending hate from others and from ourselves, we are who we are. Because, whether I like it or not . . . whether you like it or not . . . I am a Jew.

What the hell else am I going to do?

HOWARD

by Ron Howard

Let me take you back to the early 2000s—a simpler time. You see, it was 2003 when a wide-eyed, energetic young man by the name of Josh Gad burst into my life like a caffeinated toddler at a birthday party. He was twenty-two, full of ambition, and maybe just a little too full of himself. I remember this moment vividly because my daughter Bryce had started dating Seth Gabel, a wonderful guy who—by some odd cosmic coincidence—had been best friends with Josh since they were four. Yeah, four. I still don't understand how those two didn't destroy the universe by combining their energies as children.

One day, Josh, in all his cocky glory, asked me to introduce his *Saturday Night Live* audition tape. Now, you have to understand that asking me, Ron Howard, to be a part of your audition tape is like asking Spielberg to direct your high school play. But Josh was persuasive in that charming, over-the-top way that makes you want to laugh and maybe call security. So, of course, I said yes. I mean, how could I not? He'd already roped me into this fantasy where I was auditioning to direct his *SNL* tape, as if I was the one lucky enough to be in his presence.

So there I was, playing along, pretending I was vying for the chance to direct Josh's breakout moment, while he strutted around like he was already the next big thing. It was a performance, let me tell you—one that made me question whether I was in a sketch, a fever dream, or both. Spoiler alert: Josh didn't get *SNL* that year. But he did get something even better—a lifelong commitment to chasing after the most absurd and hilarious moments, all while staying true to himself (and by "true to himself," I mean never letting anyone forget how great he is).

And now, as I sit here writing this for his book, I can't help but marvel at how far Josh has come. As a family friend, let me add that it's a huge relief, because nothing was going to stop this guy, and he's much easier to be around when employed.

And as for that success, I'll just add that in this wacky show business culture, sure, you can bullshit your way into a few auditions, but you don't build a career without delivering the goods, both for collaborators and audiences. Josh has done that in many different mediums and to such a degree that it can only be chalked up to talent and the will to outwork everyone else around him.

By the way, he puts the same effort into being a state-of-the-art family man and friend.

Still, he's a unique character, and you're in a world that only Josh could create, where self-deprecation meets self-celebration in a way that's both endearing and absolutely ridiculous.

Enjoy the ride. It's Josh's world, and we're just living in it—mostly because he made us.

—Ron Howard

BOOK IV

Of Movie Magic, Something Tragic, and Stage Comebacks

GADISM

Life is a roller coaster on the side of a mountain during an earthquake at the end of a mudslide.

The harness will protect you from falling out. The rest, however, is up to God (if you believe in that sort of thing) . . .

Or Mother Nature, science, circumstance, and physics (if you believe in that sort of thing) . . .

10

CONTROVERSY
AND THE BEAST

In 2015, I took my daughters to the premiere of Kenneth Branagh's *Cinderella*. Despite the success of the *Alice in Wonderland* live-action film and *Maleficent*, this was the first live-action Disney adaptation under the stewardship of then Disney Studios president Sean Bailey that truly floored me. There was something about the adaptation that felt not only magical and familiar, but distinctly special in its own right and not just a photocopy of the original animated film it was based on. Word soon got back to me that based on the success of the film, Disney would be gearing up for other live-action adaptations including *The Jungle Book*, *Aladdin*, and *Beauty and the Beast*.

I had already been involved in creating an animated classic, but I started to wonder what it might be like to reimagine one as a live-action film. For one thing, the idea of getting to marry two of my favorite mediums (musical theater and live-action films) was an immediate draw. For another, there was a distinct challenge and opportunity to taking a familiar role and breathing new life into it in unexpected ways.

One day I received a call that there was interest in me playing a role in the live-action remake of *Beauty and the Beast*, directed by the legendary Bill Condon (of *Chicago* and *Dreamgirls* fame). I loved Bill both professionally and personally. Years earlier we had started shooting an HBO pilot based loosely on the life of a mysterious entertainment blogger, Nikki Finke, who was to be played by the great Diane Keaton. In it I played a Brett Ratner type, which was a great deal of fun, but the project ultimately didn't see the light of day. Suffice it to say, I desperately wanted to work with Bill on something, specifically a musical (given his street cred on other live-action musicals), and thought the idea of doing a Bill Condon *Beauty and the Beast* feature would be just what the doctor ordered. The role I had been hoping they were calling me up for was Lumière. After all, "Be Our Guest" is not only one of the all-time-great songs in Disney history, but in motion-picture history. I was told, however, that they had already tapped Jean Dujardin, who had won an Oscar for *The Artist* and was certainly more French than I am. It should not have come as a surprise then that the role they wanted me for was Gaston's unlovable sidekick . . . LeFou. LeFou, as anyone who has seen the original 1991 film will remember, is Gaston's idiot lackey who gets kicked, bonked on the head, and beaten repeatedly, and who, much like his boss, is also morally unforgivable. I asked to read the script, which was absolutely wonderful, but with regard to LeFou, what I got was essentially what I had remembered from the original film, down to the physical abuse he sustains and the desperate one-note adulation for his superior, Gaston. I told them unfortunately there was not enough on the page to make the role interesting for me, but that if they let me come in and work on a complete reimagining of the character in collaboration with them, I would be keen. I figured it was a long shot due to the time constraints of preproduction and the lack of a desire to blow up one of the main characters months before production. Much to my surprise, however, they were completely game. Over the course of a few sessions, Bill and I sat down and built the character back up from scratch.

The first difference that I discussed with Bill was that I was keen to make this version of LeFou less of a bumbling idiot. While animated films allow and in fact benefit from bonks, clunks, smacks, and pratfalls, the same doesn't quite land when a real grown man in a period wig is doing it. Therefore, we instead began exploring deeper and more sophisticated attributes to further dimensionalize LeFou. For example, I thought it might be interesting to make

him more of a psychoanalyst and counselor to a Gaston, who (in the new draft) was now clearly suffering from war-related PTSD. In my mind, this new dynamic gave the relationship a different wrinkle from the original animated film. It also offered a unique way that would work better for the more fleshed-out version of these characters, subsequently providing a catalyst for comedy. Along those same lines, we discussed that LeFou's humor should come not from idiocy but from being well-versed and slightly more sophisticated than his partner in crime. Rather than two bumbling idiots, it felt fresher to me to have one big bumbling idiot and a devoted servant who did everything in his power to make his friend feel and look smarter than he could ever possibly hope to be. The final and most significant change I pitched was that LeFou would have a redemption at the end of the film and ultimately break with Gaston. Bill (one of the most collaborative directors I've ever worked with) was keen to do all of it, and so we dug in and built a LeFou that would hopefully stand in stark contrast to his counterpart from the animated film, and in many ways be surprising to the audience.

One much more casual (but ultimately seismic) conversation we had was about the specific nature of LeFou's devotion to Gaston. In the course of our discussions, we tried to distinguish whether or not LeFou loved Gaston or was in love with Gaston; two very different ways to play the character. We ultimately landed on the side of LeFou was truly in awe of Gaston, and that was not driven by any sexual desire whatsoever but rather a deep-seated love, appreciation, and belief in this person he had served alongside in battle for many years. Gaston was everything LeFou thought he wanted to be, and a macho version of what LeFou could never be. What we never once discussed, however, was focusing at all on LeFou's sexuality, which frankly was not a thing to really explore in a random comedic character in the film . . . or so I thought.

The five months of production were some of the most fun and thrilling I've ever had as an artist. There is nothing like shooting a live-action musical . . . except perhaps doing a live musical onstage. The cast was exquisite from top to bottom, with Emma Watson, Dan Stevens, Luke Evans, Kevin Kline, and myself being the primary live actors in the movie, as well as one of the greatest voice-over ensembles in history, including Sir Ian McKellen, Dame Emma Thompson, Ewan McGregor (who ultimately would take over the role of Lumière, presumably because British is close

enough to French), Stanley Tucci, Audra McDonald, and Gugu Mbatha-Raw all playing the enchanted staff.

Our first reading was one for the ages, featuring a flawless Emma Thompson taking the mic and singing through the iconic "Beauty and the Beast"

ballad. Shortly there-
after, we recorded the
music, thus fulfilling a
lifelong goal of mine to
work with EGOT leg-
end Alan Menken, best
known for his work on
Beauty, *The Little Mer-*
maid, and *Aladdin*.

Alan and his amazing team truly let Luke Evans and me off-leash and
allowed us to do some insane things with the song "Gaston," including
letting me end it with a silly riff about being illiterate. Our brilliant choreographer Anthony Van Laast then took what we had laid down on music
tracks and worked with us to create a new dance that would pay homage
to the original but be updated to reflect the new slightly less physically
abusive relationship between Gaston and myself. The dance would reflect
more of an emphasis on inflating Gaston's ego as opposed to deflating
LeFou's face. The song took the better part of a week to shoot and Bill
allowed us to sing live, thus giving him the option to top anything we had
previously recorded. Working alongside Luke proved to be one of the great
pairings of my career, creating an odd couple in size, behavior, and per-
sonality. Every time he would zig, I would zag.

One thing that simply would not zag was my ability to ride a horse.
While Luke had previously shot numerous films on horseback, the closest
I had been to a horse was at the South Florida track. I was given lessons
at a ranch close to the studio and introduced to my horse for the film,
Buddy . . . who was less of a buddy and more of an asshole. The first time
I got on him, he literally threw me off. I went crumbling to the ground,
thankfully not hurting myself (outside of the severe bruising of my ego).
The staff couldn't even bother to help me, they were laughing so hard.

One day on set as we were shooting our intro into the "small pro-
vincial town" that is Belle's village, Luke and I were blocked to ride in

on our horses and stop on our mark at the cobblestone entrance. When the director called action, Luke and I entered the scene as scripted. Luke stopped on his mark with his horse. My horse, on the other hand, decided to gallop off past the cameras and past the crew into the catering area. We did the scene again, and this time, the horse decided to go the other way and take me back through the entrance and away from the village entirely. This went on all day. I finally looked at Bill and said, "Please write me off this fucking horse." And so, in a subsequent scene in which Gaston and I are meant to ride off to the Beast's castle at night, I was initially supposed to be on horseback. Because of my horse being a passive-aggressive dick, however, if you watch the film closely, I instead remain safely on the ground. Then in the next shot, when the villagers take off, it is Luke, our fellow actors, and a rather thin last-minute Josh Gad stunt double horse rider taking off into the night.

The cast was like family to me. Emma Watson soon became like a little sister. I was in awe of how she handled the pressures of the film essentially riding on her back, always asking all the right questions and attempting every step of the way to ensure that her Belle was as forward-thinking and active in the story as possible, not simply being a damsel in distress. Emma is one of the smartest and most articulate actresses I've ever worked with, sometimes intimidatingly so. Her breadth of knowledge goes far beyond the world of film and speaks to broader interests involving women's rights, education, equal opportunity, and poverty. I marveled at how a girl who had gotten her start as a superstar at such a young age could simultaneously balance the responsibilities she had as an artist with the responsibilities she had as a humanitarian. Every day she would ask me about a book she had read and every day I would have to make the choice to either lie to her and tell her I had indeed read the complete works of Hanya Yanagihara and Miguel De Cervantes, or bow my head in shame and admit that despite my near-decade age advantage, I had apparently read only one-quarter of the books Emma Watson has read.

If Emma was my little sister and Luke was my partner in crime, Dan was my mischievous frat brother. Dan is seriously one of the funniest and driest personalities I've ever known. Making him laugh is the reward that keeps on giving, because he is such a British sophisticate that I usually break him by being a crass American "sod" or "twat," which I believe are both British for "jackass." Dan had to wear the craziest shit I've ever seen in my life, including jagged stilted legs like a weird circus clown and an unbreathable mask, as the movie originally intended for the Beast's face to be a practical effect, which to those of us who have seen it in action is the stuff of nightmare fuel. At night, after we all went home, poor Dan would have to stay and do motion-capture, which basically involves the actor sitting perfectly still in a chair and doing all of his dialogue into a series of cameras with dots on his face. Then he would have to do exaggerated facial expressions, which would all eventually be augmented in digital work intended to make his practical mask more lifelike in post. Eventually, the mask was completely replaced with CGI, which makes me sad because of all the work Dan did inside of the mask, but simultaneously makes me laugh my ass off because, as I always told him, he deserved to be punished for leaving *Downton Abbey* early and traumatizing all of us who fell in love with his character and had to watch him die violently on Christmas Day.

As filming was ending, we started to learn the choreography for the final dance number at the ballroom. At rehearsal one day, our choreographer told me that he and Bill had had an idea that I would have a brief, tiny moment dancing with another male celebrant. I thought it was cheeky, and as described to me, a sweet and small moment that would just be there to allow for interpretation as people saw fit. Nothing more, nothing less. Again, because I was a side character, I didn't want to suddenly throw the weight of sexuality on this character that in no way was driving the film, but the moment (as described to me) seemed harmless enough—a fun blink-and-you'll-miss-it little beat as our fantastical story is coming to its end. We shot the sequence, all felt great about it, and we wrapped things shortly thereafter.

Around the time the movie was gearing up for its big promotional push, I got a phone call from Bill to tell me that the talking points should not include any references to LeFou's sexuality, which was perfectly fine with me because we had intentionally discussed not making his sexuality a thing to begin with. Then one day, as I was preparing to go out and promote the movie, my rightfully perplexed publicist, Melissa Raubvogel, sent me a quote from an interview with Condon that had just run in an LGBTQ magazine called *Attitude*.

"LeFou is somebody who on one day wants to be Gaston and on another day wants to kiss Gaston. He's confused about what he wants. It's somebody who's just realizing that he has these feelings. And Josh makes something really subtle and delicious out of it. And that's what has its payoff at the end, which I don't want to give away. But it is a nice, *exclusively gay moment in a Disney movie*." [emphasis mine]

The quote in and of itself was delightful, beautiful, and perfect . . . but for those three fateful words: "EXCLUSIVELY GAY MOMENT."

One doesn't need a master's degree in PR crises to understand the potential fallout of saying the words *exclusively gay* and *Disney* in the same breath in a country defined by culture wars. I knew what would happen next even before the first of what would become a barrage of phone calls came my way. From the second I read the quote, I was very aware that the only thing moving forward that people would want to discuss was LeFou's and Disney's first "exclusively gay moment." I was baffled. Never once was the moment in this film described to me as something that we were going to hang a lantern on and pat ourselves on the back for. In fact, if it had, I never would have agreed to the seemingly sweet and innocuous moment. It was both too little and not enough to be anything more than it was . . . a fun little character moment open to interpretation. Had the audience defined it as a sweet, exclusively gay moment, I would have been delighted! But the second we pointed it out and seemingly congratulated ourselves, we had invited hell and fury (an insane but predictable response to the moment, for the record). More than offending your regular cadre of trolls and bigots, however, I was mostly concerned that putting anything more on this small moment was a disservice to those who had been waiting years for actual gay representation in a film like this. I for one certainly didn't exactly feel like LeFou was who the queer community had been wistfully waiting for. I can't quite imagine a Pride celebration in honor of the "cinematic watershed moment" involving a quasi-villainous Disney sidekick dancing with a man for half a second. I mean, if I were gay, I'm sure I'd be pissed.

Then, on the other end of the equation, we had created a firestorm activating those always looking for controversy to hang their hats on; they suddenly made LeFou and *Beauty and the Beast* a platform for their prejudice and hate. All because of a HALF-SECOND DANCE! And the craziest part was I, a straight man, was now the face of this controversy I had only just learned about.

I called Bill and asked him about it. The poor guy felt awful and said that he had felt put on the spot when they asked about the moment. As a gay man giving an interview to a queer-focused magazine, he wanted to (and had every right to) share his pride for some form of representation in the film, and had simply blurted it out and now couldn't reel it back. I completely understood, but nevertheless didn't quite know how to shoulder the enormous burden of being the one to now have to talk about this unexpected lightning rod of an issue. I had wanted the movie to speak for itself and suddenly it was about everything *but* the movie and my performance. Everywhere I went, I was being questioned by every single outlet about the "exclusively gay moment." Nobody wanted to discuss anything else. Even my costars were pretty much all asked primarily about the moment.

The studio, and in particular Sean Bailey, Alan Horn, and Alan Bergman (three of the all-time greats), were unbelievably supportive and allowed me the freedom to respond meaningfully and freely. What we all wanted, however, was to get people to talk about the film. I would therefore try desperately in every interview to answer questions about the moment but also redirect the conversation back to the movie itself where I could. No matter how hard I tried to strike that balance, however, the conversation would inevitably turn back to the controversy. Everyone wanted to use the issue for broader conversation, and I was constrained because my job was to simply promote the film and try to avoid anything that would overtake that conversation. That soon changed, however, when things took an ugly turn.

Weeks before the release, word started trickling down that various regions, including Kuwait, Russia, Malaysia, and even a movie theater in Alabama, were banning the movie because of the *half-second* dance moment. The irony of course being that these same regions were apparently all in on a movie whose central concept is posited on the acceptance of *literal bestiality*, but two men dancing would be entirely unforgivable. I went from being baffled to just plain old fucking pissed. My sentiment went from avoidance to full-throated anger. It was no longer a silly story about a moment taken out of context, but now a catalyst for bigotry. For me, that was a bridge too far. Certain censors were demanding that the moment be cut out of the film or they would refuse to show the movie. Once again, much to their credit, Disney took the position that those places demanding such action would not be catered to and would have to either show the film in its entirety or tell their eager audiences that they couldn't watch it because two jovial men dance with each other for about the amount of time it takes to inhale a breath.

The faux rage and fever-pitch controversy of course predictably died down the second the movie was released, and everyone looked at each other and said: "Wait, that's it? That's what all the fuss was about?" In fact, some theaters literally had people standing and applauding the moment, not to celebrate it as a monumental achievement, but rather to remind the haters that love and acceptance will always be more powerful than hate and closed-mindedness. I remember being in one such theater and being absolutely awestruck at the communal celebration of the beat. I felt a sense of unexpected pride and joy that after all of the negative hoopla, the movie's intended audience was not only fine with the moment, but fully embraced it—to the tune of $1.2 billion and crossing (at the time of its release) into being one of the top ten highest-grossing films by the end of its run.

11

BUT WAIT, THERE'S MORE!

My career is similar to an Indonesian seismograph: lots of peaks and valleys. I have done movies that have gone on to become top-twenty highest-grossing films of all time . . . and movies that have barely broken single digits at the box office. I have done failed series that should have been hits based on the level of talent involved (looking at you, *1600 Penn . . .*) and passed on series that went on to become modern-day classics (looking at you, *Modern Family*).

Actually, looking more at what my bank account might have otherwise looked like, Modern Family.

The truth is, nobody ever knows what is going to work and what isn't and if they tell you otherwise, they are lying to you. I have never once gone into a film, TV, or theater project thinking to myself, "Oh wow, this is really bad, let's make it." There has always been some reason or other that I gravitated toward it, whether creative or otherwise. I have also learned over the course of my life that doing something strictly for money is a career killer and will always backfire. Similarly, I have found that doing something that feels safe will oftentimes cause creative stagnation and can be equally disruptive to career longevity.

You also never know what projects will become long after you're done with them. For instance, in some cases, movies that didn't necessarily light up the box office have become cult classics, like *The Wedding Ringer* with Kevin Hart and *Pixels* with Adam Sandler. Both of those films did well enough at the box office, but it wasn't until they hit home video and digital that people really started to discover them in a bigger way. Similarly, on the TV side, shows that I thought would be instant hits because of the auspices involved also only became beloved years after their cancellations, from the Billy Crystal FX series *The Comedians* to the king of social satire Armando Iannucci's follow-up to *Veep*, *Avenue 5*. The point is, there is no such thing as a "sure thing."

Well, almost no such thing . . .

The first time I heard about a sequel to the *Frozen* phenomenon was when John Lasseter and Jennifer Lee invited me to the 2015 Disney shareholders event in San Francisco. I had no clue why I was invited, and it was literally only minutes before I walked out onstage that John and Jenn told me Bob Iger would be announcing the film with me that day. In full

disclosure, I was terrified by this news. Outside of *The Rescuers Down Under* and *Fantasia 2000*, the studio had never done a big-screen sequel to one of its hits— and let's face it, neither of those films had exactly lit up the box office. To make matters even harder, it was generally a foregone con-

clusion that musical sequels were a recipe for disaster. I'm sure none of you go to sleep at night listening to the cast recordings of *Bring Back Birdie, Annie Warbucks,* or *The Best Little Whorehouse Goes Public.* The batting average of original movie musical sequels is even worse (sorry, *Grease 2*).

As much as I trusted Bobby and Kristen Anderson-Lopez, I was not sure how they would contend with this apparent curse. As for me, I felt it was important to not simply rehash the same traits and comedic elements from the first movie. I'd been thinking a lot about my daughter's tearful plea at the dinner table when she was four that she didn't want to grow up, and I was very interested in the idea of Olaf growing up. If Olaf in the first *Frozen* was a newborn, I was tickled by the idea of Olaf now being an inquisitive toddler. He'd be obsessed with learning everything he could, collecting pieces of trivia along the way—even if a great deal of it was useless. I sent my ideas to Jenn and Chris Buck and they were thrilled with that direction. Over the course of the next few months, the creatives literally sat down with a shrink and tried to get under the hood of each of the central characters (a lot of which is detailed in great length in the incredible behind-the-scenes *Frozen II* documentary on Disney+, *Into the Unknown: Making Frozen II*). The first track I laid down for the sequel was a song that was ultimately cut from the movie, "Unmeltable Me," in which Olaf attends a fancy state dinner in honor of Elsa and sings about the virtues of being unmeltable. The song was both meant to help explain why Olaf no longer had a flurry over his head and also to set up the unthinkable tragedy that would eventually occur at the end of the second act. The song itself, which you can hear on the *Frozen II* deluxe soundtrack, is a keen example of the early development process on films like this. It was a product of a story still finding itself, driven more by a need to advance the plot rather than give us insight into a character or his/her state of mind.

Quick funny sidenote: At the time, the only thing I had recorded fully for the movie was this insane little number. I remember running into one of the Disney Animation folks while I was getting coffee one day and saying, "Hey, how's Frozen II *looking?" He responded with, "As is usually the case at this point in the process, it's a mess looking for some shape, but your song killed." I said, "Oh, that's awesome!" He said, "Yeah, but just so you know, it's been cut. Have a great day!"*

On a personal note, during the very early days of the film, none of us knew what the hell the movie was about. As with the original *Frozen* film, we weren't handed a draft of a script, but rather given a basic summary by Chris, Jenn, and producer Peter Del Vecho of the major beats and arcs for our characters and the larger story. I remember back in those days, we had more of a villainous presence in the film. There was a scary monster man in the forest with antlers named Gunnar Natura—he was the leader of the Northuldra and he seemed to be the bad guy. But it was revealed at the end that it was really King Runeard (Anna and Elsa's grandfather) who had stolen his magic and was impersonating him, leading to a confrontation with Elsa during the redefining transformation. The transformation of course is the only thing that remained through the final cut of the film. There was also a great deal of cool mythology and Scandinavian lore in the film, but all in all, I was (and, reading all that back, still am) confused as hell. As with the first film, the cast never recorded with each other, but Kristen, Idina, Jonathan, and I would constantly call one another asking if anyone could explain the movie, and not a single one of us could summarize what *Frozen II* was about. (Although, to be fair, that was the same with the first *Frozen* early on as well.) The creatives do a very good job of keeping everything under lock and key and only giving us what they think we need to execute our roles.

One thing that left no nuance, however, was the first scene I ever recorded for the film.

I got to the studio and Jenn slow-rolled me into the day's material. As I looked at the scene, the first thing I saw was "Olaf begins to flurry away." I read further. "Anna sobs" and "Olaf looks to her for help." I looked at Jenn. "Wait—are we . . . ?" With tears in her eyes, she nodded her head and said, "Yes."

"WAIT! WHAT?!"

Olaf, the lovable, huggable snowman, was going to DIE (a plot point that had coincidentally never been shared with me prior to the recording).

That would be like Mark Hamill showing up to set on his first day and George Lucas being like, "So, I know I haven't had a chance to share this with you yet, but today you will be losing your lightsaber and your hand. Oh! And also Darth Vader, the big villain from the first film, is your pops! AND ACTION!"

Jenn and I started recording the dialogue and I couldn't get through it without sobbing. Those first recordings were brutal, and I remember feeling that we were doing something that was going to pack a serious punch. At the time, I don't even remember fully knowing if the plan was to bring him back at the end, but the opportunity to force Anna out onto her own without the love and support of everyone she had always relied on felt right, profound, and necessary, so I was all in, even if it meant that I might never get to play the little guy again. By the end of the recording, there wasn't a dry eye in the room. I remember getting a FaceTime call from my wife during the session and her response to seeing my puffy and red eyes was "Jesus, what the hell are they doing to you over there?" She couldn't tell if we were recording a sequel to *Frozen* or *Sophie's Choice*. Over the course of the next few months, I would come in and out of the studio while working on other projects, also recording along the way in London and Australia. Because I was coming in and out, I truly had no grasp of what we were doing and felt super discombobulated.

The first time I knew we still had a long road ahead was when I asked Jenn how the first test screening went. Jenn is many incredible things, but a good liar is not one of them. She put on a brave face and said, "The adults loved it, but the kids were very confused and very, very sad."

Uh-oh.

Just for context for the reader, when you're making a children's film, it's usually helpful if the kids leave happy and not with suicidal ideations.

Apparently, one of the major issues was that Olaf's death scene was causing absolute havoc with the younger viewers. They were apparently sobbing, screaming, and fully traumatized by the extended sequence and the tone of the scene—and it didn't help that in the first version, Olaf himself was scared and confused by what was happening (similar to Peter Parker turning into flesh dust at the end of *Infinity War*). The scene was truly stunning, but in its commitment to the brutality of Olaf's naïveté about all things, including dying, we had made our intended audience scared for Olaf, rather than emotional. As Jenn said to me: "Bob [Iger] put it best: Olaf is a child. You can't just willy-nilly kill a scared child, because the children watching will see themselves in him." While there had been discussion about removing the moment entirely, Jenn thankfully fought to do an altered version in which Olaf isn't scared, but instead is at peace and comforts Anna before he leaves. It was one of the light bulb moments and creatively brilliant pivots that Jenn and the Frozen team are known for at this point. I almost think they work better under duress rather than with a smooth production process. The truth is, animation is one of the only forms of visual art that allows you to do and redo again and again until you get it all right. In live action, you'll get reshoots here and there where you need them, but in animation you get to literally redo an entire film if need be. For example, *The Emperor's New Groove* (originally known as *Kingdom of the Sun*) was initially a period drama involving a plot to capture the sun, with a ton of original music by Sting; with eighteen months to go, *Ratatouille* was completely reimagined, with new director Brad Bird using only two lines of dialogue and two shots from the previous, nearly completed version; and *Toy Story 2* originally took place in Taiwan and was about Buzz getting recalled (please give me that movie!). The beauty of animation is, you can explore to fail and then succeed through the lessons of your failures. Through it all, I was also blown away that Jenn was simultaneously writing and directing the movie, all while now running the entire animation studio after the departure of John Lasseter.

As the story continued to progress, one of the sequences to come out of story meetings was a moment in which, earlier in the movie, Olaf is left alone in the enchanted forest. Bobby and Kristen had once again struck gold by writing a song in which Olaf is clueless about the unforgiving and dangerous magic of this new environment he's in. The real comedy, however, was that the whole thing would also work as a metaphor for how an innocent and wide-eyed optimist would look at our current world and its nonstop cycle of chaos and despair and assume that he is just too naïve to understand any of it. The song was to be called "When I Am Older." In the dialogue leading up to the scene, Olaf is looking around for the cause of some of the eerie noises happening all around him. The scene as written is that Olaf calls out, "Anna? Elsa? Sven?" hoping to get an answer back to assuage his fears. I think because I had literally gotten no sleep the night before after doing a night shoot, I was in a particularly unhinged mood. I looked at Chris and Jenn and said, "I'm going to try something. It will scare you and make no sense, but I want you to just go with me and see what happens." They looked at each other, terrified. Once again, I started the scene:

"Anna? Elsa? Sven?"

Then I paused and said "Samantha?" I started laughing my ass off and followed it up with "I don't even know a Samantha."

I was certain that the bit would ultimately be cut, seeing as Chris and Jenn were seemingly laughing in the booth not at the bit, but at the fact that I appeared to have gone off the deep end. To my shock and surprise, when I next came in to record the song with Bobby and Kristen, they both looked at me and said, "By the way, Samantha is now not only in the film, but it got such a big laugh that we're adding a moment in which you look into a giant gaping cave during the number and once again shout out 'Samantha?'"

And that is how the single most random bit in the Frozen franchise was born.

The final thing I ever recorded for the movie was literally two or three months before release. The movie was still a bit dense on plot, and at that time, an adult character was recapping some things for the audience, but it simply wasn't working, so someone pitched doing a funny recap instead and giving it to Olaf. Jenn pitched me the idea and I loved it. The beauty of Olaf's comedy is he can say very honest things without an edit button, and everyone forgives him for it because he is ultimately a child. Chris and Jenn put me in the booth with the new dialogue and immediately regretted it. The initial dialogue was simply me doing one or two quick bits from the original film and then moving on:

OLAF: *"I bet you're wondering who we are and why we're here. It's really quite simple. It began with two sisters. One born with magical powers, and one born powerless, with her love of snowmen, infinite."*

As we continued, however, I was more interested in the color commentary not included, specifically around the issue of parental loss. I quickly pivoted from the script and started to improvise:

OLAF: *"Well, at least they have their parents."*

I took a long beat, then changed my tone from optimistic to horrified.

OLAF: *"THEIR PARENTS ARE DEAD!"*

As with all of my most insane *Frozen* bits, I was certain the studio was never going to go for it, but lo and behold they did, and that last-minute recap became one of the biggest comedic highlights of both films. The joy of sitting in a theater and watching parents and children lose their minds at something I never could have imagined ever making the final cut always gives me the greatest satisfaction when doing these films. My Frozen journey is so special because of the level of confidence the creative brain trust has in me, entrusting this beloved snowman to me, regardless of where I take him . . . which is usually down an insane rabbit hole.

After three years of hard work and development, we shared *Frozen II* with the world in November 2019, almost five years to the day after we had given the world the first film. Somehow, the creative team had not only done it again but the audience reception somehow proved even more ecstatic, and the movie became the highest-grossing film in animation history at that time, surpassing even *Frozen*. The press tour for the film was also a true joy because it was the first time the cast and I got to actually be together and celebrate the film. However, one of my clearest memories was flying to Disneyland together (to light the Christmas tree) in a helicopter and all being slightly concerned with a sudden drop and a very strange motor sound. We all silently looked at each other with dread and fear, wondering if this was about to be the inspiration for a modern-day take on *La Bamba*. Our deaths probably would have done wonders for the box office, but I think we're all pretty grateful we didn't die on our way to light a Christmas tree in Anaheim.

On a separate stop, this time in London, Groff and I went out to a renowned gay nightclub in Charing Cross and watched as Idina brought down the house singing some of her most iconic songs. Groff and I of course joined her up onstage for "Let It Go." Despite rarely recording these movies together, Menzel, Groff, Bell, and I truly are family at this point and, at the time of this writing, chomping at the

bit as we gear up to commence work on the next films in this beloved franchise, a journey that is bound to continue to explore the unknown and reveal new and exciting things about Anna, Elsa, Kristoff, and Olaf. While I can't say much more than that, what I can say is . . . you ain't seen nothing yet.

12

A MURDER, AN ICON, A PANDEMIC

Some of the fondest memories I have are from working on my eclectic myriad of projects. I could write an entire chapter about one of the most fun summers of my life shooting *Pixels* with Adam Sandler in Toronto, which essentially became a summer camp for us and our families as we did activities every day and night together.

Or about the time I was invited over to Peter Dinklage's apartment where he, his lovely wife, and I all watched the episode of *Game of Thrones* **SPOILER ALERT** where Tyrion kills his father with a crossbow as his dad sits on the toilet, and Peter, sitting next to me on his small couch, surreally narrated a play-by-play of everything that happened behind the scenes and his subsequent frustration for what was left out of the sequence (apparently quite a bit). I could describe an evening in which Ashton Kutcher and I, on the set of *Jobs* (one of two Steve Jobs movies that essentially came out around the same time like an Apple version of *Armageddon* and *Deep Impact*, but instead of asteroids, our commercial subject matter was a computer engineer), were invited to a Russian billionaire's home in Silicon Valley for dinner and told we could literally request anything on Earth and it would be prepared  for us—almost like a dare. Hence, per my request (and presumably via an endless refrigerator filled with every dead consumable creature on Earth), a sea bass was presented to me in a beautiful reduction sauce. I could talk about being on the set of *New Girl* and creating Bearclaw (a weirdo hornball with a thick southern accent who crushes hard on Jess), which I thought would single-handedly destroy the show because of how insane I had made the character, only to have people still come up to me on a daily basis and call me by a character name I only played three times during a 176-episode run. I could talk about meeting my now dear friend Anne Hathaway for the first time in a scene in which she opens a door and accidentally completely disrobes in front of me. I could talk about doing a private screening of my NBC sitcom *1600 Penn* at the White House for then President Barack Obama, during which he roasted his former speech writer and our show's cocreator, Jon Lovett, by doing one of the funniest tight-five takedowns I've ever witnessed. I could talk about late nights on set with my idol Billy Crystal as we talked about the history of Hollywood, comedy, and our mutual idols, all while pretending to get stoned in a grocery store. If you will indulge me, however, I would love to instead focus on three professional experiences that stand out to me for a number of reasons, whether as milestones in my career or as significant moments that created ripples I will forever carry with me long afterward.

Murder on the Orient Express

Perhaps the greatest cast I have ever worked with was on this project. I've always been a fan of Sir Kenneth Branagh, both as an actor and as a director. I was also incredibly eager to do something that felt completely different than anything else I had done before. Subsequently, when the opportunity presented itself for me to play one of the ensemble members of an extraordinary Agatha Christie classic directed by the legend himself, I immediately jumped at the opportunity.

At the time, there was another project that I was supposed to do, which sadly I had to pass on because of my commitments to *Orient Express.* Coincidentally, that project was to star opposite Margot Robbie in Craig Gillespie's *I, Tonya* about Nancy Kerrigan's fateful assault in 1994 involving famed skater Tonya Harding. In the film, I was meant to play Shawn Eckardt, the bumbling idiot mastermind behind the assault of Kerrigan. Due to scheduling, I had to drop out, which paved the way for the brilliant Paul Walter Hauser to have a breakout performance. (In the history of projects that got away, this is one that I am beyond grateful did. It put Paul on my radar as a brilliant performer and inspired me to build an entire movie around him based on our mutual love for the late Chris

Farley, a movie I will soon be directing for Warner Bros./New Line. But, back to *Orient Express*.)

Coming off numerous comedies and spectacle films, I had wanted to find something juicy to sink my teeth into from an acting perspective. And the cast that Branagh had assembled was the acting equivalent of *The Avengers*: Michelle Pfeiffer, Willem Dafoe, Penélope Cruz, Johnny Depp, Lucy Boynton, Daisy Ridley, Manuel Garcia-Rulfo, Tom Bateman, Sir Derek Jacobi, Olivia Colman, Dame Judi Dench, and my CMU classmate and recent *Hamilton* Tony Award winner, Leslie Odom Jr. Basically, everyone on the film was either a dame, a sir, a decorated award winner . . . or me. I knew Branagh was a full-throated professional and was ecstatic about the process. What I didn't quite realize is how quickly the process would begin.

I had just landed after a fifteen-hour flight. I figured my driver was going to take me directly to my hotel so that I could take a nap or, at the very least, freshen up. Instead, we drove directly to the soundstage at Longcross Studios (a former industrial military armory or hangar or God knows what). I was then promptly taken to wardrobe, where I was placed in a period overcoat and brought over to a desolate, eerie, and empty soundstage where only one train caboose sat in the center of the room. Waiting for me on the small caboose was Sir Ken, trademark moustache glued to his face, with a notepad and pen. As I nervously sat opposite him, trying to assess what the hell was happening, he began to grill me in character as the famed Hercule Poirot (Belgian accent and all). For the next twenty minutes, I was asked question after question about my involvement in the crime on the train and had to improvise answers based on the work I had already done. "What were you doing the night of the murder?" "How long had you worked for your deceased employer?" "What was your business on the train?" On and on we went, until finally, he broke his accent and, as the director, said, "Excellent work!" It was one of the most terrifying and exhilarating experiences I have ever had. One of the many amazing things about Ken is that he is so playful as a director because he approaches it from the perspective of an actor. It didn't matter who you were, nobody messed around on that set, including Johnny Depp.

At the time, Johnny had some ongoing public issues that slightly clouded his involvement in the film (although perhaps not as much as Armie Hammer on the next Poirot movie). Having said that, he was one of the sweetest and kindest people I've had the chance to work with. Because so many of his scenes in the movie involved me, the two of us became fairly close during the shoot. In the film, Johnny plays shady American businessman Edward Ratchett, and I play his seemingly devoted secretary and liaison, Hector MacQueen. Aside from a few conversations here and there with Poirot and some of the other passengers, we essentially are never apart. That became true off set as well. At lunch, he would often invite me into his predictably enormous trailer to watch TV with him. "TV" in this case, however, meant old YouTube videos. I had watched these clips years earlier with the rest of the world, but they were still somehow foreign and hilarious to Johnny Depp. OG videos like "Charlie Bit My Finger," "Evolution of Dance," and "David After Dentist" blew Johnny's mind, and he shared them with me as if I too had been off-planet for a few years. Then he would get excited and have someone in his entourage (apparently custodians of the Depp files) pull up bloopers of him falling off a galloping horse while shooting *The Lone Ranger*. He would rewind the moment again and again and be overjoyed by the hilarity of nearly dying. I will say, his laughter was infectious. What I truly loved about Johnny was this ability to revert to almost being a child again. I honestly think it's what makes his performances so imaginative. By choice or circumstance, I don't think he ever grew up, and that ceaseless childlike wonderment fills every one of his choices on-screen.

On the weekends, the cast would get together and play a game called Werewolves, a group activity that, much like the game Mafia, involves fifteen or more people sitting in a circle in which two people are killers and everyone in the group must identify them before they pick off all of the innocent bystanders. The game was a perfect team-bonding experience for all of us, due to the murder-mystery nature of our film. Penélope Cruz introduced it to us and to this day, she is still the most remarkable person I've ever seen play it. She is so disgustingly good at convincing everyone she is innocent that even if you were one hundred percent certain she was the killer, she would still somehow successfully encourage you to accuse someone else. Sometimes, other local London casts would come over and we would play together. For instance, we had the cast of *Jurassic World* and even some of the Star Wars folks play with us. It was always an absolute delight.

From day one, all of us got along famously. Among my quickest and closest friends on set, outside of my college classmate Leslie, were Daisy Ridley and Tom Bateman. Unfortunately for Daisy, I have been and remain a die-hard Star Wars fan. From the age of five I can remember watching the films obsessively and reenacting some of the most iconic moments. In fact, that passion is what ultimately would drive me to eventually write, produce, and star in a sequel to one of my other all-time-favorite films, *Spaceballs*.

Fun little sidenote: One day, during a half-hour pitch of our Spaceballs *sequel's story beats to the legendary Mel Brooks (who had openly never really watched any of the Star Wars movies since the original), I went through every single intended beat of our new film and illustrated how it would speak directly to the new films as his classic had the old ones as he sat silently and listened intensely. At the end of my tireless presentation, Mel took a deep breath and in his signature crackly voice exclaimed, "Well, Josh, it really sounds like you've got your finger on the pulse!" I have never laughed so hard.*

But alas, I digress! Back to Daisy.

As I was saying, as anyone who has known me for the better part of forty years can attest, I have been a die-hard Star Wars fan for as far back as I can remember. Unfortunately for her, Daisy had just done *The Force Awakens*, and I made it my never-ending duty to find out everything I could about the seventh film in the Star Wars series, to the point that I started filming "gotcha" videos where I would corner Daisy in an unsuspecting manner and try to publicly shame her into giving me spoilers. Much like Daisy, Tom Bateman was also an enormous joy to be around. He is like a physically fit Falstaff, always the life of the party and a genuinely gregarious and hilarious human being, as well as a brilliant actor. It was thrilling to watch Daisy and Tom fall in love on that set, because they were both smitten with each other from the first day they laid eyes on each other. Every time they were together, they would laugh uproariously or share the sweetest of looks, or simply bask in each other's presence. Eventually those on-set glances and flirtations would culminate in matrimonial bliss. Theirs was and is one of the truest romances I've ever seen, and it is such a joy to know that our film was the catalyst for their marriage.

There wasn't a single member of our ensemble who didn't become close during those cold months in London. The one thing that truly bonded the cast, however, was our sheer terror in the presence of Dame Judi Dench, who is of course film, TV, and stage royalty. There is a regalness to her that

simply silences anyone who might dare strike up a conversation.

Anyone with sense, that is.

Early one morning, as all of us sat in the makeup trailer, I approached the dame. It was about 5:00 a.m., she had a hot towel on her face, and her makeup chair was reclined. I sauntered over to her, this woman I had never met in my entire life, and whispered softly into her ear, "Dame Judi Dench? More like Dammmmmn Judi Dench!" She removed the towel from her face, looked me up and down, and passed her verdict: "Oh, you're trouble."

Her wrap gift to me was a throw pillow with the words: "Back off 2 inches Josh Gad."

I feel blessed to have worked with Judi twice, although not as blessed the second time, which involved me eating through the Earth while shitting the remains out of my asshole like a fire extinguisher.

You win some, you lose some.

Marshall

This one is probably one of my lesser-known films on your radar, but it's possibly the most meaningful to me because of the subject matter and my costar. Along with the rest of the world, I had been blown away by Chadwick Boseman's early work in films like *42* and *Get On Up*. It wasn't, however, until I saw him in *Captain America: Civil War*, in which he was introduced as the iconic Marvel superhero T'Challa, aka the Black Panther, that I realized he was a legitimate *movie star*. Every time he was on-screen, across from some of the biggest actors in the world, you just couldn't take your eyes away from him. So, when I was offered the chance to star opposite him, I jumped at it. It also helped that the script was based on the incredible true story of a Jewish lawyer named Sam Friedman and his collaboration with a young Thurgood Marshall and the NAACP in the 1940s. Together, they successfully defended a Black man wrongfully accused of rape by a rich white couple in Connecticut.

The movie, directed by Reggie Hudlin, is a wonderful film with a stellar cast including the brilliant Sterling K. Brown and my frequent collaborators Dan Stevens and Kate Hudson (whom I worked with on *Wish I Was Here* and the unreleased animated DreamWorks film *Me and My Shadow*). What truly made that experience so memorable, however, was the short time I got to spend with one of the finest spirits I've ever known.

The production, which was shot in Buffalo, got off to a somewhat choppy start because Chad had something wrong with his stomach that he was being treated for in LA. It wouldn't be until almost three years later that I would realize the medical issue was in actuality colon cancer, and that Chad was somehow shooting our film in the early stages of the disease that would ultimately take his life. Anyone who knew Chad will tell you that there was a fierceness in his eyes and a passion in his soul. He lived for his craft, and that commitment to character made everyone around him better. When you were in the presence of Chadwick Boseman, you felt like you were sparring with one of the great American actors. His full-bodied approach to his performances was so studied, so brilliantly articulated, and so fully realized, that you felt you were in the presence of the namesakes he had been tasked with bringing to life: Jackie Robinson, James Brown, or—in this case—Thurgood Marshall.

This gravitas didn't mean, however, that he wasn't a blast to be around. When our shooting days were over, we would often take a stroll around the quiet blocks of Buffalo, discussing everything from martial arts to health regimens to spirituality. Sometimes we would talk about the nature of self-reflection and meditation, two things that unfortunately remain far too foreign for me. Oftentimes, Chad would bestow onto me lessons from Eastern philosophy and medicine (two things I sadly could never have imagined were probably at the forefront of his thoughts during his struggle with his disease at the time). He was always interested in other perspectives and ideas that weren't the status quo. There wasn't a subject he wasn't well acquainted with and there wasn't a debate he couldn't win. I would often engage him in philosophical conversations that I would inevitably regret having because he was so much more articulate and convincing in his arguments than I could ever be. Whether we debated the greatest living basketball player or the key to a great buffalo wing (seriously, a real debate we had—and for the record, his opinion was that it comes down to the right level of crisp mixed with the right consistency of vinegar tang in the sauce), he would always end the conversation by convincing me that his perspective was ultimately the right one. Not surprising, considering he was, after all, a famous alum of speech and debate, although our paths unfortunately never directly crossed (as he was a few years older than me). There was also something very wise about Chad. I don't mean that as in just smart, although he was one of the smartest people I've ever known, but I mean that as in he was beyond his years. He was the greatest proof I've ever encountered that perhaps we have been here before. You simply couldn't be around him and not think, *Man, this guy is an old soul.*

Because of the subject matter of the film, we would often engage in conversations about what it meant to be Black and what it meant to be Jewish and what the intersection of both of those things meant. Chadwick, after all, knew firsthand the struggles of Blacks historically, having made a career out of portraying some of the most iconic people of color to ever overcome prejudice and hate and, despite their obstacles, go on to become some of the greatest musicians, athletes, and lawyers of all time. Of course he himself shattered through his own glass ceiling, showing an entire skeptical world that not only was there a place for Black superheroes, but a Black superhero could be just as if not more commercially and critically viable than the more "mainstream" superhero counterparts. Chadwick was equally curious as to what it meant to be Jewish and was especially drawn to my grandparents' experiences during the Holocaust. I often find myself wishing that Chad was here to help navigate this complicated world we live in right now, because as always, I know if anyone had the answers, it would be him. Some of my favorite memories on any set during the course of my career are those memories of getting to spar and do scene after scene with one of the finest actors of the twenty-first century. Many of our scenes

would be two-handers in which Chad and I could put on our acting gloves and go a few rounds (as our characters often tore each other down in order to build each other back up and come to a mutual understanding). Let's be clear, though: every act-

ing battle between us was always a TKO in his favor . . . but I am better for having gotten my ass kicked by him.

We would often talk about other things we wanted to do together. We had an idea for a time-travel comedy that would allow him and me to travel to a period of social strife and do a biting and hilarious piece of satire that would present us both as fish out of water. Even within comedy, Chad wanted to push the boundaries and not play it safe. After we completed the movie, we kept in touch and continued to discuss when we would next work together once he was done with his insane Marvel commitments. Then came the global pandemic that would shut down the entire world. You know, that small little blip.

On April 6, 2020, less than a month into our new solitary and terrifying lives, Chadwick texted me out of the blue:

Catch the Rain

If you are in Los Angeles, you woke up this morning to the rare and peaceful sound of a steady precipitation. If you're like me, maybe you looked at the week's forecast and found that it's supposed to rain for three straight days; not without breaks of sunlight and reprieves of moist gloom, but yeah it's gonna be coming down like cats and dogs. Great. We're stuck inside these damn quarantines because of the Covid, and now we can't even get no sun in Cali. Come on now!

But now that the rain has stopped and today's storm has cleared, I urge you to go outside and take a DEEP breath. Notice how fresh the air is right now, after our skies have had a 3 week break from the usual relentless barrage of fumes from bumper to bumper LA commuters, and now today's rain has given the City of Angels a long overdo [sic] and much-needed shower. Inhale and exhale this moment, and thank God for the unique beauties and wonders of this day. We should take advantage of every moment we can to enjoy the simplicity of God's creation, whether it be clear skies and sun or clouded over with gloom. And hey, if the air is this clear right now, and it does rain tomorrow, I might even put jars and bins out and catch the rain. Throw that in the water filter and I have a water more alkaline than any bottled brand out there.

FYI, if you do that, just make sure that your jars are far away from roofs, gutters and overhead trees. All three could be poisonous, and a filter might not be able to clean your water from that type of contamination.

It was beautiful. While we would frequently text, it had never been with such thoughtful and lengthy insights like this. I didn't even know how to answer because it was such a profound statement of gratitude and of simply stopping to quite literally smell and give thanks for the rain. I was amazed, as I often was, by Chad's ability to see things that others couldn't. Here I was miserable that I was stuck in my house with no end in sight, and to add insult to injury, I couldn't even go outside because of the rain. Yet to Chadwick, that same set of circumstances was simply a gift, one more beautiful milestone in our short, sweet journey on this planet Earth.

Our final exchange was on June 2, 2020. Feeling the rage and heartbreak of everything that was happening as a result of the horrific death of George Floyd, I wrote Chad:

Here. That is all. That is the message. Here. To listen. To fight. To work. Miss you. Hope you and the fam are safe and sending you much love as we all need it. Love you.

I never knew the response I got back would be the last words I would ever hear from my friend:

Love you too brother Gad. 🖤🙏

Two months later, on August 28, I received a phone call from Kate Hudson. She was sobbing uncontrollably and the only thing I could make out was "He's gone. Chad's gone." I didn't understand. Was there a Chad whom we had worked with that was sick? Which Chad could she possibly be talking about? It wasn't until I looked down at my phone and saw the breaking-news alert that my confusion turned to shock. Nothing would allow me to make sense of the words I was reading. How was a guy only slightly older than me, who was the embodiment of health, suddenly dead? I was shocked into a stupor. About an hour later, I started sobbing uncontrollably. I, like so many others, felt robbed. I felt robbed of a friendship, I felt robbed of a talent, I felt robbed of a legacy cut far too short. How had he kept this secret from so many people? How could the doctors not save him? How long had he been sick? Who was to blame? I needed someone to blame. He had too much left to do. He had too much left still to achieve. This was supposed to be his beginning, not his fucking end.

WHY?!

In that moment I finally understood what my childhood acting teacher, James Michael, meant decades earlier, by asking that fateful word of yourself in order to make yourself cry in a scene.

WHY?

It is a word that truly captures our place in the universe. We are a species that seeks to know all answers and when we truly don't have them, it breaks us. I was broken. I did not have an answer and it hurt so fully. No matter how many times I would ask "Why?" it wouldn't bring back my friend.

At his memorial, which was one of the most touching farewells I've ever attended, you could feel Chadwick all around. There were drummers pounding ferociously to remind of us of his energy and his presence. There were beautifully poetic words spoken to remind us of his enduring legacy and the importance of the time he did have. And there were his family and friends who were all there celebrating the one person in the world who never needed to ask "Why?" but instead always found peace and solace in that which was uncertain. When I stumbled back upon his text to me about the rain later that day, it all suddenly made so much sense. Chad knew he didn't have much time left.

That urgency gave him the motivation to embrace every last second of every last day he had. I do not envy his pain, I do not envy his exhaustion, and I do not envy his limitations while he battled his disease, but I do envy his bravery. It is a bravery I myself may never know. It is the bravery to work even when confronted with real mortality. It is the bravery to fight even when told that there is nothing left to fight for. It is the bravery to be surrounded by darkness and still see nothing but light. It is the bravery to hear everyone around you saying "Why?" and calmly answer back . . . "Why not?" Perhaps if we all started looking at things not for the inconvenience and frustrations they cause us, we could all stop hiding from the rain and instead simply start to catch it.

A Pandemic

Some might question why I would choose to include such a dark and lonely period to reflect upon in this chapter, but the truth is, I might have learned just as much about myself and my wants and desires during that year-plus period than during any other big milestone in my life. The time that the pandemic afforded me to reflect upon my wants, desires, hopes, dreams, and priorities was unique in that all I had was the opportunity to reflect. For starters, the pandemic did something that my career often doesn't: allowed me to simply be home with my family from morning to night. During the early days of the pandemic, I, like many of you, created a routine to break up the monotony. We would start with breakfast, then take a walk or bike ride, then read a book, then play games like Phase 10, Yahtzee, Rummikub, Monopoly Cards, and too many other games to mention. Each night, we would camp out in the living room and I would introduce an iconic movie from my childhood to my daughters. One night it would be *Raiders of the Lost Ark*, the next night *The Breakfast Club*. Pretty soon, as I heard from other parents that they were struggling to find things to do with their kids in the early days of the pandemic, I decided on a whim to start reading children's books on Twitter Live and IG Live, allowing kids and parents to gather around for ten minutes or so as I would read everything from *The Very Hungry Caterpillar* to *The Giving Tree* to *Olivia Goes to Venice*. The joy and relief it would provide families was astounding to me and gave me purpose at a time when, like many others, I was struggling to find any (outside of being a dad). The opportunity to simply transport kids and parents to other worlds, albeit briefly, reminded me of my fond memories as a child growing up watching LeVar Burton's *Reading Rainbow*. Little did I know that a ten-minute daily reprieve for parents would only just begin to scratch the surface of my desire to keep people full of hope and joy during those trying first months.

Shortly after the book readings, I began speaking with Jennifer Lee about how we might be able to create short content utilizing the brilliant animation team at Disney Animation to give people at home even the tiniest bite-sized bits featuring Olaf. Under the direction of the insanely talented Hyrum Osmond (the primary animator behind Olaf in the Frozen films), we created twenty minimalist shorts called *At Home with Olaf* that were created entirely by an animation team working exclusively from their homes. I recorded all of the sounds and noises on a microphone from my home office and Hyrum would coordinate animation over Zoom meetings. The shorts gave kids something new to look forward to every day and the whole thing was capped off with an original song written by Bobby Lopez and Kristen Anderson-Lopez called "I Am with You," a beautiful and touching ballad that spoke so profoundly to the theme of being together even when we are far apart. That thematic idea would prove to be quite inspirational for my next pandemic-era enterprise.

It became apparent very quickly just how much help was needed by so many people due to interruptions in the workforce, health issues, and other major issues due to Covid-19. For the first few months, I felt helpless and kept sending money to organization after organization, not knowing how to get others to try to help some of the incredible groups providing relief to millions in need. One day while watching one of my favorite eighties movies, *The Goonies*, I looked at my wife and said, "Man, these movies give me so much joy, I wish there were a way to parlay that into something useful during this awful period." Almost as a joke she said, "Well, I'm sure the cast has plenty of time on their hands right now. You should get them together." While she may have *meant* it as a joke, it soon became my obsession. Years earlier I had watched a reunion special where Oprah had brought the entire surviving cast of *The Sound of Music* together. I vividly remember how much joy it brought me to see them all come out and recount their memories on the set of one of cinema's most iconic movies. I started to wonder if I could re-create that feeling in a way that would bring many of my favorite stars and filmmakers together again even though they were all separated and sheltering at home. That night it was all I could think about. The next morning, I reached out to my colleague and friend Jeff Cohen, who played the iconic character Chunk in *The Goonies* and is now one of our industry's finest entertainment lawyers. This is the email I sent:

First of all, I hope you and your family are staying healthy and sane during this impossible time. I'm thinking about doing something that can both be entertaining and healing as we navigate this fucking nightmare and wanted to see what you thought. I have been toying with something that I think can generate eyes and dollars for some of the very important organizations and funds desperately in need in order to navigate this nightmare. My idea, should you be interested, would be to host a fireside reunion chat with different casts on something like zoom and record it and share to raise money to combat Covid 19. As you may expect, were I to do this, I would want to start with you and your co-stars from The Goonies. I think it could be fun, hilarious and most importantly, helpful to the community writ large.

Jeff wrote back and said he and Ke Huy Quan, who had played Data, were both in. Soon after, I started tracking down one Goonie after another, like some insane fan willing to go to the ends of the digital Earth to find them. The next ones to say yes were Josh Brolin and Sean Astin. Soon after that, I was able to confirm Corey Feldman and Martha Plimpton. Finally, after some intense searching (because she had moved away from acting), I was able to track down Kerri Green and confirm my final Goonie member. My original intention was to simply reunite the kids from the film, but now that I had them I thought to myself, *Why not reach out to the surviving adults too?* Soon, Joe Pantoliano and Robert Davi, aka the Fratelli brothers, were both in. With the cast in place, I decided, what the hell, why not reach out to the writer, my friend Chris Columbus, whom I had worked with on *Pixels*? Chris immediately said yes.

With every yes came a new challenge to myself. Before long, I had decided to pursue director Richard Donner and producer Steven Spielberg, who both immediately committed as well. Finally, I reached out to the only missing piece I could think of—singer-songwriter Cyndi Lauper, who also said yes. With everyone in place, I now needed a show worthy of bringing them all back together. While I originally toyed with a simple sit-down interview where everyone came out at the same time, I soon pivoted and decided that the most compelling and exciting way to build the show out would be to introduce one guest and then bring out the next and slowly build to the point where it almost becomes insane how many surprises we had in store for the audience. I figured this would not only build interest in real time but also motivate our viewers to donate, because of how excited they were throughout the telecast. I would first talk about the organization we were fundraising for, introduce a link, then talk about my love for the film, and finally bring out the first guest. I wrote a sketch for Sean Astin and me to do together, and then used that to introduce the rest of the Goonies one by one. I also decided that I would keep as many surprises from everyone involved as possible, so that they would be as excited and shocked as the viewers. That is why when Steven and Donner eventually come on, you can see everyone is shell-shocked. Other moments I built in were not only having the cast and creative team walk down memory lane and tell stories no one had ever heard before but also reenact some of the most iconic scenes from the film as well. The final piece of the puzzle was to come up with a name for the show that would excite, connect, and reflect the nature of what we were trying to do. After a few days of throwing around titles like *The Reunion Show*, *The Gang's All Here*, and *Together Again*, I finally wrote down two words that shouldn't go together but somehow made all the sense in the world for this enterprise: *Reunited Apart*. On April 27, 2020, we premiered our first episode of the show and it was viewed by over three million people, raising thousands of dollars in the process for an incredible organization called the Center for Disaster Philanthropy.

Over the next few months, I was able to reunite the casts of some of my favorite movies of all time, including *Back to the Future*, *Splash*, *Ghostbusters*, *Ferris Bueller's Day Off*, *Wayne's World*, *The Karate Kid*, and, the episode to end all episodes, *The Lord of the Rings*, which raised over $2 million and was seen by over seven million people. To this day, people come up to me on a daily basis to tell me how much this online YouTube series got them through the most trying days of the pandemic. The truth is, it honestly got me through it as well. Having the chance to sit down

with everyone from Bill Murray to Michael J. Fox to Tom Hanks to Mike Myers and Dana Carvey discussing their work in my favorite films of all time, while raising hundreds of thousands of dollars for some amazing causes, gave me purpose at a time in which I needed it the most. At a certain point, people began branding me as the hardest-working pandemic entertainer, which is a badge of honor I wear with great pride. During that year-plus stretch, I worked harder than I've ever worked to make people laugh, think, and engage, even though I never made a dime while doing it. Yet I have never felt more fulfilled putting my talents to good use than I did during this hellish communal experience we all lived through. It made me fall back in love with what I do.

When you are not working for a paycheck but rather working to genuinely make people happy, it resets the fundamentals of why you do what you do and reminds you that being able to entertain is not only a gift . . . but very often an honor. Entertaining millions of people when they also needed it the most was one of the great honors of my life.

13

HOMECOMING

Coming back to Broadway had always been in the cards. I knew I wasn't done with it, but I was also terrified of trying to live up to the historic precedent of *The Book of Mormon*. Over the years, I had flirted with numerous projects, including a revival of *A Funny Thing Happened on the Way to the Forum* and a staged production of *A Confederacy of Dunces* alongside my *Beauty and the Beast* director, Bill Condon, and even a musical adaptation of the classic Steve Martin film *The Jerk*, but for scheduling and family reasons, I could never find the right window for a lengthy run of a show. After a decade away, however, the time felt right to finally make my return.

In late 2019, director Alex Timbers, whom I had previously talked with about doing *Forum*, told me that he had a script he wanted to send me based on a project he had done off-Broadway years earlier called *Gutenberg! The Musical!* about two nursing home employees who use all of their money to stage a one-night-only workshop of their new passion project: an original musical based on the life of Johannes Gutenberg, the inventor of the printing press. The conceit of the show is that these two amateur writers/performers play all the roles in order to try to sell the concept to a would-be producer in the audience. That show had apparently inspired Nick Kroll and John Mulaney to team up with Timbers years earlier on their first Broadway collab, the *Oh, Hello Show*. Despite the show sounding hilarious and obviously having many fans, my immediate reaction to the pitch for *Gutenberg* was that it felt way too niche and far too meta for what I was looking for, but I promised him I would listen to the album and read the script before ruling anything out.

Much to my surprise, I found the whole thing deliriously funny and beyond stupid in all the best ways. I called Alex up and said, "Look, this is really funny. I have a bunch of thoughts, but the only person I could ever imagine doing it with is Andrew [Rannells, whom I had worked with on *Mormon*]." I essentially wanted to get the gang back together again . . . even if it was a two-person gang.

Alex thought it was an inspired idea and told me he would reach out to him directly. (Little did I know at the time that the son of a bitch had already sent him the material and was playing a game of 4D chess in which he already had us both wrapped around his finger.) Andrew and I agreed that before we made any decisions, we would need to hear the script out loud and do a workshop . . . of this weird show about a workshop. So, we all cleared our schedules, booked a rehearsal space in Los Angeles, and over the course of a week learned all of the songs and worked on the script alongside Alex, the two writers (Anthony King and Scott Brown), and the musical director T. O. Sterrett. The reading was an enormous success and by the end of the week, we decided that we would take the next steps. That was the first week of March 2020. I'm sure you know what happened next.

Two years later, with the show out of sight and out of mind, I once again received a call asking me if I was still interested in making my return to the stage opposite Rannells in *Gutenberg*. By this time, J.J. Abrams and an impressive group of producers had joined the project and were looking to mount it on Broadway in the fall of 2023. After one more reading and a long chat with my wife and children, I agreed to return to Broadway for a twenty-week limited run. The rehearsal schedule was insane. Andrew and I would go to New York for one week at the end of June, learn all of act 1, take a three-week break, and then come back for two more weeks of rehearsal before moving into the theater for tech.

I was terrified. Unlike for Andrew, dancing and I do not go hand in hand. It had also been over a decade since I had done a stage musical, and I was (shall we just say) not in fighting shape. I immediately started working again with my *Book of Mormon* singing teacher, the legendary Liz Caplan, and built my vocal muscles up to endure the grueling eight-show-a-week schedule. Rehearsals with Alex, Andrew, and the creative team were truly the most hilarious and wondrous of my career. It was so thrilling to be able to build something from the ground up with such a small group and have everyone working side by side to achieve the same goal. Having been professionally separated from Rannells for a decade, I was curious how our chemistry and our working relationship would go all these years later. We had always kept in touch and discussed various possibilities for a reunion (includ-

ing for one hot second a re-vival of *The Producers*), but this would officially be the first time we teamed up again. It became very apparent after one day in the room that for some unknown reason this handsome Nebraska Catholic boy and this chubby South Florida Jew had been destined to be comedy partners.

I like to say that when it comes to comedy, Andrew is a sniper rifle, and I am a

machine gun. His targeted approach and my sloppy chaos are a comedy marriage built in heaven. We balance each other and work off one another in ways that complement each other so easily. It embarrasses us greatly to hear people compare us to some of the great comedy duos like Nichols and May, Lane and Broderick, Martin and Short, and Abercrombie & Fitch, but we do not take the comparisons lightly and feel blessed to share that rarefied air. In all honesty, I think we still have a ways to go to be in that category, but dammit if we don't hope to one day be worthy of such comparisons.

One of the great challenges of *Gutenberg! The Musical!* was the central conceit of the show that the two main characters, Bud and Doug, would use trucker hats to distinguish between the twenty-plus characters in their workshop that they are putting on for the producers. I am not a coordinated young man and knowing when and how to switch two hats, let alone *forty-two* hats, gave me serious agita. I would literally sneak hats home at night and make my poor employee and friend Taylor Stuewe do the hat choreography and dance choreography until both of us would collapse to the ground. Meanwhile, Rannells would do it once and have it fully down.

The second complication of the show's premise was that Andrew and I would not only be responsible for playing all of the roles in the actual

show, but also all of the stagehands responsible for moving the sets around and placing props where they needed to be before and after each number. I would often sit in a corner and ask myself why I had chosen to make my Broadway comeback the single hardest assignment I could find. During rehearsals, I would literally have to change shirts at intermission because I would sweat through them during each run.

Andrew and I also weren't certain if the comedy was working or not, because we had been performing it solely for the benefit of the same eight people in the rehearsal space day after day. Alex therefore decided that the best thing to do was to bring in some guests and do the show for them inside of the small dance space. Let me tell you, there is nothing more terrifying than doing a big, broad two-person musical with the audience a mere five feet away from you. It was, however, the perfect antidote to any fears we might have had that the comedy wasn't going to play, as the small audience went nuts for what we were doing. A small audience watching something for free in a rehearsal space, however, is very different than an eleven-hundred-seat Broadway theater.

As opening night fast approached, I started to wonder what brand of crack I had been smoking before I committed to coming back to Broadway in a two-person original musical, while all of Broadway was still recovering from the setbacks of the pandemic. The topic of discussion every day during rehearsals was which new show was closing and how poor Broadway attendance had been since 2020.

I started to spiral. What if the show was a flop? What if nobody came? What if I couldn't sustain my vocal and physical health for one *week* of shows, let alone five months? What if I had a heart attack onstage from dealing with all of the fucking hats? From night one, however, all of that fear and stress disappeared, and it became immediately apparent that we had somehow created a tonic to New York's doldrums. People started calling our show the *Ted Lasso* of Broadway, a feel-good comedy that wanted nothing more than to make people smile. The show, after all, is about dreamers and the dreams they set out to conquer ("eat," as we call it in the show), regardless of the obstacles they may face.

I really feel in my heart that that message connected in such a deep and profound way for so many people who are constantly immersed in cynicism and the never-ending cycle of shit that seems to define the twenty-first century. In many ways, that has become my mission statement as an artist: to continue to make people laugh and to give them hope at a time in which they need it the most. There is so much cynicism in our world and a lot of times I feel like the content we as artists partake in is equally cynical and oftentimes nihilistic, which can feel cool and edgy, but when you get back to the basics, isn't it equally compelling to give people a sense of escapism and optimism when they are already surrounded by such a barrage of shit all the time?

One interesting wrinkle to arise during early previews was that a joke that had been killing in our first few performances was completely derailed overnight by world events nobody could have ever anticipated. Early on in the show Bud and Doug talk the audience through the machinations of musical theater and the tropes that must be included in order to create a great musical. One such expectation for any big musical, they explain, is that it should have a serious issue to tackle, and our serious issue is antisemitism. We then explain further: "History tells us that Germans do not like Jews. And these days, it seems like it may not just be Germans." The joke, while cutting, brought the house down every night. Every night, that is, until October 7, 2023. That day, over a thousand Jews were massacred by Hamas terrorists in Israel, resulting in the largest loss of Jewish life since the Holocaust. Immediately after the event, I knew that the second the line came out of my mouth that we were fucked, and boy, was that an understatement. The "joke" not only fell flat, but was met with audible gasps. I got off the stage and Rannells and I immediately wrote our writers and our director.

For the next few nights we tweaked it, but the bigger problem was that one of our characters was a little psychotic child who wore a hat that said, in large black font, ANTISEMITE (trust me, it worked in the show!). No matter what we did, every time I played that character and put on the hat, I was met with hostile and/or perplexed stares. We had little time and resources to change what is a significant part of our plot and story and couldn't simply cut the character wholesale. Finally, one day we gathered around and somebody had the pitch that while people couldn't laugh at antisemitism right now, perhaps they could laugh if she was a little Nazi girl. Alex miraculously got us new hats for that night. We changed the line to "Our serious issue is Nazis. History tells us that Nazis are kind of the worst." Finally, people started laughing again, but it wasn't yet a seismic laugh, which I knew we could get, so I pitched the boys a joke using the Indiana Jones films, which seemingly always go back to the Nazis. The next performance I said: "History . . . and every Indiana Jones film except for *Crystal Skull* tells us that Nazis are kind of the worst." We finally found the right recipe, and a joke area that was causing us serious concern was suddenly the catalyst to give the audience permission to laugh at everything that would soon follow. It was such an incredible example of creative collaboration at its best. Sometimes when your backs are against the wall, you simply have to break down the wall.

The show officially opened on October 12, 2023, to rave reviews. It became one of the few breakout hits of 2023, resulting in numerous accolades, nominations, and record-breaking attendance for the James Earl Jones Theatre, but perhaps the greatest joy I associate with being a part of this show is a story that our writer Anthony found on Reddit one day, which he forwarded to Andrew and me. It is from a profile named Prestigious_Hawk1218 and is a daily reminder of why I do what I do. After losing his father to stage-four lung cancer, this person needed a pick-me-up and decided to buy a ticket to our show, hoping to have his spirits lifted. He talks about sitting in the audience and thinking about his father's passing and trying to contextualize his own life and how he can continue given the enormous hole that has been left behind. Then he says that during a moment in which he was particularly reflective and introspective, the following happened:

"It's okay," I hear Andrew Rannells say. And I'm paraphrasing, but I hear him continue: "We've already succeeded. We're doing the things

we love. And if it all goes wrong, or we don't get what we want, we'll keep going. We'll try again."

It was everything I was supposed to hear. It's what was bouncing around in the vacuum my life had been for two months, but could only take root and blossom when full attention and an open heart let the idea in. This show—this silly, silly, show—had tricked my [sic] into letting my guard down. Suddenly these two people who loved each other, and had hopes and fears, and faced it all with such poise, suddenly were THERE for each other and I thought: my God why wasn't anyone CLAPPING for this moment of tenderness?

That's when the row in front of me parted. And the row in front of them. And the row in front of them. Everyone in the audience had turned to look at me.

And on stage, Josh Gad and Andrew Rannells (who I believe had been freshly walking upstage)

ALSO TURNED AROUND TO LOOK AT ME

I froze. The sound that had been ringing in my ears stopped and with a thundercrack of realization I realized that I was clapping. Horror swelled and swallowed me. From beneath the shield of my hand the theatre disappeared. Among the improv jokes and jabs, I heard Andrew Rannells say—

"Don't worry. You're the real hero."

I was mortified. I still am.

I've been back to the city to see other shows since then. It's an easy drive, and a fun I used to think escape. Now . . . I don't think you leave everything behind you when you go to a show on Broadway. The James Earl Jones Theatre saw me haunted by the ghost of my father, and he was certainly laughing with everyone else when I found my heart burst open in Act 2. It was nice to know he was there.

How lucky are we, the few, who get to provide a gift like this? I am eternally grateful that I get to not only "eat dreams" for a living, but help others aspire to do the same. Such is where I know I find myself at this point in my life. At forty-three years old, I feel I have just begun to skim the surface of not only what I want to do, but what I *can* do. It is interesting to me that for every decade of my professional life, I have returned home to theater . . . almost as a creative reset. At twenty-four, I pivoted away from pursuing TV/film and won my big break on the stage in *The 25th Annual Putnam County Spelling Bee*. At thirty, eager to avoid the traps of becoming the funny fat best friend on-screen, I blew everything up and returned to the stage in what would turn out to be the biggest breakout role of my career in *The Book of Mormon*. And now, in my early forties, needing yet another reset, in this case to imagine a new career pivot for myself that involves more than simply performing but also encompasses writing, directing, and other new frontiers, I made my return to the stage in a two-hander that miraculously showed me I am now at a place in my career where I can open my own show (based on no preexisting IP) and not only not embarrass myself, but somehow bring in sold-out houses night after night.

The stage is a place where I cannot cheat, I cannot get multiple takes, I cannot hide, and I cannot coast. It is a place where artists must reckon with their own demons knowing very well the audience, who is paying a fortune, expects to see you at your best, regardless of how tired, stressed, distracted, or hungry you are. It is a foundation built quite literally on blood, sweat, and tears eight times a week and sometimes twice a day. The theater is where it all began for me and where it will most likely end for me. It connects to the past and challenges us to look to the future. It is a cherished and sacred temple where audiences and actors both have roles to play and each night share a distinctly unique experience that will never be replicated and in most cases never be seen or heard again.

On a personal level, the theater has accompanied me, healed me, and nurtured me, as I battled anxiety, courted my wife, brought a new baby into this world, and crossed milestone after milestone in my career. It is a gift I have shared with the most important people in my life, from my Holocaust-surviving grandparents to my heroic single mother, to my beloved brothers, to my amazing niece and nephew, to my own children who have now had the opportunity to watch me build a show from the ground up. The theater is my boxing ring where I can fight my own insecurities and come out stronger each night as a result. It is a place to bury old grievances and make new memories. It is also, as it turns out, a place to revisit the past and find peace along the way.

In one particularly surreal full-circle moment during *Gutenberg*, I received an unexpected phone call one day from my estranged father. He told me he was in New Jersey and wanted to see me onstage for the first time. I'm not sure which part was the most surprising: that he called me, that he was in New Jersey, or that forty-three years into my life as an actor I realized my father had never once seen me onstage. Having not seen him in person in over twenty years, I reluctantly invited him to my show on Halloween and told him to spend the night at my place so we could catch up. After the show ended, I asked Andrew to come out with me to make it less awkward. When I saw my father again, I barely recognized him. Gone was the titan of my childhood, a man who had been the life of the party, and in his place was a frail old man whom time and mistakes had caught up with. Due to his hearing impairment (one he has had since childhood) and his broken English, he seemed to enjoy the show but not understand much of it. He looked not only worn out but fairly unkempt with an old, ill-fitting jacket, rumpled clothes, and chipped and missing teeth. I would find out later he was essentially now living off Social Security checks and what few assets he still had. He looked perplexed by Andrew and me dressed as Joan Crawford and Christina Crawford in *Mommie Dearest* attire, which we had worn as joke costumes for Halloween. After we left the theater, we went back to my place and he shared his pride with me for all of my accomplishments and the

joy he'd had while watching the show and telling anyone who would listen I was his son. Over the course of the night, we shared stories about his past, much of which I'm able to share in this book because of our reunion, and about his regrets, many of which are either too little or too late.

What I did get out of that evening, however, was a sense of closure. After forty years of seeking his approval, here I was, at the height of my success, sitting in a massive New York City penthouse apartment that the production had leased for me, and my father couldn't be prouder. Yet somehow it didn't quite live up to any of my expectations. What was worse was I had this enormous guilt, because I had a bunch of work to do and wanted to call my kids, who were on the other side of the country in Los Angeles. In that moment it occurred to me that my relationship with my father could essentially be summarized by part of the final verse of Harry Chapin's classic "Cat's in the Cradle":

I've long since retired, my son's moved away
I called him up just the other day
I said, I'd like to see you if you don't mind
He said, I'd love to, dad, if I can find the time

My dad stayed over that night. We talked for many hours about his childhood, his family, his regrets, and his struggles. The next morning I handed him all the money I had in my wallet (despite his embarrassed reluctance) and said my goodbyes. I have stayed in touch since, but I often wonder if I will ever see him again. Yet somehow, I am at peace with that, because like the gentleman who saw our show and found closure with his father's passing, so too did my show bring long-needed closure to my complicated relationship with my father. I will always love him deeply, but I am no longer searching for his love in return. I know in his own way, he has loved and always will love me, even though he made so many fundamental mistakes in his approach to being there for my family both as a husband and a father.

What my father ironically did give me was a road map for how to be the best version of a husband and father I am capable of being. I have and will continue to make mistakes in that role, but at least I have the wherewithal to know to call them mistakes. Saying goodbye to my dad that day was both bittersweet and poignant because it meant that I had finally closed one chapter of my life that had been open-ended for forty-three years. Perhaps poetically, shortly after my father left, my mother and my stepfather, the incredible man whom I have now had the privilege of calling my dad for thirty-three years, came to stay with me in my NYC apartment for the last month of my run. While I at first was reluctant to

admit to them both that I let my dad spend the night or even saw him (for fear of how they would react), I finally caved and used the opportunity to fully get so much of the pain of my childhood off my chest. As they both have throughout our journey together, they listened attentively and showed me the love and affection I so desperately needed in that moment of extreme vulnerability. The time we got to spend together that month was invigorating. It was like I was an adult version of my ten-year-old self. It was just the three of us, eating together, talking late into the night, watching TV shows (more specifically, bingeing *Jury Duty*), and going to the theater every night together, where they would sit backstage and wait for me to finish, often rubbing shoulders with icons including Will Ferrell, Martin Short, Steve Martin, and of course, their favorite of all, Hillary Clinton. Perhaps the greatest thrill, however, was knowing they were there every night to see me do my thing and reminding myself and them that dreams really do come true when you work hard enough and never give up.

A few months after finishing *Gutenberg*, I found myself back in New York City for an event at Carnegie Hall that my daughter Ava was performing at. My wife, two daughters, and I had just come out of seeing a wonderful musical called *Kimberly Akimbo*. I looked up the street and saw that we were only a few blocks away from the Eugene O'Neil Theatre, home to the still-running *Book of Mormon*. I glanced at my watch and realized there were a few minutes left in the show. When we got to the theater, the lovely security, still there after fourteen years, welcomed us with open arms and found us standing room at the back of the packed house. My girls, who had never seen the show before, looked at the actor playing Cunningham and immediately turned to me: "That was your character, wasn't it?" I gave them a terse laugh (the suggestion being *What gave it away . . . the chubby guy with frazzled black hair and glasses in the role?*). As the characters sang the final number, which eventually turns into a reprise of "Hello," I started to feel joyful tears falling down my cheeks. The tears continued as I watched my girls in turn watch the fruits of my labor playing out like a reenactment of a dream. When my little one asked me if I had happy tears, I looked down at her and said, "Yes, I sure do. I sure do." Because in that moment, as my daughters watched and laughed alongside a full and uproarious audience eager and ready to stand and applaud the tenth generation of a role and a show I helped create before my girls were even born, I had an eye-opening revelation: I didn't simply have a great career . . .

I now had a legacy.

AFTERWORD:
One Last Thing

So here we are. As one chapter closes, a new one begins, full of the same fear, excitement, anxiety, and uncertainty that seems to characterize every chapter in my life. I have lived long enough to tell at least some part of my story, but not quite long enough to tell you how it is going to end or what awaits us along the way. There are still so many aspirations I have and so many dreams yet to be realized. So far I have played many roles on this journey: child, son, brother, student, friend, enemy, speech and debate champion, nerd, class president, anxiety-stricken agoraphobe, highly functional person in society, actor, singer, drama major, lover, husband, father, Floridian, Pittsburgher, New Yorker, Californian, Tony nominee, star of stage and screen, celebrated performer, reviled performer, self-doubter, overweight person, healthy person, producer, animated sidekick, leading man, outspoken activist, armchair activist, Jew, nondenominational agnostic, Mormon, possibly gay Disney pseudo-villain, all-around pandemic entertainer, and now published writer. Who knows what roles yet remain on the horizon? Director? Businessman? Playwright? Politician? Your guess is as good as mine. For now, I am happy simply living by the motto I have lived by since I took the finals stage at the speech and debate tournament as an eighteen-year-old senior in high school . . . where there is an easy path, turn the other way and take the riskier route. In my life I have always taken chances, and by taking chances I have felt the beauty and thrill of success . . . and failure. Such is the journey of our time here on this planet from the moment we are born:

Only by flailing can we learn to crawl. Only by falling can we learn to walk. Only by failing can we learn to succeed.

So, when you put this book down, ask yourself not where you can step, but where you can leap. Tackle something you have always wanted to do, but never had the courage to try. Ask yourself a hard question and challenge yourself to answer it even if the truth is scary. Ask that person you've always had affection for on a date. Read that book that has been sitting on your nightstand for six months. Apply for that job you want but are afraid of getting rejected from. Use that saved-up money to travel somewhere you've always wanted to go. Along the way, you will surely cry, but you will also laugh. You will be scared, but ultimately grateful. You may be rejected, but you will simultaneously have had yet one more experience to learn and grow from. If it doesn't work out, you can always go back to the three-thousand-year-plus tradition of asking God what went wrong.

But . . . if it *does* happen to work out in your favor . . .

Tell them Gad sent you.

ONWARD
by Mel Brooks

Dear Josh,

I know I promised you a wonderful blurb for your new book, but after reading it, I find myself struggling to say something nice.

If I get a positive thought that's not too destructive, I'll send it along.

All the best,
Mel

ACKNOWLEDGMENTS

It's so nice to be able to acknowledge people without the stress of a ticking clock telling you to get offstage at an awards show. While the act of writing a book is at times incredibly lonely, mine was quite often a joyful collaboration with many different people in my life who came at this from both a professional and a personal lens. This journey began with my book agent, Anthony Mattero, somehow convincing me that writing eighty thousand words of something would be a good use of my and your time. Together with my longtime manager, Meredith Wechter Lane, I was presented with the incredible opportunity of teaming up with the awesome folks at Simon & Schuster's Gallery Books division and in particular my out-of-this-world writing muse Natasha Simons, who held my hand for the past year and a half while always reminding me that books take longer to finish than movies and TV. Along the way, I was blessed to have to some far superior eyes always looking out for errors, faux pas, and just plain old bad writing, including my colleagues Taylor Stuewe, Page Ryland, and Sydney Shiffman. I also want to thank Mia Robertson and the copy team at S&S for painstakingly going through my nonsense with a fine-tooth comb and making it legally sound. I also owe a debt of gratitude to my dear friends Rory O'Malley, David Lang, Seth Gabel, Matt Swerdlow, Brett Horgan, Craig Gilwit, Sam Weitzner, Danny Swerdlow, Andrew Rannells, Nikki M. James, Jennifer Lee, Gunnar Clancy, Bo Clancy, and Tim Curtis, who accepted my late-night calls and fact-checked many a personal anecdote along the way. Furthermore, I would like to acknowledge Julie Graham, Joan Marcus, and Tricia M. Baron for their help in securing some of the wonderful photos within the book. I would also like to give a shout-out to my partners P. J. Shapiro,

Melissa Raubvogel, and Lindsey Faig for their help bringing this book to life. And a very special thanks to icons Sacha Baron Cohen, Mel Brooks, Billy Crystal, Ron Howard, Idina Menzel, Trey Parker and Matt Stone, Pink, and Adam Sandler, who, as well as offering to write nice words on my behalf, would make an incredible band.

There would also, frankly, be no book without the inspiration, education, and instruction of some of the greatest teachers on Earth, all of whom made me fall in love with literature, language, and the arts, including Mrs. Lambert, Mrs. Winrow, Mrs. Morris, Mr. Redler, Mrs. Frat, Mrs. Rothschild, and the many other professors along the way who introduced my hand to paper and challenged me to be the best writer I could possibly be.

On a personal note, I would not have a book to write without my family, who clearly had an enormous impact on me along the way. From my brothers, Jason and Jeffrey, to my sister-in-law, Stacy, brother-in-law, Saadi, and his partner, Homa, and mother- and father-in-law, Marisa and Johnny, as well as my incredible nieces, Sydney, Justin, my beautiful departed Marco, and my stepsister, Monica, and her family, I have always been supported and loved as I take big swings, like tackling a Broadway show or writing a memoir. At the center of my support system, however, has always been my mother, Susan, and her incredible husband and my stepfather, Stan, who gave me the fundamentals that I now get to reflect upon and share with you. I am forever grateful for having an upbringing as beautiful and complicated as I did, because it made me who I am today and gave me the framework to be decent and kind, two attributes seemingly in short supply these days.

Finally, I would like to thank the centerpiece of my world: my wife, Ida, and our beautiful girls, Ava and Isabella. Without them, I would not have the inspiration and the drive to be the dreamer I am and the doer I hope to continuously be. They fill me with daily love and remind me that in the scheme of things, there really is no better role than that of husband

and father. Thank you so much for putting up with me as I holed up to write late into the night or interrupted playtime and vacation time for quick edits. I owe you more than you can know and will repay you by never writing another one of these again . . .

At least for the near future.